Southern Literary Studies
Louis D. Rubin, Jr., Editor

# KATHERINE ANNE PORTER'S ARTISTIC DEVELOPMENT

Robert H. Brinkmeyer, Jr.

# Katherine Anne Porter's Artistic Development

*Primitivism,
Traditionalism, and
Totalitarianism*

Louisiana State University Press
Baton Rouge and London

Copyright © 1993 by Louisiana State University Press
All rights reserved
Manufactured in the United States of America
First printing
02  01  00  99  98  97  96  95  94  93     5  4  3  2  1

Designer: Glynnis Phoebe
Typeface: Granjon
Typesetter: G&S Typesetters, Inc.
Printer and binder: Thomson-Shore, Inc.

Library of Congress Cataloging-in-Publication Data
Brinkmeyer, Robert H.
    Katherine Anne Porter's artistic development : primitivism,
traditionalism, and totalitarianism / Robert H. Brinkmeyer, Jr.
        p.   cm. — (Southern literary studies)
    Includes bibliographical references and index.
    ISBN 0-8071-1822-2 (alk. paper)
    1. Porter, Katherine Anne, 1890–1980—Criticism and
interpretation.   2. Southern States in literature.   I. Title.
II. Series.
PS3531.0752Z53   1993
813'.52—dc20
                                                    92-37039
                                                    CIP

The author offers grateful acknowledgment to the literary trustee for the Estate of Katherine Anne Porter for permission to quote material from the Katherine Anne Porter Collection in the McKeldin Library, University of Maryland. James Agee's poem "Dixie Doodle," which first appeared in *Partisan Review,* IV (February, 1938), is reprinted by permission of the James Agee Trust. Excerpts from "The Grave" in *The Leaning Tower and Other Stories,* copyright 1944 and renewed 1972 by Katherine Anne Porter, reprinted by permission of Harcourt Brace Jovanovich, Inc. Excerpts from "The Circus" in *The Leaning Tower and Other Stories,* copyright 1935 and renewed 1963 by Katherine Anne Porter, reprinted by permission of Harcourt Brace Jovanovich, Inc. Excerpts from "Flowering Judas" and "The Jilting of Granny Weatherall" in *Flowering Judas and Other Stories,* copyright 1930 and renewed by Katherine Anne Porter, reprinted by permission of Harcourt Brace Jovanovich, Inc. Excerpts from "The Grave," "The Jilting of Granny Weatherall," "Flowering Judas," and "The Circus" reprinted by permission of Jonathan Cape, publisher, and the Estate of Katherine Anne Porter. Excerpts from "Why I Write About Mexico," "The Fiesta of Guadalupe," and "A Letter to the Editor of *The Nation*" from *The Collected Essays and Occasional Writings of Katherine Anne Porter* copyright © 1970 by Katherine Anne Porter. Reprinted by permission of Houghton Mifflin Co./Seymour Lawrence. All rights reserved. Excerpts from *The Letters of Katherine Anne Porter,* copyright © 1990 by Isabel Bayley. Reprinted with permission of Atlantic Monthly Press.

The paper in this book meets the guidelines for permanence and durability of the Committee on Production Guidelines for Book Longevity of the Council on Library Resources.∞

*For D. R. C.*

# Contents

# PREFACE

In a 1963 interview with Barbara Thompson, Katherine Anne Porter commented that throughout her long career, stretching back to the twenties, she wrote from essentially the same perspective and with the same set of values. "It's astonishing how little I've changed: nothing in my point of view or my way of feeling," she told Thompson (*C*, 96). Critical studies of Porter by and large have confirmed her claim. Most present Porter as a writer who developed only in her artistic technique. In considering consciousness—how Porter viewed herself and the world and particularly how she understood human struggles with self-awareness and ethical imperatives—these studies suggest that Porter remained essentially the same throughout her career. Darlene Unrue, for instance, in her important book, *Truth and Vision in Katherine Anne Porter's Fiction,* charts out the shape of Porter's thought as embodied in her fiction almost as if all her work were written at the same time. As perceptive and persuasive as Unrue is, what we miss in her analysis is a sense of Porter's ongoing development as a thinker and observer and, going one step further, a sense of how this development affected the shape and texture of her art. Looking at what Unrue and most other Porter critics have not—the transformations in Porter's thinking and the artistic consequences of these upheavals—is what the book at hand attempts to do.

Only in the very broadest sense can Porter be seen as consistent in perspective: she possessed an inquiring and dissenting sensibility. While throughout her career she held fast to this sensibility, its focus, methodology, and underlying values underwent profound change. At one time or another in her life—and frequently at one and the same time—Porter was (or at least presented herself as) a devout Catholic, an antipapist, a left-wing radical, a segregationist, an ascetic artist, a freewheeling bohemian, and a proper southern lady. In looking at her intellectual and artistic evolution, I will touch upon the various positions and identities embraced by Porter, focusing on three developments that proved to be crucial turning points: her interest in Mexico in the twenties, her rediscovery of her Texas heritage and her embracing of a southern identity in the late twenties and thirties, and her fear and hatred of totalitarianism in the thirties and throughout the rest of her life. Although to carve Porter's career into three distinct periods based on this cluster of interests is to make the development of her work overly tidy, the three focal points provide a useful way of following and assessing Porter's evolving consciousness and her literature.

Porter's literature is usually considered within the framework of the southern literary renascence, but its geographic origin is actually problematic. As a native of Texas, a state more known for its western than its southern literary tradition, Porter stands apart from other southern writers of the renascence, almost all of whom grew up in the Deep or Upper South. Yet, given the shape and subject matter of her mature fiction, she justifiably commands a place alongside these other writers. In the last decade or so Porter's relationship with her home state has generated a good deal of critical attention, in large part because of the resurgence of interest in the southwestern literary tradition, specifically that of Texas. Whatever the reasons for this critical enthusiasm, coming to terms with Porter's place—or non-place—within the Texas tradition is a central issue for almost all the commentators. At one extreme stands Larry McMurtry, who in his 1968 essay "Southwestern Literature?" breezily dismisses Porter from his discussion: "Katherine Anne Porter was born in Indian Creek—can we then take credit for her better stories? I think not. Let those who are free of Texas enjoy their freedom." In his later, controversial evaluation of Texas literature, "Ever a Bridegroom: Reflections on the Failure of Texas Literature," McMurtry designates Porter as a Texas writer but then almost immediately suggests that there is absolutely nothing Texan about her or her fiction. McMurtry argues that in the name of aesthetics, Porter developed a literary style so purified that the heart and soul of fiction—what he identifies as "the local and the immediate"—vanished from her work. Driving his point home, McMurtry interprets Porter in light of Gertrude Stein's remark about Oakland, California: "There was no there there, she said. I feel very much the same way about the fiction of Katherine Anne Porter. The plumage is beautiful, but plumage, after all, is only feathers." If McMurtry tries to muscle Porter entirely out of the Texas literary heritage, at the other extreme James T. F. Tanner attempts wholeheartedly to annex her. The title of Tanner's recent book in the University of North Texas Press's Texas Writers Series, *The Texas Legacy of Katherine Anne Porter,* clearly signals the thrust of his thinking. On the second page he compactly summarizes his perspective: "Her wanderings over the earth notwithstanding, Katherine Anne Porter was a Texas writer first and last." Although Tanner acknowledges Porter's conflicting, often hostile feelings about Texas, he argues that her distancing from her home state was essentially a career choice that belied the deep affinities with Texas that shaped Porter's mind and art. Tanner writes that as an aspiring modern writer Porter would not have been helped by the tag of "Texas writer" (among other things, says Tanner, she would have had "to produce a full-length novel occasionally to keep her name before the regional audience"), and so she publicly—but not imaginatively—turned her back on her upbringing and her state's traditions.[1]

More persuasive and perceptive than either McMurtry or Tanner (both of whom are too single-minded in their efforts) are some recent critics who look at Porter as a Texas writer within a larger southern context. Don Graham, Janis P. Stout, and Joan Givner, for example, have argued persuasively for recognizing Porter's Texas and southern heritages. As most of

1. Larry McMurtry, "Southwestern Literature?," in McMurtry, *In a Narrow Grave: Essays on Texas* (1968; rpr. New York, 1989), 31; Larry McMurtry, "Ever a Bridegroom: Reflections on the Failure of Texas Literature," in *Range Wars: Heated Debates, Sober Reflections, and Other Assessments of Texas Writing,* ed. Craig Clifford and Tom Pilkington (Dallas, 1989), 16, 17; James T. F. Tanner, *The Texas Legacy of Katherine Anne Porter* (Denton, Tex., 1990), 2, 36.

these critics point out, Porter's depictions of Texas in her fiction and nonfiction are almost always more compellingly Deep South than Texan. Both Graham and Stout, for instance, in essays from the useful collection *Katherine Anne Porter and Texas: An Uneasy Relationship* edited by Clinton Machann and William Bedford Clark, make a case for recovering Porter as a Texas writer while at the same time discussing the ways that Porter's imaginative vision was anchored to the eastern part of the southern heartland. Commenting on how Porter portrayed Kyle, the central Texas community where she spent most of her childhood, Graham writes that "Kyle partakes of both prairie and farmland, though it's mainly prairie. But when Porter describes Kyle, it's a place of honeyed heat and as luscious as anything in Thomas Wolfe or any of the other Southern lyricists." Stout observes that when Porter depicts Texas in her fiction the "home place is reconstituted or resituated. It does not simply replicate the place where Porter grew up. Home is shifted eastward, so as to coincide more nearly with the Old South. She sets up a pattern that is repeated in less geographical ways as well, a pattern of the *unfamiliar familiar*. Thus the home place is Texas, and yet it is not Texas."[2]

While Porter's descriptions of Texas as the Deep South are in some regards fairly accurate (parts of central and eastern Texas are decidedly southern in culture and geography), they are more indicative of her stronger allegiances to a southern aristocratic and literary heritage that she did not know in Texas but that she endorsed long after she had left the region. As we shall see in Chapter 5, Porter embraced her "southernness" only after an extended and bitter period of doing just about everything she could to cut herself off from her roots. When she turned her eyes, heart, and memories to the world of her upbringing, she transformed her lower-middle-class family into aristocratic gentry fallen on hard times in a landscape that could easily be anywhere in the rural South. That she chose to identify

2. Don Graham, "A Southern Writer in Texas: Porter and the Texas Literary Tradition," in *Katherine Anne Porter and Texas: An Uneasy Relationship,* ed. Clinton Machann and William Bedford Clark (College Station, Tex., 1990), 65; Janis P. Stout, "Estranging Texas: Porter and the Distance from Home," in *Katherine Anne Porter and Texas,* ed. Machann and Clark, 89.

herself as a child of the southern aristocracy, emphasizing a class identity linked more in the popular mind with the Deep South than with Texas, suggests that Porter at some point in her career made the choice to become self-consciously southern, to embrace a personal and artistic identity that was regional rather than Texan.

A number of factors lay behind this choice. To begin with, most of the southern writers with whom Porter maintained friendships during the late twenties and early thirties when she began to become seriously interested in her heritage (Allen Tate, Caroline Gordon, and Andrew Lytle, among others) were themselves embracing decidedly southern allegiances. Much of their fiction, nonfiction, and poetry focused on questions and problems of what was perceived as the South's traditional way of life that stood opposed to the chaotic modernism of the urban and industrialized North. Clearly her friends' struggles influenced Porter's own attempts to integrate her regional roots with her artistic calling. If the group never came together to form a school of writing, Porter nonetheless certainly came to see herself as sharing with her friends a specifically southern sensibility and imagination. It was with these writers that Porter saw herself allied, not with any writer from Texas, even though, as James W. Lee has convincingly shown, other writers from Texas (none now considered major) were writing within a decidedly southern tradition. Any ties with a Texas literary tradition must have been shattered in 1939, when the Texas Institute of Letters awarded its prize for the best book by a Texas writer to J. Frank Dobie for *Apache Gold and Yaqui Silver* rather than to Porter for *Pale Horse, Pale Rider,* apparently because Dobie had stayed in Texas to live and because he wrote about recognizably Texan life—that is, western life.[3]

Porter's allegiances to a larger southern tradition were also fostered by her desires to distance herself from her humble origins. As Joan Givner has pointed out, Porter took no pride in the fact that she had raised herself from the lowly conditions of her Texas childhood. Poverty and social ostracism were not the stuff of Porter's conception of the artist's heroic calling. More appealing was the glamor of the southern aristocracy and its beautiful belles.

3. Joan Givner, *Katherine Anne Porter: A Life* (Rev. ed.; Athens, Ga., 1991), 315.

Porter began claiming a role for herself in this tradition in the early thirties. Givner writes:

> She transformed herself and her own personal history. In the place of Callie Porter, raised in poverty and obscurity, she created Katherine Anne Porter, an aristocratic daughter of the Old South and a descendent of a long line of distinguished statesmen. In this reincarnation she became one of the most celebrated personalities of the American literary scene, in demand everywhere for writers' conferences and lectures. She appeared on numerous platforms, elegantly gowned, furred, jeweled, and equipped with honorary degrees from several universities. With her magnolia skin, her velvety voice and white hair, she presented the perfect image of a southern belle, a member, as she styled herself, of the "guilt-ridden white pillar crowd."

Givner astutely observes that "Porter edited the story of her life as she might have shaped one of her short stories, rejecting certain experiences which she felt should not have happened and did not really belong to her and substituting others which seemed more appropriate."[4] In this act of rewriting and editing her life, one thinks of Amy's words in "Old Mortality": "And if I am to be the heroine of this novel, why shouldn't I make the most of it?" (*CS,* 189).

Porter turned to the cultural and literary traditions of the South to depict her heritage, and this represents her commitment to be truthful in her writing to the experiences of her interior life rather than to event and circumstance. She found in the themes and structures of the southern literary imagination the means to negotiate, rework, and transform raw experience into something much more profound—understanding. Porter's mature writing began when she embraced the southern imagination, and her literary falling off later in life came when she abandoned it. Among other things, this book explores Porter's momentous *decision* to become a southern writer and how her artistic rise and fall are integrally bound up in this deliberate choice.

Finally, I want to say a few words about my own perspective. Besides

4. *Ibid.,* 18–19, 20.

being influenced by the work of numerous Porter critics, my understanding of Porter has been shaped most profoundly by two sources: commentators on the southern literary renascence and the literary theorist Mikhail Bakhtin. Critics such as Louis D. Rubin, Jr., Lewis P. Simpson, Fred Hobson, Michael Kreyling, Anne Goodwyn Jones, Richard Gray, and Richard King have in their own ways helped me to understand the literary tradition of which Porter is most significantly a part. Bakhtin helped in providing a way to fathom the rich and complex workings of Porter's imaginative vision. Bakhtin's ideas on the monologic and dialogic imagination proved particularly helpful in grasping Porter's mature artistic vision that centered on the writer's struggles with memory. *Struggles* is no overstatement, for to engage one's memory was for Porter not simply to recall past events: it was to open oneself to the challenges of the past and to respond to those challenges. Ideally one's conscious self was always interacting with one's deepest memories, each shaping and being shaped by the interplay, the past opening up the present and the present opening up the past. "This constant exercise of memory seems to be the chief occupation of my mind," Porter wrote in a journal entry in 1936, "and all my experience seems to me memory, with continuity, marginal notes, constant revision and comparison of one thing with another" (*CE*, 449). As her words suggest, memories were not fixed and completed but always under "constant revision," as indeed was the very self doing the revising.

Having acknowledged my debt to Bakhtin, let me say further that my study of Porter is in no way strictly Bakhtinian or absolutely dependent upon his or any other theorist's observations. I have done my best to resist the tendency to build a theoretical system and then to plug Porter into it with little regard for whether she actually fits. I have tried instead to let Porter herself do most of the talking and to use insights from others to help me understand what I have heard. I hope that my book succeeds in helping us hear Porter's voice—or voices—in new contexts and with new meanings.

A number of people helped me along the way. My special thanks goes to the librarians in Special Collections at the University of Maryland's McKeldin Library, particularly Blanche Ebeling-Konig, Lauren Brown, and Ruth Alvarez, who were at all times supportive and professional in their help with my work at the Porter Collection. Dean James Kilroy of Tulane University provided funds to support a trip to the University of Maryland, as did the English department and the Graduate School at the University of Mississippi. The Graduate School at the University of Mississippi also provided a summer grant for me to write a portion of the book. Isabel Bayley, the literary trustee of the Porter estate, graciously granted permission to me to quote from unpublished material in the Porter Collection; she also provided some thoughtful commentary when she read a draft of the book. Several Porter scholars, including Ruth Alvarez, Mary Titus, and the late Thomas F. Walsh, were generous in their advice and their responses to my calls for help.

Other people closer to home also deserve my thanks. Chris Brinkmeyer did a splendid job of editing several early versions of chapters. Over numerous lunches, my colleague Jay Watson offered penetrating commentary on my ideas on Porter. Charles Eagles, a historian of southern history, was extremely helpful in providing me with sources for studying the American response to fascism and nazism during the thirties. Debra Rae Cohen edited portions of the book and was always there when I needed her to help work through a problem.

A number of people helped in getting the manuscript in order. My graduate assistant, Joyce Miller, did a great deal of the leg work, tracking down sources, checking citations, and proofreading. From a messy handwritten copy, Sara Selby, then a departmental assistant and now a professor of English at Waycross College, typed the entire manuscript. After Sara left Ole Miss, Kristen Sulser completed work on the manuscript copy, typing in corrections and additions. At Louisiana State University Press, John Easterly, Catherine Landry, and Julie Schorfheide kept a close eye on the manuscript throughout the submission and publication process and were always available when I needed advice and information. My copy editor, Angela Ray, did a professional job cleaning up my prose and putting the manuscript into its final shape.

My thanks to one and all.

# Abbreviations and Short Titles

Abbreviations of works cited in the text refer to the following editions:

BR      *"This Strange, Old World" and Other Book Reviews by Katherine Anne Porter.* Edited by Darlene Harbour Unrue. Athens, Ga., 1991.

C       *Katherine Anne Porter: Conversations.* Edited by Joan Givner. Jackson, Miss., 1987.

CE      *The Collected Essays and Occasional Writings of Katherine Anne Porter.* New York, 1970.

CS      *The Collected Stories of Katherine Anne Porter.* New York, 1965.

L       *Letters of Katherine Anne Porter.* Edited by Isabel Bayley. New York, 1990.

McKeldin    Unpublished material from the Katherine Anne Porter Collection, Special Collections, McKeldin Library, University of Maryland. Porter's letters in the collection are arranged by correspondent. Other materials, such as manuscripts and notes, are arranged in files by title and subject, although a number are listed generically as "Notes."

SF      *Ship of Fools.* Boston, 1962.

KATHERINE ANNE PORTER'S ARTISTIC DEVELOPMENT

# I
## ART AND MEMORY

One of the qualities that Katherine Anne Porter admired most in a writer was a refusal to allow dogmatism, religious or otherwise, to limit the mystery of human existence. She found such a refusal in the life and work of Virginia Woolf, a writer who, said Porter, opened herself up to life's wonder and honestly described what she discovered there. In a review of *The Captain's Death Bed* Porter wrote that Woolf "was full of secular intelligence primed with the profane virtues, with her love not only of the world of all the arts created by the human imagination, but a love of life itself and of daily living, a spirit at once gay and severe, exacting and generous, a born artist and a sober craftsman; and she had no plan whatever for personal salvation; or the personal salvation even of someone else; brought no doctrine; no dogma." Unlike the general run of writers, added Porter, Woolf "lived in the naturalness of her vocation" and "outside of dogmatic belief." This, together with Woolf's belief in the unfathomableness of life's mystery, made her "what the true believers always have called a heretic" (*CE,* 71).

An even greater heretic, in Porter's eyes, was Thomas Hardy, and in her essay "On a Criticism of Thomas Hardy" she vigorously defends—and celebrates—Hardy's independence from society's dogma, particularly that of the Anglican church. In praising Hardy, she calls him both a "Dissenter" and an "Inquirer." Rather than ending his search for truth in chambers of conformity, says Porter, Hardy took a path that "led him out of the tradition of orthodoxy into another tradition of equal antiquity, equal importance, equal seriousness, a body of opinion running parallel throughout history to the body of law in church and state: the great tradition of dissent." Porter goes on, "He went, perhaps not so much by choice as by compulsion of *belief,* with the Inquirers rather than the Believers. His mind, not the greatest, certainly not the most flexible, but a good, candid strong mind, asked simply the oldest, most terrifying questions, and the traditional orthodox answers did not satisfy it" (*CE,* 6).

According to Porter, Hardy's belief that all people possessed a mysterious core of existence where elemental forces of good and evil did battle was the underlying assumption that lay at the heart of his dissent and guided its growth and development. Human nature, to Hardy, was grounded neither in rationality nor in common sense but rather, in Porter's words, in the "deep place in it where the mind does not go, where the blind monsters sleep and wake, war among themselves, and feed upon death" (*CE,* 9). Consequently, Hardy put little faith in the stock answers proposed by church and state for the cure of humanity's ills. Instead, he embraced the overwhelming complexity of our selves and our universe and probed its mysterious depths. For Hardy, even the everyday and the mundane possessed the seeds of mystery, and all life was integrally related. "The human race," Hardy wrote in his notebook as he laid out the plans for one of his novels, "is to be shown as one great net-work or tissue which quivers in every part when one point is shaken, like a spider's web if touched" (*CE,* 8).

Porter's analysis of Woolf and Hardy makes for a perceptive gloss of Porter's own work, for clearly she saw herself writing in the same tradition of inquiry and dissent. "I always used to say that if I were English I would be the Loyal Opposition," Porter told Hank Lopez. "I am always the Loyal Opposition. *I'm the dissenting party, by nature*" (*C,* 122). In her essays and letters, she time and again stressed that the essential traits of the artist, other than natural talent and commitment to mastering technical skills, were independence and the courage to live that independence. The integrity of the artist, indeed, was determined by a commitment to resist the demands of others—publishers, readers, and anyone else who had a use for one's writing—and to answer instead, without compromise, one's own demands. "The thing is not to follow a pattern," Porter said in an interview with Barbara Thompson. "Follow your own pattern of feeling and thought. The thing is, to accept your own life and not try to live someone else's life. Look, the thumbprint is not like any other, and the thumbprint is what you must go by" (C, 86). Underscoring the necessity of the artist's independence, Porter in this interview and elsewhere discussed the dangers for the artist in joining a group or circle, even if on the surface one shared a good deal with the others. "You cannot be an artist and work collectively," she told Thompson. To Roy Newquist she stressed the freedom that marked her career: "I have never been drawn into a group; I cannot join a circle, a crowd, the thing I call a 'huddle'" (C, 86–87, 114).

Freedom was crucial to Porter because she saw her life and art—and indeed the work of all artists—as a quest for truth and understanding in a disordered and chaotic world. As Darlene Unrue has argued in *Truth and Vision in Katherine Anne Porter's Fiction,* this quest can be seen as the controlling impulse of Porter's career, its focus the discovery of the dark interior reaches of one's self and the open acceptance of—rather than the retreat from—whatever one finds there.[1] Self-knowledge was the bedrock of truth for Porter because she believed there were no absolutes, no ultimate answers or systems of order that encompassed the teeming fullness and confusion of life. In her essay on Lawrence's *Lady Chatterly's Lover,* "A Wreath for the Gamekeeper," she refuted Mark Schorer's claim that the modern industrial state had destroyed the harmonies of life and interpersonal dynamics, arguing that "the world itself, as well as the relationship between men and women, has not 'grown into confusion.' We have never had anything else, or anything much better; all human life since recorded time has been a terrible struggle from confusion to confusion to more confusion" (CE, 27). What a person knew for sure about life—and the possible ways that it might be ordered—was found in only what the person brought away from his or her own experiences. Nothing else could be absolutely trusted. "So whatever real permanence we have, we must carry around in our own bosoms. A good safe handy place for it, too, I say," Porter wrote to Caroline Gordon on December 19, 1934, in words that speak both to her life of continuous moves from one home to another and to her sense of establishing

1. Darlene Harbour Unrue, *Truth and Vision in Katherine Anne Porter's Fiction* (Athens, Ga., 1985). See particularly the introduction and Chapter 1.

a personal order (McKeldin). On her own life, in "A House of My Own" she wrote, "There was never permanency of any sort, except the permanency of hope" (*CE,* 175).

Self-knowledge, however, was as Porter knew no simple cure-all for the disorder of human existence. Indeed, the quest for self-understanding, she was well aware, itself finally led to confusion, since in the end it was impossible to know completely the workings of the self. "No one does know the truth, either about himself or about anyone else," Porter wrote in "A Wreath for the Gamekeeper." She continued, "All recorded acts and words are open testimony to our endless efforts to know each other, and our failure to do so" (*CE,* 23). Moreover, the search for self-knowledge was fraught with traps and temptations that led to self-delusion rather than to insight. Far easier than honest probing of the depths of the self was the creation of a flattering self-image that denied the evil that Porter saw lurking in the human heart. In a letter to Malcolm Cowley dated October 13, 1952, Porter wrote that "very few people want the cold facts about anything at all. . . . They prefer to go on believing what they wish, they love their prejudices and myths and legends" (McKeldin). For Porter, good and evil in the human heart were hopelessly intertwined and in collusion. To live one's life as if one were entirely good, without the taint of evil, was to embrace a dangerous self-delusion. Blinded by what Porter would consider an elevated sense of pride, a person could justify his or her every action, even actions that might unjustly bring pain and suffering to others. Characters so deluded abound in Porter's fiction.

Perhaps the most striking testamony to Porter's own resistance to recognizing the dark forces within comes in her essay "St. Augustine and the Bullfight." Here Porter reflects upon what may have been her first experiences as a spectator of bullfights in Mexico.[2] She writes that for a good while she had resisted the urgings of a friend of hers, a man named Shelley, to attend the bullfights. Bullfighting, she acknowledges, called to mind her conflicting feelings about human cruelty to animals, feelings she would just

---

2. Thomas F. Walsh has pointed out the factual errors in the essay and suggests that the work "tells us more about how [Porter] transformed reality than about reality itself." See Walsh, *Katherine Anne Porter and Mexico: The Illusion of Eden* (Austin, Tex., 1992), 199–204.

as soon not face. She preferred quite simply to believe in her humane and civilized distaste for suffering. "All forms of cruelty offend me bitterly," she writes, describing these feelings, "and this repugnance is inborn, absolutely impervious to any arguments, or even insults, at which the red-blooded lovers of blood sports are very expert; they don't admire me at all, any more than I admire them." But such feelings, she knew, were "revoltingly sentimental and, worse than that, confused" (*CE,* 98), and she goes on to describe how as a child she thoroughly enjoyed raising calves as pets, giving no thought to their subsequent fates at the slaughter yards.

Porter eventually gave in to Shelley's entreaties and accompanied him to the ring. She was shocked by what she discovered there: rather than recoiling from the sport, Porter relished it. "I loved the spectacle of the bullfights, I was drunk on it, I was in a strange wild dream from which I did not want to be awakened," she writes. "I was now drawn irresistably to the bullring as before I had been drawn to the race tracks and the polo fields at home. But this had death in it, and it was the death in it that I loved." At first Porter was ashamed of her feelings, thinking that she alone had sunk to the depths of depravity. (The bullfight aficionados, she conjectures, did not know any better; she as civilized person did.) As she reports, she still clung tenaciously to what she characterized as her "flattering view of [her]self as a unique case, as a humane, blood-avoiding civilized being, somehow a fallen angel," but at the same she faced head-on the disturbing question that undermined this view: "How could I face the cold fact that at heart I was just a killer, like any other, that some deep corner of my soul consented not just willingly but with rapture?" (*CE,* 100).

Porter says that she came to grips with her dilemma when she read in Augustine's *Confessions* the episode of a young friend of Augustine's who, after initially resisting attending gladitorial games, enthusiastically embraced them. Porter saw that, far from being unique, her bloodlust was innately human and that while it may have been both hers and the Roman boy's weakness to go to the blood sports, it was also their strength to face up to what they discovered there and not to shrink from it. What for many spectators of blood sports remains merely what Porter characterizes as "adventure" ("something you seek for pleasure, or even for profit, like a gold rush or invading a country; for the illusion of being more alive than ordinarily, the thing you will to occur" [*CE,* 92]) became for her and the Roman boy "experience," that is, an understanding of the truth embodied in one's actions, a truth that comes only with struggle, reflection, and courage. Porter's sentimental views of herself as humane and civilized collapsed before her new knowledge, but as she suggests at the end of "St. Augustine and the Bullfight," she became a stronger and better person, more aware of herself and the world about her. "Of course we are all good and evil," Porter said years later in a panel discussion. "And some of these people," she added, speaking of characters in *Ship of Fools,* "have very great strength and they overcome things and you can see that they're going to live through some terrific trials."[3] These characters gain their strength, as Porter depicted herself doing in "St. Augustine and the Bullfight," from their clear-sighted probing of human complexity and capacity for evil, their own included.

Knowledge of oneself, despite the depth of insight it gives a person, nonetheless cannot provide an overarching structure of order and stability, the type of structure one generally gains through faith in something outside the self. This limitation arises primarily from the very complexity of the self, itself a disorder and confusion of forces and identities that resist clarity and stability. In an interview with Barbara Thompson, Porter pointed out that while the workings of the universe had apparent order (planetary motion, for instance), human life had none. "Human life itself is almost pure chaos," she said. "Everyone takes his stance, asserts his own rights and feelings, mistaking the motives of others and his own. . . . Misunderstanding and separation are the natural conditions of man" (*C,* 97). Porter's words here suggest another difficulty in the unbounded faith in the self as a guiding principle: the complexity of one's motives in self-conception and self-definition. One's turn inward for guidance was never a purely simple and innocent act, and so the perceptions of what one found in the self were always colored by one's preconceptions and prejudices, thus resulting in distortion, unreliability, and instability. Moreover, as Porter knew well, much of what happens to people, and thus what they come to know, results from chance and accident, so that one's ideas of order are in a sense less the

3. E. C. Bufkin, ed., "An *Open Mind* Profile: Katherine Anne Porter Talks with Glenway Wescott and Eric F. Goldman," *Georgia Review,* XLI (1987), 773.

embodiments of universal truth than examples of the very chaos that they seek to transcend.

Despite these difficulties, Porter believed that the search for meaning and order had to be ongoing. It was better to struggle for critical insight than to surrender to life's chaos or to the myths and legends created by others. As literary artist, Porter came to see her fiction as the tool that could provide her both the objectivity and the focus for her own quest for truth. Like many other writers in the twenties, a period when, in the aftermath of the catastrophic destruction of World War I, the idealism of the Western world lay in shambles, Porter apotheosized the literary craft, coming to see writing as perhaps the only way to give human life a meaningful frame. Allen Tate, remembering the twenties in *Mere Literature and the Lost Traveller,* described the milieu of literary modernism: "Like most literary men of the twentieth century I have at times found myself confronted with the dilemma: Religion *or* Literature. This disjunction fifty years ago was widespread, and like most of my contemporaries I went with literature, without trying to think why, because in the nineteen-twenties there was a literary religion that without reflection that many of us drifted into."[4] Tate, of course, did not merely unthinkingly drift into literature—his commitment to literary endeavor was made with thoughtful conviction—and neither did Porter. For Porter, as for Tate, literature was a means to bring if not strict order then at least recognizable coherence to the sprawling mess of existence. Interestingly enough, in a 1942 statement on writing Porter described the situation of the writer in the same terms that Tate later used in *Mere Literature and the Lost Traveller* (and also, as she notes, that E. M. Forster had already used): "I agree with Mr. E. M. Forster that there are only two possibilities for any real order: in art and religion. All political history is a vile mess, varying only in degrees of vileness from one epoch to another, and only the work of saints and artists give us any reason to believe that the human race is worth belonging to" (*CE,* 459). Porter's mention here of religion as a possible structuring principle suggests the significance that religion at times had in her life, a significance, particularly concerning her relationship with Roman Catholicism (a faith to which she was converted

4. Allen Tate, *Mere Literature and the Lost Traveller* (Nashville, 1969), 3.

during her first marriage), that will be discussed in forthcoming chapters. Suffice it to say here, however, that for most of her life Porter dedicated herself to art rather than to religion in her search for understanding and order. As she told Newquist, art, unlike religion, was "strictly of this world" (*C*, 118), the only allegiance demanded by it being the artist's commitment to his or her—and not someone else's—imaginative vision. This emphasis on the concrete and on individual vision Porter generally found much more appealing to her dissenting and inquiring sensibility than rigid theological dogma.

Statements on literature's role in bringing order to life, together with those on the artist's commitment to this purpose, abound in Porter's essays, letters, and interviews, attesting to the centrality of her conception of art and the artist. Order, Porter wrote in some unpublished notes, "is the first law of art." She added that "the real end of art, its real original purpose, (for the beginn[in]g and the end, the starting point and the goal, are the same) is to create order and harmony and form out of [the artist's] share of Universal chaos" (McKeldin). In a letter dated June 2, 1953, to Donald Sutherland she underscored the differences between what she saw as the confusion of life and the coherence of art. "Art does not imitate the shapelessness of life, that is, the shapeless, fragmentary life which most individuals see," she wrote, adding later in the letter: "Life is one bloody, horrible confusion, and the one business of the artist is to know it, admit it, and manifest his vision of order in the human imagination: he simply mustn't be sloppy and he must know what he is doing and he mustn't elevate his weaknesses into dogma" (*CE*, 278). Not merely searching for order but creating it with an individual creative vision was for Porter a life's work, the activity that most enriched the human spirit. Thus, as she wrote in "St. Augustine and the Bullfight," writing fiction was for her "a wholesome exercise to my natural, incurable tendency to try to wangle the sprawling mess of our existence in this bloody world into some kind of shape: almost any shape will do, just so it is recognizably made with human hands, one small proof the more of the validity and reality of the human imagination" (*CE*, 93).

At the end of the letter to Sutherland in which she discussed the artist's quest for order, Porter wrote that she was writing "in a fearful hurry" and so her words were somewhat incomplete. Nonetheless, she told Sutherland, he could take her words as an "expression of a principle of my being" (*CE*, 278). Porter's observation here underscores the extent to which her identity, together with her sense of purpose and fulfillment, was integrally bound up with her art and her conception of the artist. In a 1962 interview on the NBC television show *The Open Mind*, the moderator Eric F. Goldman asked Porter about the meaning and security her literary craft gave her. She responded: "I think it gives all the meaning that I need, and it probably does give meaning to my life because I can't imagine life without it." She added, taking up a point made by Glenway Wescott, who was also being interviewed, that her literary endeavor provided her with the foundation of her ethics—expressed quite simply as "the ethics of doing a good, self-respecting job."[5] Art, she frequently said, was a vocation, not a job but a calling, a means of living. "For the real artist," she said to Barbara Thompson, "it is the most natural thing in the world, not as necessary as air and water, perhaps, but as food and water" (*C*, 86).

As secure as Porter sounds here and elsewhere in defining herself as an artist, it is clear that at the same time she experienced conflicting feelings about her artistic calling. If art was the center of life, it was also a terrible burden, one that she saw drawing her away from the adventures of life that she also desperately sought and cherished. As she wrote in a letter on December 1, 1931, to Eugene Pressly, writing for her was an ascetic enterprise, "requir[ing] a hair shirt and a determined putting away of the things of the world" (McKeldin). Porter was deeply influenced by Flaubert, Joyce, and other modernist writers who made a religion of their art, and her commitment to and sacrifice for art and aesthetics echo theirs. In describing his trials with *Madame Bovary,* Flaubert speaks for many modern writers, including Porter:

> I am leading an austere life, stripped of all external pleasure, and am sustained only by a kind of permanent frenzy, which sometimes makes me weep tears of impotence but never abates. I love my work with a love that is frenzied and perverted, as an ascetic loves the hair shirt that scratches his belly.
>
> Sometimes, when I am empty, when words don't come, when I find

5. Bufkin, ed., "An *Open Mind* Profile," 794.

I haven't written a single sentence after scribbling whole pages, I collapse on my couch and lie there dazed, bogged in a swamp of despair, hating myself and blaming myself for this demented pride that makes me pant after a chimera. A quarter of an hour later, everything has changed; my heart is pounding with joy. . . . There exist even higher emotions of this same kind: those which are devoid of the sensory element. These are superior, in moral beauty, to virtue—so independent are they of any personal factor, of any human implication. Occasionally (at great moments of illumination) I have had glimpses, in the glow of an enthusiasm that made me thrill from head to foot, of such a state of mind, superior to life itself, a state in which fame counts for nothing and even happiness is superfluous. . . . we must (regardless of material things and of mankind, which disavows us) live for our vocation, climb up our ivory tower, and . . . dwell alone with our dreams. At times I have feelings of great despair and emptiness—doubts that taunt me in the midst of my simplest satisfactions. And yet I would not exchange all this for anything, because my conscience tells me that I am fulfilling my duty, obeying a decree of fate—that I am doing what is Good, that I am in the Right.[6]

At the same time that she embraced the asceticism of the modern artist, Porter yearned for a sensuous, nonascetic life, and she thus found herself being pulled in two directions—toward immersion in the fast-paced and hard-living life-style of literary bohemianism and toward the isolation and self-withdrawal of the committed artist.[7]

Porter's obsessive desires may have had much to do with her position as a woman artist in a patriarchal society. Her ascetic conception of the artistic enterprise, from this perspective, may be understood as a distorted

6. Gustave Flaubert to Louise Colet, April 24, 1852, in Flaubert, *The Letters of Gustave Flaubert, 1830–1857,* trans. and ed. Francis Steegmuller (Cambridge, Mass., 1980), 158–59.

7. Porter's struggles can be understood within the larger issue of female identity that Jane Krause DeMouy finds central to Porter's imaginative vision. As DeMouy establishes, to achieve identity women in Porter's fiction must make a basic choice between love (security) and work (independence). See DeMouy, *Katherine Anne Porter's Women: The Eye of Her Fiction* (Austin, Tex., 1983). For a further discussion of Porter's conflicting feelings about the demands of the artistic calling and female identity, see Mary Titus, "The 'Booby Trap' of Love: Artist and Sadist in Katherine Anne Porter's Mexico Fiction," *Journal of Modern Literature,* XVI (1990), 617–34.

version of the selflessness and self-sacrifice demanded of women by the Western patriarchal tradition—distorted because Porter turns the very ascetic practice that has long silenced women and held them in place into an instrument of power for establishing a voice. That Porter could not forever happily embrace such demanding asceticism—she wanted to be simultaneously a literary "saint" and a glamorous lady—embodies the general confusion in self-image that Givner finds in Porter. "Porter was torn between wishing to be an accomplished, independent woman, speaking authoritatively on literature and world events," Givner writes, "and wishing to be a charmingly capricious belle, sought after for her beauty and arousing chivalrous thoughts in every male breast" (C, xiv). Further underscoring Porter's confusion are the women artists Porter looked to for her own identity. Givner observes that while Porter wrote enthusiastically about the work of other women writers (for instance, she composed essays on Virginia Woolf, Willa Cather, and Katherine Mansfield), she did not look to them for models of literary life. Rather she turned for inspiration to, in Givner's words, "the artists of the stage, such as Sarah Bernhardt, Lillie Langtry, and Isadora Duncan, whose combination of talent and beauty earned them a large following of fans and lovers" (C, xiv). If publicly Porter projected the image of the glamorous artist, first as literary bohemian and later as southern belle, an artist whose personal life was as rich as her prose, privately she knew that intense living and intense writing remained for her a binary opposition, an either/or rather than a both/and proposition. No doubt such an opposition, which owed much to the pressures of the dominant male-centered culture, at times had a crippling effect on Porter's creative imagination and her literary output.

In a 1962 interview with Maurice Dolbier, Porter looked back over her life, saying that she had had a good run for her money, "a free field in the things that matter: the will to be an artist and to live as a human being" (C, 77). The *and* in her comment is ambiguous: on the one hand, *and* as a connective suggests that Porter's two desires were successfully integrated into one; on the other, *and* underscores the distinctness of the two desires, suggesting that they stand forever in opposition. Whatever Porter meant here (her interviews, as is well known, are frequently untrustworthy sources of biographical information and must therefore be read cautiously), much external evidence suggests that her career is best understood by the latter interpretation. In a revealing statement repeated several times in letters, Porter spoke of the two places on earth, themselves manifesting her dual desires for immersion in and withdrawal from life, where she would prefer to live: a cosmopolitan city or the deep wilderness. To Leonie Adams, Porter wrote on September 15, 1949: "I always knew there were only two habitable spots on the globe—the greatest world capital you can find or the deepest most inaccessible country. The howling desert, the heart of the jungle, or the middle of your favorite Babylon" (McKeldin). There was no acceptable middle ground between these places, no reconciliation of her two wills. All other places, she said, were suburbs, havens of intolerable middle-class domesticity and mediocrity.

Porter's difficulty in forging a satisfactory personal and artistic life is tellingly portrayed in her own struggles with what might be called domesticity, that is, with her relationships with men and their demands upon her. Although she frequently spoke of the ascetic demands of artistic life ("Now, I am all for human life, and I am all for marriage and children and all that sort of thing, but quite often you can't have that and do what you were supposed to do, too," Porter told Barbara Thompson, speaking of the artistic calling [C, 86]), Porter throughout her life was almost continuously involved with men, as lovers and husbands. (She was married four times.) Psychoanalytically, much could be, and has been, made about Porter's love life. Avoiding this thicket of interpretations, I want to suggest that Porter's numerous relationships demonstrate at their simplest her desire to wring the most from life, to live intensely and fully, in spite of the rigorous demands of the artistic vocation. But Porter's relationships with men almost always ended unhappily, and though there are of course many reasons for these failures, one factor surfaces repeatedly, particularly in her marriages: Porter's refusal to give herself entirely to a relationship for an indefinite length of time. Even when Porter's relationships were going well, her demands for privacy and private space no doubt created a strain. Albert Erskine, whom she was about to marry, certainly must have been taken aback by what Porter wrote to him on February 3, 1938: "All my life, darling, I have failed apparently to grasp the real meaning of marriage, being a firm advocate of separate room and bed; have thought the custom of two persons sleeping together barbarous to the last degree; have felt that to share a room with *anybody,* school mate, fellow voyager, or whatever, was appalling." Although Porter went on to say that her concerns for privacy "don't seem to mean much where we are concerned" and that she was pleased with the huge bed the carpenter was then making in which she assured him she would sleep with him, she also said that she wanted in their house a huge dressing room, adding "I know already, darling, that if we ever quarrelled I couldn't possibly sleep with you, and you probably wouldn't want me to" (McKeldin). In a June 5, 1948, letter to her nephew Paul Porter, Porter characterized her affairs of the heart as belonging to "the Stroke of Lightning (*coup de foudre*) or 'love at first sight and the hell with theories' school." She went on to explain: "In this, one beholds (and the circumstances may be of the most ordinary, the time any hour, the place anywhere, the only fixed rule being that it must happen with absolute suddenness, when one is thinking of something, almost anything else); an Object irrevocably becomes a Subject—in my case, of course, male—which is instantly transfigured with a light of such blinding brilliance all natural attributes disappear and are replaced by those usually associated with archangels at least" (*CE,* 111).

Such transformations naturally never lasted forever, partly because infatuations are destined to fade but also because Porter could abandon only for so long her commitment to art and its ascetic demands. Despite frequently being displaced for a while by the intensity of emotional fervor during her relationships, Porter inevitably experienced a resurfacing of the calling to write, which wreaked predictable havoc upon her personal— and interpersonal—life. Speaking of her former husbands, Porter told Josephine Novak that "they couldn't live with me because I was a writer and, now and then, writing took first place. If I can't work, I'm as good as dead, and sometimes the only way I could write was to go away for a while. Everything I have ever written was written in that way—I had to leave home and disappear for a while, and when I came back I would have quite a lot of husband trouble. They felt neglected. I don't blame them." Porter concluded her reflection: "To be an artist—No marriage was worth giving up what I had. I am so glad I was really strong enough to make those decisions" (*C,* 137).

In confronting this wrenching tension between a desire to immerse herself in life and a need to withdraw from it, Porter came to see literary endeavor as a marshaling of the forces and energies of the consciousness, an attempt to discover and express a vision of wholeness. She agreed whole-heartedly with Thompson's observation in her interview with Porter that "the practice of any kind of art demands a corralling and concentrating of self and its always insufficient energies" (*C,* 94), and in her letters she re-peatedly spoke of her need for such concentration and the life of solitude that fostered it. Writing to Cyrilly Abels on June 18, 1959, she characterized what she saw as the necessary withdrawal from life as "hermitting." She spoke of it as "a getting back to that center where I live." "I've been torn apart for so long," she added, explaining what she hoped to accomplish in her isolation, "but I can re-assemble myself, it[']s been done before!" (McKeldin). In her correspondence and notes, Porter frequently described the difference between loneliness and solitude, stressing that the two should not be confused. "Loneliness," she wrote in some notes on a proposed essay on the subject, "is the changeless condition of human life, and each one of us meets it and comes to terms with it as he may." Solitude, in contrast, "is an occasional necessity, a human situation brought about by the individual being for reasons and purposes of his own, if he is lucky and has an end in view." A person faces up to loneliness; a person emerges whole with soli-tude. Driving home her point, Porter added: "Solitude is the nearest thing to heaven on earth that I shall ever know. . . . [It] is a situation absolutely necessary to all growth, all work—for any work means prolonged periods of blessed solitude, silence, time to recollect" (McKeldin). In these same notes Porter equates solitude with freedom, not merely freedom of thought and expression, but most crucially freedom from people and their demands.

If withdrawal from life embodied a centripetal marshaling of the self, then immersion in life embodied a centrifugal dispersion. Engaging life with intensity, while gratifying a person's emotional and social desires, for Porter nonetheless stood as a threat to undo whatever unity and order the self had structured in its isolation. Porter frequently complained about the lack of focus and the scattering of her energies that seemed to characterize her life. So sharp are many of these complaints that in a number of her letters Porter appears to have lost control of things, gripped by overpower-ing forces and pressures. Her life was so full of distractions, she wrote on

March 17, 1963, to Abels, that it was "no good trying to locate the exact set of steel teeth that are tearing my life to pieces." After spending her mornings trying to get her papers and correspondence in order, she told Abels, "I am too shattered to work in the afternoon, anyway. My mind is just a pulp. . . . I'm never going to be able to live or work anywhere—ever again. There is simply no place for me to go, no end to the awful strain and pull in so many directions I can't even count them anymore" (McKeldin). Here and elsewhere strong verbs—*tear, shatter, pull, scatter,* for example—underscore the struggles in which she saw herself engaged.

The dispersion of the self was for Porter in part owing to the very nature of life itself, its chaos and confusion. To give oneself entirely to life, and particularly during times of social upheaval and unrest, was to become part of the disorder, making the focus necessary for art doubly difficult to achieve. Although Porter certainly relished the energy and excitement of the twenties (much of which she spent in New York City and Mexico, two hotbeds of rebellious spirit), she also was well aware that the nature of the times took its toll on artists and their art. It was, she said in the introduction to the 1940 edition of *Flowering Judas and Other Stories,* "a period of grotesque dislocations in a whole society when the world was heaving in the sickness of millenial change." She added, "We none of us flourished in those times, artists or not, for art, like the human life of which it is the truest voice, thrives best by daylight in a green and growing world" (*CE,* 457), a world, in other words, not in the throes of confusion.

Maintaining the self's integrity amid forces of dispersion was also, Porter knew, a particularly vexing problem for women. Despite her at times conflicting and strained attitudes toward women's issues and feminism, Porter was keenly aware of the patriarchal and cultural forces that herded women into identities less of their own choosing than of the male-dominated society's. One such identity, as identified by Thompson in her interview with Porter, was the helpmate—a woman who is called upon to help others in any number of situations, with the result that her own core identity is scattered in all directions so that it lacks the focus that promotes growth and creativity. "It seems to me that a great deal of the upbringing of women encourages the dispersion of the self in many small bits," Thompson observed. Porter agreed with Thompson's assessment and went on to point out that her own struggles with the role of helpmate had drastically affected her creative output, particularly in the length of time it took her to complete *Ship of Fools:* "You're brought up with the notion of feminine chastity and inaccessibility, yet with the curious idea of feminine availability in all spiritual ways, and in giving service to anyone who demands it. And I suppose that's why it has taken me twenty years to write this novel; it's been interrupted by just anyone who could jimmy his way into my life" (*C,* 95). One of the recurring complaints in Porter's letters is how much she feels put upon by the demands of others—husbands, lovers, friends, admirers, editors, critics—parasites all in Porter's final analysis.

All great literature, I think it is fair to say, arises from tensions and conflicts within the artist's mind, dilemmas that the artist consciously or unconsciously attempts to work out in art. Without these tensions, literature usually remains flat and forced, perhaps a marvel on the surface but empty of passionate feeling at its core. These internal tensions in the artist, however, can become so wrenching as to disable, paralyzing the imagination rather than nourishing it. There can be little doubt that the tension Porter felt between a desire to immerse herself in life and its adventures and a desire to withdraw from chaos into the stability of solitude and artistic creation was at times so severe that it hindered her creativity. The extremity of this conflict is one but not the only reason for Porter's relatively small canon, particularly small for a writer whose career spans close to six decades. And yet if this tension was sometimes debilitating, it was also procreative. Indeed it was, I believe, a crucial element in the development of Porter's mature ideas on the artist and artistic creation, ideas centering on the significance of memory. These ideas in turn led Porter into a renewed interest in the world of her upbringing and of the South, paving the way in the mid- to late twenties for the creation of her most powerful and significant fiction.

Porter's interest in memory's place in self-identity and the literary imagination in large part embodies her efforts to resolve the tension she felt between life and art.[8] If Porter knew that giving herself entirely to life's

8. Several critics have done extensive work on Porter and memory. See particularly Robert H. Brinkmeyer, Jr., "'Endless Remembering': The Artistic Vision of Katherine Anne Porter," *Mississippi Quarterly,* XL (1986–87), 5–19; Edward G. Schwartz, "The Fic-

adventures dispersed the self, thereby discouraging growth and reflection, she also knew that an utter withdrawal from the community into the isolated self could be disastrous for the writer: the artist could be entrapped by a prideful solipsism that limited his or her interest in other people and other views, as well as the ability to understand them. Solitude, she knew, was needed for reflection and creativity, but a life entirely solitary was, as James Ruoff reports her saying, "as enervating as alcohol or drugs." "Any such alienation from society is death," she told Ruoff. "You may live in an attic, and you'll probably have fine company if you do, but first you have to become a human being" (C, 65).

A focus on memory gave Porter the means to celebrate the necessity of solitude and self-reflection without denying the importance of an intense life in the larger world. Porter came to believe that people possess a secret core identity formed and shaped by memories. A person's immediate experiences in the world—that is, returning to her terms from "St. Augustine and the Bullfight," one's adventures—initially had little, if any, bearing on his or her deep self. These occurrences, as she said in a January 5, 1932, letter to Eugene Pressly, "keep the surface of life so horribly and meaninglessly in motion" but do not enter what Porter called "real life" and the "undistracted center" (McKeldin). Only much later, when the consequences and significance of these adventures can be known through the hard work of reflection and comparison—that is, when adventures become experiences—do the events of a person's life profoundly affect his or her inner self. "Surely, we understand very little of what is happening to us at any given moment," Porter told Thompson, speaking of this process of maturation. "But by remembering, comparing, waiting to know the consequences, we can sometimes see what an event really meant, what it was trying to teach us" (C, 88). Thus, while writers must work most crucially with their inner lives of meanings and memories and must withdraw into

tions of Memory," *Southwest Review*, XLV (1960), 204–15; Mary Titus, "'Mingled Sweetness and Corruption': Katherine Anne Porter's 'The Fig Tree' and 'The Grave,'" *South Atlantic Review*, LIII (1988), 111–25; Eudora Welty, "The Eye of the Story," *Yale Review*, LV (1966), 265–74; and Ray B. West, Jr., "Katherine Anne Porter and Historic Memory," *Hopkins Review*, VI (Fall, 1952), 16–27.

solitude to do it, they cannot completely ignore their everyday lives in society, for ultimately these events will be shaped into the experiences that make up the self and what it knows. For this reason, writers must not shy from adventures but must embrace them. Only a life enriched in the present can lead to a life that will be more deeply enriched in the future when the significance of events finally is understood.

Besides the effort to resolve this tension between embracing and withdrawing from life, the emergence of memory in Porter's mind as the foundation of self-knowledge and artistic endeavor also demonstrates her dissatisfaction by the mid-twenties with what might best be called the literary priesthood—a central legend of literary modernism based on the belief that order and meaning were possible only in the artifact, with the artist as sanctified creator. One of the distinctive characteristics of the twentieth century's literary priesthood, as Hayden White points out in his essay "The Burden of History," is the underlying assumption of the potential of the historical imagination, and, by extension, of memory, to undermine, if not destroy, a person's efforts both to structure a meaningful life and to create a vital art. White mentions a number of writers, mostly Continental (Gide, Ibsen, Malraux, Sartre, Joyce, Kafka, Lawrence, Woolf, to name several; the only American cited is Edward Albee), who embraced a thoroughgoing antihistoricism that called not for a pious respect for the past (an action they believed led to the repression of sensibility and imagination) but instead for its obliteration (an act that freed the artistic spirit). In White's brief discussion of several writers, a number of specific criticisms of the historical consciousness emerges: that history teaches nothing because it can justify anything (Valéry); that history is merely what a person wills to remember and therefore is, in White's words, "at best a myth, justifying our gamble on a specific future, and at worst a lie, a retrospective rationalization of what we have in fact become through our choices" (Sartre); and that history represses a person's instinctual life, condemning one to a life of pale abstraction under the rule of a false morality (Nietzsche). White sums up his observations by suggesting that most of the writers he discusses would agree with psychologist N. O. Brown's view that history is a dangerous fixation that "alienates the neurotic from the present and commits him to the unconscious quest for the past in the future." For these writers, White continues, "history is not only a substantive burden imposed upon the present by the past in the form of outmoded institutions, ideas, and values, but also *the way of looking at the world* which gives to these outmoded forms their specious authority." [9] Freeing the imagination from the tyranny of the past and of memory thereby emerges as one of the central thrusts of the twentieth-century literary consciousness.

For Katherine Anne Porter in the early twenties, flush with her determination to cut herself off from her Texas upbringing and to side with antitraditionalist, modernist forces (literary and political), such antihistoricism had a strong appeal. Her fiction from this period, to be examined closely in the next chapter, reveals this modernist orientation toward tradition and history. And yet, like a number of southerners with whom Porter came to identify, writers who left their homeland in the twenties and thirties to pursue their careers in the cosmopolitan cities of America and Europe, Porter eventually discovered that strict allegiance to the literary priesthood was not entirely fulfilling. Like these other writers, Porter became disenchanted in large part because of the very disorder of the times that she embraced. Once affirmed as the embodiment writ large of her own rebelliousness, the chaotic times eventually came to be seen as misrule, a force less of procreation than of destruction. For Porter and the writers with whom she aligned herself, many of whom grew up in communities where the transforming forces of the modern industrial state had not toppled the old ways of southern life based on myth and tradition, the order achieved in the literary artifact proved fulfilling only for a while. In his perceptive discussion of Porter in *The Literature of Memory: Writers of the Modern South,* Richard Gray cites a passage from one of Robert Frost's discussions of poetic order to describe what he sees in Porter's fiction: it is, says Gray, using Frost's words, "a momentary stay against confusion." [10] Gray's observation here, used in an overall discussion of Porter's ideal of an open and perceptive consciousness, also suggests the limits Porter saw in the artistic quest: art yielded only momentary, not permanent, stays against confusion.

9. Hayden White, "The Burden of History," in White, *Tropics of Discourse: Essays in Cultural Criticism* (Baltimore, 1978), 27–50, esp. 39 (N. O. Brown quoted on 39).

10. Richard Gray, *The Literature of Memory: Writers of the Modern South* (Baltimore, 1977), 196.

Porter eventually came to believe that the single-minded pursuit of art, encompassing the denial of history and memory and the repudiation of any transcendence outside that gained from the literary artifact, limited the richness and potentiality of life. A central dilemma for Porter now became how to reinvigorate her life, incorporating the richness of her memories and her modernist identity and ideals.

In her essay "Reflections on Willa Cather," Porter observed that in looking back on the twenties she felt it was fortunate that she was already thirty years old when the decade began. With her youth behind her, she said, she had been in a better position than some of the younger writers to make her way through the tumultuous years. "I had had time to grow up," she wrote, "to consider, to look again, to begin finding my way a little through the inordinate clutter and noise of my immediate day, in which very literally everything in the world was being pulled apart, torn up, turned wrong side out and upside down; almost no frontiers left unattacked, governments and currencies falling; even the very sexes seemed to be changing back and forth and multiplying weird, unclassifiable genders. And every day, in the arts, as in schemes of government and organized crime, there was, there had to be, something New" (*CE,* 33–34). Porter's declaration that during this time she sought "to consider, to look again, to begin finding my way," describes her turn away from a faith in the literary religion to a belief in the redeeming powers of memory. Her new interest in her own consciousness of her past, an interest that would be central to her life and art for the rest of her days, initiated within her a profound interest in and reappraisal of her Texas upbringing and what she came to embrace as her southern heritage. By the mid-twenties she was for the first time writing stories set in the South and drawn from the people and experiences of her childhood. These stories stand in marked contrast with her earlier works: of the four stories she completed before 1925 ("María Concepción," "Virgin Violeta," "The Martyr," and "Magic"), three are set in Mexico and one in New Orleans. Also, as Givner points out, all but "The Martyr" have identifiable sources (traditional tales or contemporary stories that Porter had heard) that lay outside Porter's immediate experience.[11]

11. Givner, *Katherine Anne Porter: A Life,* 161–62, 171–72, 197.

Her first draft of "Holiday" (written in 1924, although the final version was not published until 1960) along with the publication of "He" (1927) signaled the new direction of Porter's art and vision, drawing upon memory for inspiration and meaning. Both stories were set in a countryside resembling Texas, the land of Porter's childhood. A number of Porter's best works soon followed, which not only transmuted the writer's own Texas memories but were themselves explorations of the integral relationship between memory and growth. These works include "The Jilting of Granny Weatherall," "Old Mortality," "Pale Horse, Pale Rider," "Noon Wine," and the sequence of stories and sketches "The Old Order." In the early thirties, moreover, Porter began work on a novel that was to follow the exploits of her family from the time of its original landing in America. The work—it remained unfinished, with parts being incorporated into other works—Porter tentatively entitled, significantly enough, "Historical Present." She titled its first section "Legend and Memory." Most of her best works from the thirties until her death—most important, "Flowering Judas," "Hacienda," "The Leaning Tower," and *Ship of Fools*—explore episodes embedded in her memory and depict characters grappling with the past in order to derive understanding of the present.

Porter's exploration of memory places her in the company of a number of other modern southern writers who made similar if less extreme quests. As Lewis P. Simpson has observed, much of modern southern literature bristles with the tension between a perspective derived from memory (an openness to tradition and stability) and one derived from modern experience (a resistance to tradition and stability). To resist the modern forces that were transforming southern society—remaking a community of myth and tradition into one of history and science—many southern writers developed what Simpson calls an "aesthetic of memory." Almost by necessity did southern writers turn to memory to maintain a sense of the transcendent and the mysterious. Modernity's onslaught was that overwhelming. Simpson describes the radical interpretation of history that underlay the modern impulse by saying it "is the looking upon everything—man, nature, place, time, and God—as subject to the dominion of history. Not history as story; on the contrary, of history as an ineluctable process or series of processes, which may be regarded either as teleological or blankly purposeless."

Simpson adds, "In this situation, memory became, not a spiritual heritage, but a 'life's work.'"[12]

It is this turning to memory that most distinguishes writers of the southern literary renascence from the modernist writers discussed by Hayden White in "The Burden of History." If the modernist writers sought to escape what Nietzsche called the "malady of history" through their literary religion, southern writers sought to transform it, to see history not as a process, using Simpson's words, "teleological or blankly purposeless," but as a narrative, as a story that spoke tellingly to people, giving them insight into themselves and underscoring their free will and the meaningfulness of their lives. The modernists celebrated the power of the immediate moment and of the consciousness freed from the historical, arguing that the present moment cannot be experienced in all its fullness if impinged upon by the past and that the consciousness cannot reach its full potential if held in check by values derived from the past. Southern writers, in contrast, believed that the present moment was empty of meaning if not shaped by the past and that unless the consciousness became profoundly historical it floundered directionless, guided more by chance than by purpose. John Peale Bishop, speaking for a number of southern writers, argued for understanding the past in the present, suggesting that the present moment in effect disappears if it is not perceived as being informed by the past. "Without a past," Bishop wrote in "The South and Tradition," "we are not living in the present, but in a vague and rather unsatisfactory future."[13]

By the early thirties Porter had fully developed her own "aesthetic of memory" and had made the exploration of memory the central focus of her thinking and art. Discussions of the significance of memory to the human and the artistic experience now began appearing with regularity in her nonfiction. One of her most telling discussions comes in a journal entry written in Paris in 1936. The key passage begins: "Perhaps in time I shall

12. Lewis P. Simpson, *The Brazen Face of History: Studies in the Literary Consciousness in America* (Baton Rouge, 1980), 240, 241.

13. Friedrich Nietzsche, "On the Uses and Disadvantages of History for Life," in Nietzsche, *Untimely Meditations,* trans. R. J. Hollingdale (Cambridge, Mass., 1983), 120; John Peale Bishop, "The South and Tradition," in Bishop, *The Collected Essays,* ed. Edmund Wilson (New York, 1948), 13.

learn to live more deeply and consistently in that undistracted center of being where the will does not intrude, and the sense of time passing is lost, or has no power over the imagination" (CE, 449). Although these lines do not say so, Porter soon makes it clear that this "undistracted center of being" resides in the wholeness of memory, a realm of mystery and meaning. The entry continues:

> Of the three dimensions of time, only the past is "real" in the absolute sense that it has occurred, the future is only a concept, and the present is that fateful split second in which all action takes place. One of the most disturbing habits of the human mind is the willful and destructive forgetting of whatever in its past does not flatter or confirm its present point of view. I must very often refer far back in time to seek the meaning or explanation of today's smallest event, and I have long since lost the power to be astonished at what I find there. This constant exercise of memory seems to be the chief occupation of my mind, and all my experience seems to be simply memory, with continuity, marginal notes, constant revision and comparison of one thing with another. (CE, 449)

Engaging one's memories was for Porter the means for discovering and creating meaning and thus for initiating growth. Meaning arises only when events are seen in a context derived from the active workings of memory, and this context is never final, since one's memories are continuously being added to by the accumulation of events in one's life and diminished by the willful act of forgetting. For this reason, understanding comes, as Porter says, with the "constant exercise of memory." Thus she comments, "All my experience seems to be simply memory."

To engage one's memory was for Porter not an act of passive recall or a submersion into nostalgia. It was, rather, an engagement with a mysterious and ever-changing realm of meanings we all carry within us, in a real sense an encounter with another and secret self. Walter J. Ong's observation, in an essay on voice and belief in literature, that a person's "own 'I' is haunted by the shadow of a 'thou' which it itself casts and which it can never fully exorcise" seems particularly relevant to Porter: for her this shadowy "thou" is a person's memory, and only by entering into an open and free dialogue with this secret self does a person mature and achieve understanding, both of the self and of the world. To ignore or repress memory is to limit growth and potential, for in doing so people close themselves off from the multiplicity of life's meanings, thereby consolidating their own already established and self-assured understanding of reality, an understanding rooted in the belief that the individual consciousness stands alone, without a secret thou, unified and self-sufficient. Porter, on the other hand, sought what Mikhail Bakhtin calls a dialogic (as opposed to a monologic) relationship with self, a relationship that acknowledges the existence of another self within and actively engages this self in a dialogue where voices freely interact and provoke, but do not impose, new meanings. Such a relationship, writes Bakhtin in *Problems of Dostoevsky's Poetics,* leads to "the discovery of the *inner man*—'one's own self,' accessible not to passive self-observation but only through an *active dialogic approach to one's own self,* destroying that naive wholeness of one's notions about self that lies at the heart of the lyric, epic, and tragic image of man. A dialogic approach to oneself breaks down the shell of one's image, that shell which exists for other people, determining the external assessment of a person (in the eyes of others) and dimming the purity of self-consciousness."[14]

Achieving a dialogic relationship with the inner self—and indeed with the world at large—was for Porter crucial not only for personal fulfillment but also for artistic creation. As we have seen, Porter saw literature on one level as the author's attempt to construct and communicate meaningful ways to understand the chaotic nature of life. "Literary art, at least," she wrote in "St. Augustine and the Bullfight," "is the business of setting human events to rights and giving them meanings that, in fact, they do not possess, or not obviously, or not the meanings the artist feels they should have—we do understand so little of what is really happening to us in any given moment" (*CE,* 94). To overcome limited vision and to know "what is really happening to us," the artist must actively search out his or her memory, listening and responding to the mysteries of the secret self, while at the same time bringing pressure upon those very mysteries, by the insights and knowledge of the artist's present life. Neither the conscious self nor the self

14. Walter J. Ong, "Voice as Summons for Belief," in *Literature and Belief,* ed. M. H. Abrams (New York, 1958), 84; Mikhail Bakhtin, *Problems of Dostoevsky's Poetics,* ed. and trans. Caryl Emerson (Minneapolis, 1984), 120.

of memory should be allowed to become final and unchallengeable. Rather they should be forever engaged in a dialogue that challenges each to respond to the other, a dialogue of ongoing creation and re-creation that never lapses into monologue. Eudora Welty, herself deeply concerned with memory and imagination, wrote of this type of dialogic interplay in *The Optimist's Daughter,* saying that as long as memory is "vulnerable to the living moment"—that is, under constant revision according to a person's present situation—"it lives for us, and while it lives, and while we are able, we can give it up its due."[15]

Porter believed that this dialogue with memory required the artist actively to search out, compare, and re-create events and feelings in ways that, while frequently departing from strict verisimilitude, provoked larger meanings to surface. In " 'Noon Wine': The Sources," Porter described this process, writing that "in this endless remembering which surely must be the main occupation of the writer, events are changed, reshaped, interpreted again and again in different ways" (*CE,* 468) in the pursuit of significance and understanding. The creative act, as she liked to describe it, was a magical confluence of sources, or voices, from the memory: "Now and again thousands of memories converge, harmonize, arrange themselves around a central idea in a coherent form, and I write a story" (*CE,* 449). In "Three Statements about Writing," she writes that in her art "memory, legend, personal experience, and acquired knowledge" come together "in a constant process of re-creation" (*CE,* 451).

Openly exploring one's memories and feelings to reach a true understanding of their significance, Porter knew, was a tortuous and hard-fought task. Much of Porter's mature fiction, from the mid-twenties on, centers on this theme, and many of these works typically depict characters who strive to forget or rationalize unflattering aspects of their selves and their histories. To do so, however, according to Porter, is to spurn the fullness of life in all its mystery, and Porter shows that these characters' repression of memory and their refusal to enter into a dialogue with its voices are the major causes of the emptiness and desolation of their interior lives. Although she rarely admitted it publicly, Porter knew perfectly well that she herself was prone

15. Eudora Welty, *The Optimist's Daughter* (New York, 1972), 179.

to such weakness, that she had a disturbing tendency to repress unpleasant emotions and memories. As Mary Titus has shown, Porter's memories were never essentially nostalgic. Rather, "home and the grave, fulfillment and absence, nurturing and death [were] bound together."[16] She also knew, though again she was loath to admit it, that closing herself off from the disturbing aspects of her memories severely impeded her development as a person and as an artist.

Just as damaging for individual growth and expression as the repression of memories is allowing memory to harden into a final and complete voice that cannot be challenged. Rather than engaging the memory in a dialogue that pressures both memory and self, thereby opening both to larger visions, a person in this situation falls prey to memory, his or her present self silenced before the sacred realm of the past. In his essay "Epic and Novel," Mikhail Bakhtin characterizes this orientation toward the past as "epic," and his words on the world of epic also speak crucially to the potentially dominating world of memory:

> Tradition isolates the world of the epic from personal experience, from any new insights, from any personal initiative in understanding and interpreting, from new points of view and evaluations. The epic world is an utterly finished thing, not only as an authentic event of the distant past but also on its own terms and by its own standards; it is impossible to change, to re-think, to reevaluate anything in it. It is completed, conclusive and immutable, as a fact, an idea and a value. . . . . One can only accept the epic world with reverence; it is impossible to really touch it, for it is beyond the realm of human activity, the realm in which everything humans touch is altered and re-thought.[17]

In this situation the realm of memory is entirely withdrawn from contact with present reality. The most pervasive way of isolating memory in its own completeness is the romanticizing of the past, a fault to which Porter knew

16. Titus, "'Mingled Sweetness and Corruption,'" 117.

17. Mikhail Bakhtin, "Epic and Novel," in Bakhtin, *The Dialogic Imagination: Four Essays,* ed. Michael Holquist, trans. Caryl Emerson and Michael Holquist (Austin, Tex., 1981), 17.

that all people, and particularly southerners, including herself, were given. "The past is inhabited by the demon of romance," she wrote in a review of Sacheverell Sitwell's *The Gothick North: A Study of Medieval Life, Art and Thought,* "and the poet must tread circumspectly in fear of that ominous shade" (*BR,* 91). It is this danger of the romanticized past smothering the creative imagination that Porter perhaps had in mind when she wrote in some notes for a planned essay entitled "Notes on a Decade" that "the past can be a viper" (McKeldin). When the past so overshadows the present, there can be no meaningful dialogue can occur between a person and his or her memory because the world of memory is perceived to contain all meaning and value. The only possible encounter between a person and this valorized past is the measuring of the self and the contemporary world alongside the realm of memory to see how far present reality has fallen from the ideal.

A particular danger for the artist, besides that of romanticizing the past, is the romanticizing of the artistic calling and the quest for order. If Porter in part turned to a literature of memory in reaction against the literary priesthood and the worshiping of the literary artifact, she also knew that a person could just as easily uncritically embrace the pursuit of order through the historical imagination. Porter came to see that while the artist's descent into memory was on the one hand an effort to forge order and understanding, it was on the other a pursuit that ultimately undid, or at least pointed to the undoing of, the very order it had created. Because the artist's engagement with memory was dialogic, it was unfinished and ongoing. The order forged at any particular moment was open to dialogue and challenge in the next, and the failure to maintain a dialogue was for the artist to sink into a dangerous stasis of solipsism and self-aggrandizement. So for Porter, if artistic creation on one level embodied a movement from confusion to order, a move that shaped events into experience, in the end it also represented a move back to disorder, with events again needing to be reshaped into experience. The irony that marks Porter's best work in large part rests on this awareness that artistic endeavor is never complete, that the very forces of memory that construct the work are also those that deconstruct it, challenging the artist to continue the quest for understanding.

# 2
## THE EARLY YEARS IN MEXICO

When Katherine Anne Porter recalled the literary environment of the twenties, she frequently contrasted herself with those American writers who spent a good deal of time in Europe, those literary exiles frequently designated as "the lost generation." In his overview of these writers, Malcolm Cowley in *Exile's Return: A Literary Odyssey of the 1920's* discusses not only their similar artistic visions but also the strikingly similar direction of their lives. "Until they were thirty most of them would follow a geographical pattern of life," writes Cowley, "one that could be suggested briefly by the names of two cities and a state: New York, Paris, Connecticut. After leaving Greenwich Village they would live in Montparnasse (or its suburbs in Normandy and on the Riviera), and some of them would stay there year after year in what promised to be a permanent exile. Others would go back to New York, then settle in a Connecticut farmhouse with their books, a portable typewriter and the best intentions." Cowley stresses that the bohemian life of Greenwich Village during this time, which had a profound impact on the lives and careers of most of these writers, represented not merely a style of life but also a doctrine, a system of ideas that if never formally written down was nonetheless known and embraced by just about everyone. One of these ideas Cowley identifies as "the idea of changing place," or, more specifically, "They do things better in Europe." Cowley explains the rationale behind this idea: "England and Germany have the wisdom of

Old cultures; the Latin peoples have admirably preserved their pagan heritage. By expatriating himself, by living in Paris, Capri or the South of France, the artist can break the puritan shackles, drink, live freely and be wholly creative." Late in *Exile's Return* Cowley notes some of the writers from the period who did not fit precisely into the pattern he saw for the literary decade, three of whom were southerners: William Faulkner, Thomas Wolfe, and Katherine Anne Porter. Porter, he notes (in the only sentence she receives in the book), "was a newspaper woman in the Southwest before she went to Mexico and worked for the revolutionary government; Mexico City was her Paris and Taxco was her South of France." [1]

Cowley's observation on Porter suggests that even if she did not flee to Europe, she was an exile nonetheless, her trips to Mexico demonstrating her desire for expatriation from her homeland. Porter saw the pattern differently. In a letter to Cowley dated March 16, 1965, Porter wrote simply: "I went to Mexico because I was not going into exile, but I was going back to a place I knew and loved" (McKeldin). For Porter, her time in Mexico was less a departure from than a return to her home country, and she mentioned to Cowley her ties to Mexican culture stemming from her Texas upbringing. Nor did Porter like seeing herself as cast among a generation of writers designated as "lost." As she admitted in some notes she made on the twenties, she certainly belonged chronologically with the writers of the lost generation, but that was about it. "But again," she wrote, "as we did not have the Twenties in Mexico, nor professional exiles, so we did not have a lost generation, either. I was never in exile for a day, nor was I ever in the least lost for a moment. I got myself into some very odd corners, and some disconcerting scrapes, and quite often I wondered how in the world I managed to land where I was, and [was] sometimes doubtful as to how I was going to get out again, but I knew where I was, and what I was doing, and I knew why" (McKeldin).

What brought Porter to Mexico, at least initially, was magazine work. In 1920 she accepted a position with a promotional magazine, *Magazine of*

---

1. Malcolm Cowley, *Exile's Return: A Literary Odyssey of the 1920's* (New York, 1951), 6, 61, 291.

*Mexico,* and while in Mexico collecting material she began contributing to other publications as well, including the *Christian Science Monitor* and *Century*.[2] Porter's excursions to Mexico should not be understood as being merely mercenary, however, for she had a strong interest in the country before she went there on assignment. This interest, as we have already noted, in part stemmed from her upbringing, particularly from her proximity to Mexico as a child and the time she spent in San Antonio, a city that, as Porter noted in an outline for an article on her relationship to writers of the twenties, had a large Mexican population, including a number of political exiles (McKeldin).[3] Just as significant, perhaps even more so, were Porter's experiences during her stay in Greenwich Village in 1919 and 1920. During that time Porter got to know a number of Mexican artists who were living in the city, most notably Adolpho Best-Maugard, a painter interested in primitive Mexican design. Recalling her fascination with Best-Maugard's ideas and work, Porter wrote of him in a letter to Monroe Wheeler on July 7, 1965, saying that he had developed "a system of design he had invented himself based on ancient Mexico designs from buried cities, mostly Mayan. Though Aztec and other tribes contributed motifs" (McKeldin). With Best-Maugard, Porter worked for a while on a textbook of his artistic principles and method, and at his invitation she wrote the story for a Mexican ballet that he and Castro Padillo were working on for Anna Pavlova and the Diaghilev ballet. Through her work with Best-Maugard, as Givner notes, Porter learned much about Mexican history and folk culture and also about the revival of interest in primitive art by contemporary Mexican artists.[4] These interests, together with the revolutionary upheavals then reshaping Mexican society (Porter at this time was expressing strong leftist sympathies), primed her creative and intellectual energies, and she was overjoyed when she was offered the opportunity to travel to and write about Mexico.

2. For discussions of Porter's decision to travel to Mexico, see particularly Givner, *Katherine Anne Porter: A Life,* 145–47, Unrue, *Truth and Vision,* 13–18, and Walsh, *Katherine Anne Porter and Mexico,* 4–6.

3. Porter claims in these notes to have made trips to Mexico as a child; however, I have seen nothing to substantiate these claims, which may be more of Porter's mythifying.

4. Givner, *Katherine Anne Porter: A Life,* 146–47.

Porter's experiences in Mexico apparently catalyzed her mature writing career. Before "María Concepción" (1922) and the other stories of Mexico that would follow, Porter had already done a fair amount of writing, but most of it was occasional and/or slight—newspaper articles, several children's stories, and a ghostwritten book, *My Chinese Marriage*. In large part as a response to her Mexican adventures amid revolutionary turmoil and artistic revival, Porter's writing took a new direction, one of greater depth and richness. "I think my first trip to Mexico by myself set me off," she told Roy Newquist, speaking of this change in her writing. "I ran into things, heard things, saw people. One might think my New York experiences would have been the catalyst; but New York never impressed me particularly. I went back to Mexico and began to be really interested in motives and to make stories" (*C,* 107). Crucial to her artistic development, and provided by her Mexican experiences, was what Porter called, in some notes apparently on writers in the twenties, "a point of reference," that is, a foundation of value by which she could judge and measure her feelings and thus come to understand them, herself, and other people from a perspective not centered entirely on the self. Writers of the lost generation were in Porter's eyes indeed lost because they lacked this foundation. In the same notes Porter wrote that these writers "lacked richness because they had cut away from themselve[s] all that traditionally gave meaning to human sorrow, to love, to all experience. They had no point of reference except their own unsupported emotions." So adrift, without the means to understand what happened to them, Porter went on, they "remained strangely inexperienced," their primary emotion self-pity. "How sorry they were for themselves, each one for himself and no one else," Porter wrote. "They had no time for pity or charity to each other" (McKeldin). For Porter, however, herself given to self-pity (an emotion with which she would struggle her entire life), her interest in Mexico, and particularly in the plight of the Indians and in the primitivism that underlay their lives and artistic expression, provided her with the reference point to organize and understand and finally to write about her experiences and values.

The fullest statement Porter made on the influence of her early experiences in Mexico came in a 1923 letter to the editor of *Century,* later published as "Why I Write About Mexico" in her *Collected Essays and Occa-*

*sional Writings.* The letter opens with Porter's simple statement, "I write about Mexico because that is my familiar country," affirming her lifelong ties with the country and her view that her time in Mexico was best understood as a homecoming, a move toward order and stability, rather than as an exile, a move toward freedom and unrestraint. Whatever confusion she felt in her efforts to understand the complex country and the revolutionary turmoil it was undergoing, Porter continued, was cleared up after a conversation with an old Indian woman. (Porter later admitted that the conversation was invented.) Porter writes that she and the woman had just witnessed a street battle between government troops and Maderistas insurgents. As they stood together watching the bodies being collected, the woman spoke, "It is all a great trouble now, but it is for the sake of happiness to come." After the woman crossed herself, Porter asked her, "In heaven?" "No, on earth," the woman replied, her voice full of scorn. "Happiness for men, not for angels!" For Porter, the old woman's answer captured the spirit of the country and what was happening there, and it became for her the center of reference that she used to order her thoughts and observations. Mexico suddenly came into clear focus: "From that day I watched Mexico, and all the apparently unrelated events that grew out of that first struggle never seemed false or alien or aimless to me. A straight, undeviating purpose guided the working of the plan. And it permitted many fine things to grow out of the national soil, only faintly surmised during the last two or three centuries even by the Mexicans themselves. It was as if an old field had been watered, and all the long-buried seeds flourished" (*CE,* 355).

As becomes evident in the rest of the letter, Porter's now-focused perceptions of Mexican folk culture become for her the foundation by which during the early twenties she would construct her understanding of her self and her art. In the next paragraph she asserts her admiration for and identification with what she calls "the renascence of Mexican art," a renascence she describes as "a veritable rebirth, very conscious, very powerful, of a deeply racial and personal art" (*CE,* 355–56). To underscore her affinities with this movement, Porter says that she returned to Mexico to study its art—a statement not altogether true—and that her interest in it derives not from any "artificial influence," by which she means, one gathers, not merely from academic or intellectual curiosity (knowledge for knowledge's sake).

Rather, she goes on, since she is a writer, her interest in Mexican art stems from its imaginative vision, a vision she says she shares. "I recognized it at once," she writes, "as something very natural and acceptable, a feeling for art consanguine with my own, unfolding in a revolution which returned to find its freedoms in profound and honorable sources." As Mexican artists incorporated the wisdom of the folk and the beauty of native arts—aspects of the artists' racial heritage—so too would Porter. Of her own work on Mexico, Porter writes: "I cannot say, 'I gathered material' for it; there was nothing so mechanical as that, but the process of absorption went on almost unconsciously, and my impressions remain not merely as of places visited and people known, but as of a moving experience in my own life that is now a part of me" (*CE*, 356). Through her experiences in Mexico and her writing about it, Porter suggests here, Mexican culture became a crucial aspect of her identity and her creative vision.

In the letter's final paragraph, Porter suggests that what she clearly sees as her Mexican identity has actually been with her all along. She opens the paragraph by returning to the idea with which she began her letter—that Mexico is familiar country—but now she takes the identification even further: Mexico is her native country, or at least one area of it. After distancing herself based on origin not only from mainline American culture but also from the bohemian world of Greenwich Village with her claim that "New York is the most foreign place I know," she describes the many cultures from which she derived: the French-Spanish people of New Orleans, the Cajuns of southwest Louisiana, the German colonists of Texas, the Mexicans of San Antonio. All these people, she says, are every bit as American as members of the predominant white culture, and it is clear that she now casts her lot with them. "Literally speaking, I have never been out of America," she declares, "but my America has been a borderland of strange tongues and commingled races, and if they are not American, I am fearfully mistaken. The artist can do no more than deal with familiar and beloved things, from which he could not, and, above all, would not escape. So I claim that I write of things native to me, that part of America to which I belong by birth and association and temperament, which is as much the province of our native literature as Chicago or New York or San Francisco. All the things I write of I have first known, and they are real to me" (*CE*, 356).

Porter's identification with Mexican culture and her establishment of it as her reference point to structure her values and beliefs might be interpreted as a turning to memory and history for creating order and meaning. And yet, because Porter's interest in Mexico arose primarily from her fascination with the primitivism that she saw underlying Indian culture and native arts, her looking to Mexico embodies in a real sense just the opposite—the obliteration of memory and history. The primitivism that so intrigued Porter celebrated a life-style given to free expression of instinctual desires and deeply felt emotions, with its social structure based more on the cycles of nature than on the linear chronology of history and the constructs of private memory. Primitivism embraced memory, but not memory as we generally think of it—that is, the deliberate recall of specific events that are reworked and reinterpreted from the perspective of a person's present life. Primitive memory was racial, not personal, a memory paradoxically of instincts, and thus of the blood, and of cultural traditions and legends. So powerful was this racial memory that the structures of thought and interpretation derived from personal experience and memory lost value and power. While integrally linked to the past and tradition, primitivism nonetheless erased the past as history because the past was not conceived historically—individuals acting in a specific time and place—but culturally and mythically: community order and belief, timeless and immutable, forever affirmed. Thus, although the Indians, as Porter put it in some of her notes on Mexico, were "irrevocably bound by their very navel cords to the past," they remained, as Porter wrote in other notes, "profoundly ignorant of [their] history, though there is a wide surviving body of legend and tradition" (McKeldin). In *Outline of Mexican Popular Arts and Crafts,* Porter described what she saw as the stability, arising from shared memory and tradition, of primitive Indian culture: "There is no groping for motives, no divided faith: [the Indians] love their past with that uncritical, unquestioning devotion which is beyond logic and above reason. Order and precision they know by heart. Instinctive obedience to the changeless laws of nature, strait fidelity to their own inner sense of fitness mark all they do."[5]

5. Katherine Anne Porter, *Outline of Mexican Popular Arts and Crafts* (Los Angeles, 1922), 39.

Porter's identification with the culture of Mexico, her "familiar country," then, represents a turning away from memory rather than a turning to it, even though she cites her childhood experiences to support her claims. At this point in her career Porter looked for inspiration to the power and beauty of a primitivist vision that dismantles the structures of the intellect and the systems of thought derived from it, particularly those of social and religious order that disrupt native culture and the racial (as opposed to individual) memory that underpins it. Of course, this turning to primitivism created in Porter a good deal of tension and questioning, for she herself was not a primitive (and would not "drop out" to try to live like one) but an educated modern writer. Indeed, underlying all of Porter's nonfiction and fiction from this early period in her writing is a tension, in varying degrees of intensity, between her primitivist sympathies and her modern vision, or between her primitivist point of reference and her resistance to it.

Perhaps the purest statement in her nonfiction of her primitivist ideal as manifested in Indian culture comes in "Children of Xochitl," a typescript of a travel piece, eventually published in a shorter version in the *Christian Science Monitor,* describing life in the village of Xochimilco.[6] The sketch opens with a statement expressing the primitive erasure of history, endorsed by Porter as narrator: "Xochimilco is an Indian village of formidable history, most of which I learned and have happily forgotten." The narrator's focus is on the village's traditional life, not its history, and as she tells us, this life is under threat of being overrun by modernism and Roman Catholicism (whose rituals undermine primitivist faith). For now, however, it stands in fragile equilibrium with the forces that impinge on it. "Spared that fate," the narrator writes, speaking of village life and the threat of its being transformed, "no doubt it will continue as it is for a dozen generations longer."

As described by the narrator, life in Xochimilco is simple and serene, even in work. "Everywhere is a leisurely industry, a primitive cleanliness and rigor," and nowhere to be found are people suffering from the psychological stresses associated with modern urban society. "There are no neu-

6. The discussion here draws from the unpublished typescript, which is located in the Katherine Anne Porter Collection at the McKeldin Library, University of Maryland. The shorter version was published as "Xochimilco," *Christian Science Monitor,* May 31, 1921, p. 10.

rotics among them," the narrator writes of the village women, in words that speak equally as well for the men. "No strained lines of sleeplessness or worry mar their faces. It is their muscles, not their nerves, that give way in old age; when the body can no longer lift and strain and tug and bear, it is worn out, and sits in the sun a while, with the taste of tobacco in the mouth. It counsels and reminisces, and develops skill in tribal witchcraft. And dies. But the nerves did not kill it." People in Xochimilco are close to nature because they work the soil and more generally because they organize their lives around nature's rhythmic cycles. The narrator's words on the village women suggest this naturalness, as does her observation on a boatman she sees: "He lives as a tree lives, rightly a part of the earth."

The simple life of Xochimilco has persevered primarily because of the town's isolation, what the narrator characterizes as "a voluntary detach-ment, not hostile, from the ruling race of their country." But as the presence of the tourists indicates, indeed the presence of Porter herself, whose article on the village in all likelihood only increased outside pressure on the life there, such isolation is far from secure. Although in the words of the nar-rator "there are flat roofed houses in [the village] that have resisted destruc-tion since the days of Cortez," the resistance to time and history by the people themselves may not be so unyielding, and indeed there are sugges-tions that it is not. If, as the narrator notes, the people of Xochimilco "get all material for their needs from the earth," they nonetheless are not eco-nomically isolated, for they conduct a busy trade in vegetables and flowers with the rest of Mexico. This commerce implies a much more complex economic structure than mere subsistence living, a suggestion borne out when the narrator describes a party taking place on canal barges: "There are many types of Mexican youth and age—young school teachers and clerks, stenographers and shop keepers, with a scattering of the more wealthy folk; there is every type of girl from the modern young person in the flannel walking skirt, to the more reactionary type who wears a fluffy dress with a pretty scarf over her shoulders. It is the Mexico of industry and work and sober family virtues, the respectable, comfortably well off people whom we see here for the most part; all of them happy, bent on a day of leisure and recreation in their incomparable playground." In spite of the narrator's enthusiasm for what she sees as the happy mixing of Xochimilco's people, the very fact that a party would be seen as mixing, suggesting stratifications of class and wealth, a perception bolstered by the descriptions of the partygoers' different styles of dress and professions, indicates that Xochimilco's traditional life is under a good deal of pressure, particularly from its youth.

The other major threat to Xochimilco's primitive life is Roman Catholicism, a usurping religion. If village life exists in an uneasy balance with the outside world, so too does the primitive religious life, still alive and rooted in Aztec culture, coexist with Catholicism. Although the Indians are now Catholics, they still look to ancient Aztec gods for guidance and protection, as one of the village elders explains to the narrator. A Catholic church in the village, for instance, is protected not only by four patron saints—the Virgin of Guadalupe, Our Lady of Lourdes, Our Lady of Pity, and Our Lady of Help—but also by the Aztec goddess Reina Xochitl, described by the narrator as "goddess of the earth, of fruit, of abundance, who discovered pulque—especially the strawberry flavored kind!—and also made known the many other uses of the maguey plant, by which the Indians can live almost entirely." As the village elder explains the powers of each patron, the tension between the two religious traditions becomes unmistakable. Pointing with grave formality to each of the Catholic saints, the elder says: "This one gives health after sickness, this one discovers lost things, this one is powerful to intercede for the Poor Souls (in Purgatory)[,] this one helps us bear our sorrows." When asked about Xochitl, however, the elder turns and flings "his arm toward the wide portal, where the smell of the clean open world defied the grey mould of centuries prisoned in damp stones. 'Xochitl sends rain. Xochitl makes the crops grow—the maguey and the maize and the sweet fruits and the pumpkins. Xochitl feeds us!' " He then explains the relationship of Xochitl to the Catholic saints: "She is saint of the body. . . . These are saints of the soul."

The elder's comments, in the context established by the narrator, who is in no way a neutral observer (her comment at one point that the Indians in Xochimilco "have suffered the benefits of Christianity to an unreasonable degree" indicates her bias), provide the most telling critique that Porter at this point in her life leveled at Catholicism: that in its focus on spirit and the afterlife, Catholicism denied the life of the body, compelling the faithful to turn away from nature and the everyday world. As the narrator makes clear in her observation that "the clean open world" associated with Xochitl defies "the grey mould of centuries prisoned in damp stones" of the church, she sees Catholicism as an embodiment of the terrible burden of history, a prison separating those within from the abundance of the natural world and its cycles. The Indians' worship of Xochitl works against the life-denying thrust of Catholicism, keeping the Indians in touch with the body and the world. The balance between the two religious traditions, however, is clearly strained and uneasy.

In Porter's other nonfiction from this early period, the tension between primitive Indian culture and outside threats is even more pronounced, with the folkways of Indian society suffering under progressively greater pressure from forces of change. Nonetheless, Porter still looked to primitivism as her reference point, and in so doing she established a stark binary opposition between primitive and modern cultures that provided her with a framework with which to interpret her experiences and observations. In "The Mexican Trinity" (1921), for instance, Porter as narrator spends the first half of the essay describing the utter confusion of Mexican politics and social disorder and her own difficulties in understanding it all. After criticizing those reporters who visit Mexico for a few weeks and think they are thus experts on the social scene, the narrator describes her own situation: "I have been here for seven months, and for quite six of these I have not been sure of what the excitement is all about. Indeed, I am not yet able to say whether my accumulated impression of Mexico is justly proportioned; or that if I write with profound conviction of what is going on I shall not be making a profoundly comical mistake." What she calls "the true story of a people" is what she seeks, but she is unsure how to go about finding it. The complete true story, she says, is to be found neither in official documents nor in popular discourse. "The life of a great nation," she writes, "is too widely scattered and complex and vast; too many opposing forces are at work, each with its own intensity of self-seeking" (CE, 399–400).

Despite her complaints, the narrator eventually sorts out the confusion of the Mexican revolution, but only when she looks at the fate of the Indians and their culture. By establishing the primitive Indian culture as her focus, as the firm base of reference against which the turmoil of Mexico can be interpreted, the narrator is able to bring order to disorder. Once she understands that the revolution has passed the Indian by, she sees that the social forces driving Mexican society work to enslave the Indian, despite whatever claims to the contrary those behind these forces make. She writes that "leagued against the Indian are four centuries of servitude, the incoming foreigner who will take the last hectare of his land, and his own church that stands with the foreigners" (*CE,* 402). By keeping her focus on what is happening to Indian culture, she now sees that the country is under the control of "the Mexican trinity": land, oil, and the Catholic church. These powers, she ends her essay by saying, "hold this country securely in their grip" (*CE,* 403).

Of the three powers in the Mexican trinity, the Catholic church comes under particularly fierce attack by the narrator. She depicts the Church as a greedy monolith, the protector of its own wealth rather than of the bodies and souls of the people. "If the Church is to have wealth, it needs land," she writes, and she then goes on to describe the political machinations the Church employs both to evade the land reform laws prohibiting Church ownership of land and to convince the peons not to accept the land that under the law is now rightly theirs. The Catholic clergy, she writes, "are pulling their old familiar wires, and all the bedraggled puppets are dancing with a great clatter. The clever ones indulge in skillful moves in the political game, and there are street brawls for the hot-heads." The Church itself is less a spiritual body than a political one, "solidly entrenched as it is in its growing strength, and playing the intricate game of international politics with gusto and skill" (*CE,* 402, 403).

Most striking here is less the nature of the criticisms—they are fairly standard anti-Catholic fare—than the fact that at the time she wrote these words Porter was herself a Catholic. Porter's relationship with the Church, as we shall see, and indeed as we have already seen suggested, was throughout her life troubled and turbulent. Her shifts in attitude toward the Church and her faith stand as significant indicators of the changes that her prevailing ideology of self and world underwent. Porter was converted to Catholicism in 1910 during her marriage to John Henry Koontz, himself a Catholic. Very little is known about Porter's feelings during this time about the Church and her conversion—other than the fact that she apparently greatly admired the priest who instructed and baptized her, Father Thomas Hennessy—because in later life Porter said little about her marriage to Koontz, frequently not even mentioning it in biographical accounts, and also because she characteristically claimed that she was a born Catholic. Despite the absence of firm information, it seems clear that by the time Porter left Koontz in 1915, whatever zeal, if any, she had felt toward the Catholic church had cooled considerably. Her religious enthusiasm would wane further in the years immediately following. By the time she was living in Greenwich Village, as we have already noted, hers was more a religion of the literary artifact than of the Virgin Mary and her Son.[7]

Certainly, then, when Porter went to Mexico in 1920 her Catholic faith was anything but central to her imaginative vision. Moreover, her experiences in Mexico, and particularly her adoption of primitivism as her frame of reference, drastically shaped her perceptions of the Church. From her new "Mexican" perspective, the matter of the Church became less spiritual than social and political. What concerned her now, at least as revealed in her writing, were issues not of individual faith (such as religious doubt and the ethics of one's actions) but of the political implications of Church doctrine and of the institutional power of the clergy and the Church hierarchy. These issues surfaced most tellingly in Porter's depiction of the Church's relationship with Indian culture.

The fullest expression in her nonfiction of the Church's antagonistic role with primitive Indian culture, suggested in "Children of Xochitl" and stated explicitly in "The Mexican Trinity," comes in her sketch "The Fiesta of Guadalupe." Here the tension between the Indians' primitivism and their Catholic faith emerges as the central metaphor for understanding the plight of Indian culture and, more generally, of all Mexico. "The Fiesta of Guadalupe" describes the pilgrimage of Indians to the shrine of Mary Guadalupe, erected where an Indian centuries before had beheld the Virgin, and the fiesta that is celebrated there. Fittingly, at least for Porter, who as narrator maintains a harsh anti-Catholic stance, the shrine stands atop a barren

7. For Porter's views on Father Hennessy, see Givner, *Katherine Anne Porter: A Life*, 100. Walsh has suggested that in all likelihood Porter "had rejected Christian dogma and probably religion itself before coming to Mexico." See Walsh, *Katherine Anne Porter and Mexico*, 18.

hillside, towering over and entirely cut off from the teeming land beneath it (*CE,* 398). The cathedral below the shrine is associated with remoteness, lifelessness, and a cold spirituality, all of which seem to sap the life and color out of all those who enter it. "Great is the power of that faded virgin curving like a new moon in her bright blue cloak, dim and remote and immobile in her frame above the soaring altar columns," the narrator writes (*CE,* 396). For her the power of the Virgin lies not in healing (Mary's image in the shrine is professed by the faithful to have such powers) but in drawing worshipers to her, in moving the strong and mighty to kneel before her as the meek and humble.

The pilgrims, as described by the narrator, are "tired" and "burdened." They are "bowed under their loads of potteries and food and babies and baskets, their clothes dusty and their faces a little streaked with long-borne fatigue" (*CE,* 394). Despite the trials of the pilgrimage—literally the demands of the long journey most have undertaken and more generally the burden of their faith that draws them away from the sustenance of the earth—the Indians still exhibit a wholesomeness that suggests that the restorative powers of their primitive traditional culture still flourish. As the Indians in "Children of Xochitl" interwove their primitivism with their Catholicism, worshiping Xochitl as well as their patron Catholic saints, so here too the Indians bring to the Virgin a faith shaped in part by their primitive heritage. The fiesta that takes place outside the cathedral embodies this heritage. It is a festival driven by what Mikhail Bakhtin calls "the carnivalesque," a joyful celebration of folk culture, particularly in its release from the hierarchies and structures that normally order people's lives. In words that certainly apply to the scene at Guadalupe, Bakhtin in *Rabelais and His World* discusses the tensions between the official ceremonies given by the ruling bodies of church and state and the open festivals celebrated by the people in the marketplace: "As opposed to the official feast, one might say that carnival celebrated temporary liberation from the prevailing truth and from the established order; it marked the suspension of all hierarchical rank, privileges, norms, and prohibitions. Carnival was the true feast of time, the feast of becoming, change, and renewal."[8] Although the fiesta at

8. Mikhail Bakhtin, *Rabelais and His World,* trans. Helene Iswolsky (Bloomington, Ind., 1984), 10.

Guadalupe honors the Virgin and the established Catholic church, its driving force is the carnivalesque, and thus on some deep level the fiesta at the same time celebrates the liberation of the human spirit from the order that the Church imposes.

The clothes of the pilgrims, gaily colored and decorated, represent the vitality of the carnivalesque and stand in striking contrast with the subdued colors of the interior of the cathedral, where the dim light washes everything into paleness. The narrator notes the distinctive costumes that mark each tribe: "Women wearing skirts of one piece of cloth wrapped around their sturdy bodies and women wearing gaily embroidered blouses with very short puffed sleeves. Women wearing their gathered skirts of green and red, with blue *rebosos* wrapped tightly around their shoulders. And men in great hats with peaked crowns, wide flat hats with almost no crown. Blankets, and *serapes,* and thonged sandals. And a strange-appearing group whose men all wore a large square of fiber cloth as a cloak, brought under one arm and knotted on the opposite shoulder exactly in the style depicted in the old drawings of Montezuma" (*CE,* 394). In contrast with the formal ritual inside the church, with "the drone of priests' voices in endless prayers" (*CE,* 396), the street scene outside the cathedral gates is tumultuous and overflowing. "A clutter of babies and dolls and jars and strange-looking people lined the sidewalks," the narrator writes, "intermingled with booths, red curtained and hung with paper streamers" (*CE,* 394). Life in the streets, in the marketplace, is the life of the people—Bakhtin's carnival. At its center is the frenzied dance of religious ecstasy that, as the narrator notes, recalls "the ancient Dionysian rites" and, for both dancer and observer, "links one's imagination, for the moment, with all the lives that have been" (*CE,* 395).

Whatever carnivalesque forces are at work in the joyous celebration of the fiesta are utterly silenced within the sphere of the church, harnessed by the cold reverence of the mass and, perhaps even more strikingly, channeled into what the narrator sees as the false hopes for health and regeneration offered by Christ and Mary Guadalupe at their shrine atop the hill. The Indians let out no joyful songs and do not give themselves to any ecstatic dances in the procession up the hill. Instead they trudge slowly, "in silent groups, pursued by the prayers of the blind and the halt and the lame who have gathered to reap a little share of the blessings being rained upon the children of faith" (*CE,* 397). The scene at the shrine, where the Indians crowd around Mary Guadalupe's image, touching the glass that protects it and hoping for the Virgin's intercession, haunts the narrator. Whereas the dance at the fiesta had celebrated the vital and rejuvenating energy of the body and nature, at least in the Dionysian force underlying it, the ceremony for regeneration at the shrine represents a turning away from the richness of life to the sterility of the heavens. "I see the awful hands of faith," the narrator writes, "the credulous and worn hands of believers; the humble and beseeching hands of the millions and millions who have only the anodyne of credulity. In my dreams I shall see those groping insatiable hands reaching, reaching, reaching, the eyes turned blinded away from the good earth which should fill then, to the vast and empty sky" (*CE,* 397–98).[9] The narrator closes the sketch by saying that the religious feelings of the pilgrims are not hers. What she brings away from her pilgrimage to the shrine of Mary Guadalupe is not a pious adoration for Mary and Jesus, but a haunting vision of the Indians "kneeling in scattered ranks on the flagged floor of their church, fixing their eyes on mystic, speechless things. It is their rugged hands I see, and their wounded hearts that I feel beating under their work-stained clothes like a great volcano under the earth and I think to myself, hopefully, that men do not live in a deathly dream forever" (*CE,* 398).

In these final words the narrator underscores what she sees as the barrenness of Catholicism, a "deathly dream" that stands opposed to the enriching primal forces of life—the wounded hearts of the Indians that nonetheless still beat "like a great volcano under the earth." Here the opposition between Catholicism and primitivism is much more severe and rigid than in the earlier "Children of Xochitl." In that piece Catholicism and primitivism intermingled in an uneasy balance, with the Aztec goddess and the Catholic patron saints worshiped together. Although Xochitl is associated with the world outside the church—the elder looks out the door when he speaks of her—her presence, in the very fact that she is a patron of the church, is felt inside it as well. Despite their Catholic faith, the Indians

9. "The good earth which should fill then" is a correct transcription from *The Collected Essays. Then,* however, seems clearly to be a printer's error for *them.*

remain children of the Aztec goddess, and one surmises that Porter had in mind the type of religious worship she found in Xochimilco when she wrote in some notes on Mexico that "Catholicism and the old Indian faith are so intermingled it is very difficult to say where one begins or leaves off" (McKeldin).

There is little intermingling of Catholicism and the Indian faith in "The Fiesta of Guadalupe," with the boundary separating the two— literally the iron fence surrounding the churchyard—sharp and pronounced. While the festivities of the fiesta are clearly endorsed by Church authorities (the cathedral's bells ring, "sharply, with shocking clamor" [*CE,* 395] as the dancers dance), the celebrations are nonetheless prohibited from church ground and are thus marginalized. The ceremony within the cathedral and the procession to Mary Guadalupe's shrine illustrate the overwhelming power of the Church to contain the carnival forces of folk culture and to promulgate the "deathly dream" of Catholicism. Unlike the Indians in "Children of Xochitl," those in "The Fiesta of Guadalupe" appear to be, particularly in light of the narrator's final observations, less the inheritors of Aztec culture (there is no mention of the ancient Indian gods in the sketch) than the prisoners of the Catholic church.

The rigid opposition between primitivism and Roman Catholicism that structures "The Fiesta of Guadalupe" is precisely that which underlies Porter's two most significant stories from this early period of her writing, "María Concepción" and "Virgin Violeta." In each, a young woman struggles with what Darlene Unrue rightly identifies as the "dark and primitive self." Here the elemental life of the body and of nature is pitted against the confining strictures of Catholicism.[10]

"María Concepción" opens with the tension between the traditional life of the Indians and their Roman Catholic faith existing in a strained but relatively stable balance, much as it was in "Children of Xochitl." The title character, a young, recently married and now pregnant Indian woman, embodies this balance. She is, on the one hand, a devoted Christian who has

10. Unrue, *Truth and Vision,* 13. During this period, Porter also worked on a story, "The Dove of Chapacalco," much of which focused on a decadent priest's victimization of Indians. The story remained unfinished. For a discussion of this story, see Walsh, *Katherine Anne Porter and Mexico,* 50–56.

crawled many times before the shrine at Guadalupe Villa and who spent her own money for the license allowing her marriage to take place inside the church (rather than outside it, where most Indians took their vows since it was less expensive). On the other hand, she is also a woman with a deep instinctual life that teems with the richness of nature. Although the intensity of María Concepción's faith separates her in some ways from the traditional life of the village (she refuses, for instance, the traditional medicinal cures concocted by Lupe, the village's medicine woman), she nevertheless remains an active member of the village and glows with natural splendor. In the story's opening scene, the narrator writes that "her straight back outlined itself strongly under her clean bright blue cotton rebozo. Instinctive serenity softened her black eyes, shaped like almonds, set far apart, and tilted a bit endwise. She walked with the free, natural, guarded ease of the primitive woman carrying an unborn child. The shape of her body was easy, the swelling life was not a distortion, but the right inevitable proportions of a woman" (CS, 3). María Concepción straddles both traditions, giving herself entirely to neither. She is a good Catholic who remains closely tied to nature and an instinctual woman who puts her faith in the otherworldly. On her errand in the opening scene, she walks carefully down the middle of the road, which indicates her balancing two ways of life. She remains close to nature, walking with the grace and demeanor of an earth goddess, but not too close: she specifically avoids the "maguey thorns and the treacherous curved spines of organ cactus" (CS, 3), images in the story of nature's primal power.[11]

María Concepción's balanced life flies apart when her husband, Juan, runs away with his mistress, María Rosa, and when her baby dies shortly after birth. In response to her shattered life, María Concepción forsakes the traditional life of the village and her own instinctual life for that of the Church. Her commitment to Catholicism becomes consuming. The time that she once spent in the village, talking "with the other women as they sat along the curb, nursing their babies and eating fruit, at the end of the market-day," she now spends in church, "lighting candles before the saints,

11. Unrue gives a fine discussion of "María Concepción" and Porter's primitivism in *Truth and Vision*, 16–26.

kneeling with her arms spread in the form of a cross for hours at a time, and receiving holy communion every month." She bitterly spurns offers from the villagers to help her deal with her loss. When Lupe offers her charms for preserving María Concepción's baby after the child's death, María Concepción says to her, "May you rot in hell with your charms." Later when she hears that Lupe has been praying for her, she tells the medicine woman: "Keep your prayers to yourself, Lupe, or offer them for others who need them. I will ask God for what I want in this world" (CS, 9).

In wholeheartedly embracing the ways of the Church, María Concepción turns from the vital forces of her instinctual interior life. She shows no emotion when Juan leaves her or when her baby dies, instead repressing her raging feelings of anger and grief with the power of her Catholic faith. Physically, she is a changed person: whereas once she exhibited a natural grace and liveliness, now she has a sickly pallor. "She was gaunt," the narrator says of her, "as if something were gnawing her away inside, her eyes were sunken, and she would not speak a word if she could help it" (CS, 10). Elsewhere the narrator comments that "her face was so changed and blind-looking" (CS, 9) that had she not been so devout the villagers would have suspected her of being possessed by the devil. "She is mere stone," says Lupe (CS, 9), bluntly suggesting the loss of María Concepción's human feelings and her place among the living.

Outwardly María Concepción may appear stonelike, but inwardly her emotions still rage, repressed by the rigor and resolve of her Catholic worship. When Juan and María Rosa return to the village, however, her emotions burst forth from their constraints. On her way to the market, María Concepción abandons the road to cut across the fields on her own. Before long she realizes that she has not been traveling toward the marketplace but toward María Rosa. In a moment of blinding insight, she gives herself completely to her pent-up emotions:

> At once she came to her senses completely, recognized the thing that troubled her so terribly, was certain of what she wanted. She sat down quietly under a sheltering thorny bush and gave herself over to her long devouring sorrow. The thing which had for so long squeezed her whole body into a tight dumb knot of suffering suddenly broke with shocking

violence. She jerked with the involuntary recoil of one who receives a blow, and the sweat poured from her skin as if the wounds of her whole life were shedding their salt ichor. Drawing her rebozo over her head, she bowed her forehead on her updrawn knees, and sat there in deadly silence and immobility. From time to time she lifted her head where the sweat formed steadily and poured down her face, drenching the front of her chemise, and her mouth had the shape of crying, but there were no tears and no sound. All her being was a dark confused memory of grief burning in her at night, of deadly baffled anger eating at her by day, until her very tongue tasted bitter, and her feet were as heavy as if she were mired in the muddy roads during the time of rains. (*CS,* 13–14)

A woman now of nature rather than of the Church, María Concepción looks not to God for guidance but, as Willene and George Hendrick point out, instead becomes her own goddess, passing judgment on María Rosa and carrying out the sentence.[12] Her shelter now is not the altar but the thorny bush beside which she huddles—an image of nature's spirit and law. To these María Concepción now turns for justice. She seeks restitution in the here and now rather than in the afterlife. With her murder of María Rosa, a sin by Catholic judgment, María Concepción takes the first step in rejoining the traditional Indian community.

She takes the second step when she returns home to Juan. When Juan hears what she has done, he immediately acts to protect her from the inevitable investigation. Although he performs no formal ceremony, Juan's actions resemble just that—a ritual readmitting of María Concepción into the home and married life. María Concepción's first act upon returning is to get down on her knees and to crawl "toward [Juan] as he had seen her crawl many times toward the shrine at Guadalupe Villa" (*CS,* 14). Juan then proceeds with a rite of purification: he cleans the blood off the knife with which she has killed María Rosa and then discards the clothes she was wearing. María Concepción bathes and puts on one of her old dresses, described as "soiled" (*CS,* 15), suggestive of her return to a life closer to the earth. They then finish their ceremony by lighting candles and sharing a meal, eating "from the same dish, after their old habit" (*CS,* 16).

12. Willene Hendrick and George Hendrick, *Katherine Anne Porter* (Rev. ed.; Boston, 1988), 18.

María Concepción's full acceptance back into the larger community comes with her questioning by the gendarmes and the villagers' defense of her. The gendarmes represent a code of justice based on the power of the state, a code alien to that of the traditional community. To the villagers, María Concepción's killing of María Rosa is just retribution for María Rosa's adulterous acts. Instead of disrupting the village's order, the killing reestablishes it, returning María Concepción to her rightful place as wife to Juan. To protect María Concepción from the gendarmes' charges, the villagers crowd "around her, speaking for her, defending her, the forces of life were ranged invincibly with her against the beaten dead. María Rosa had thrown away her share of strength in them, she lay forfeited among them." So protected, María Concepción feels "guarded, surrounded, upborne by her faithful friends," and when she looks into their faces, their eyes return "reassurance, understanding, a secret and mighty sympathy" (*CS,* 20). The gendarmes stand helpless before the villagers and the woman they protect. They leave without arresting María Concepción, even though they are certain that she killed María Rosa.

With the departure of the gendarmes, María Concepción and Juan take María Rosa's baby home to start their new life together, the order of family and community restored. That night María Concepción receives communion not from the Catholic church, whose rituals drew her away from the vital forces of her deepest self and of the traditional community, but from the natural order of earth and sky, of which she is now contentedly a part: "The night, the earth under her, seemed to swell and recede together with a limitless, unhurried, benign breathing. She drooped and closed her eyes, feeling the slow rise and fall within her own body. She did not know what it was, but it eased all through. Even as she was falling asleep, head bowed over the child, she was still aware of a strange wakeful happiness" (*CS,* 21). With this final scene, "María Concepción" celebrates the deep-seated powers of the instinctual self and the traditional community to resist the usurping forces of modern civilization.

The primitivist victory is less clear-cut in "Virgin Violeta." As she had in "María Concepción," Porter here establishes a tension between Catholicism and the innate, primitive self, and she uses this tension to reveal the limits and distortions of Catholic faith. But in this later story, set in a modern, not a traditional, community, the recognition of the primal forces of self and world is more problematic, involving alienation rather than integration. What people do with their primitive urges in a premodern society structured by traditions that openly recognize and indeed celebrate such feelings is one problem; what they do with these emotions in a modern society structured to repress and deny them is quite another. "Is not civilization the agreement, slowly arrived at, to let the abyss alone?" asks Lacy Buchan in Allen Tate's *The Fathers,* speaking of the dark reaches of the human heart.[13] As "Virgin Violeta" suggests, those who break the agreement and embrace these dark forces risk suffering damaging neuroses rather than initiating healthful growth. Crucial to this more problematic situation is the attenuation of the carnivalesque in modern society. No longer a powerful unifying force within the community, as it was in "María Concepción," carnival joy resides in "Virgin Violeta" merely in falsely romantic daydreams of wonder and beauty. These dreams, the story suggests, are as dangerous and illusory as those structuring modern culture.

The character in "Virgin Violeta" who wrestles with the conflicting pulls of the instinctual self and repressive society is a fifteen-year-old convent-educated Indian girl. Violeta's dilemma centers on her confusion about how to handle her quickly developing feelings of love and desires for romance in light of her strict Catholic education. At the convent she learned "modesty, chastity, silence, obedience, with a little French and music and some arithmetic" (*CS,* 23), but such teachings say little about her surging inner life. Violeta thus remains torn and confused "because she could not understand why the things that happen outside of people were so different from what she felt inside of her. Everybody went about doing the same things every day, precisely as if there were nothing else going to happen, ever; and all the time she was certain there was something simply tremendously exciting waiting for her outside the convent" (*CS,* 23–24). Although, as the narrator says, "she had the silence and watchfulness of a young animal," she also lacks, because of her religious education, an openness to the "native wisdom" of her sexuality (*CS,* 20).

13. Allen Tate, *The Fathers,* rev. ed., in Tate, *"The Fathers" and Other Fiction* (Baton Rouge, 1977), 185–86.

Violeta's emerging desires lead her to dream of a future beyond the confines of the convent when she will be strikingly beautiful and free to do as she pleases. Her dreams express carnival élan. Her new life, she imagines, will be "like a festival," an echo of the fiesta that takes place outside the cathedral gates in "The Fiesta of Guadalupe" and of the joy of life that underlies its festivities. "She wanted to wear red poppies in her hair and dance," the narrator writes. "Life would always be very gay, with no one about telling you that almost everything you said and did was wrong. She would be free to read poetry, too, and stories about love, without having to hide them in her copybooks" (CS, 24). Such carnival joy, she knows, has no place within the convent, and so she feels thwarted by the Church, her secret life imprisoned and stunted: "She wanted to stretch her arms up and yawn, not because she was sleepy but because something inside her felt as if it were enclosed in a cage too small for it, and she could not breathe. Like those poor parrots in the markets, stuffed into tiny wicker cages so that they bulged through the withes, gasping and panting, waiting for someone to come and rescue them. Church was a terrible, huge cage, but it seemed too small" (CS, 26). But if the Church confines her inner life, her "carnival" dreams distort it, manipulating the generative forces of the self into unrealistic dreams of unending goodness and happiness.

Despite her romantic longings for a life outside the Church, Violeta has not denounced Church morality and teachings and indeed is still strongly under their sway. She is thus torn by both constraint and longing, with the disturbing interplay reaching a crisis when she sits at home with her sister, Bianca, and Bianca's boyfriend, Carlos. From afar Violeta has for some time been secretly smitten with Carlos, her romantic dreams focused on and driven by his youthful beauty and the romantic poetry he writes. When Violeta sees Carlos flirting with Bianca, strong emotions surge within her. Until now her dreams of love and romance have been untested and unchallenged, generated in the safety and solitude of the convent. Now, however, Violeta must deal with her feelings in the here and now, in the flesh—a far more difficult and complex endeavor. She struggles to control her feelings, turning to her Catholic faith for help. When she imagines voicing her love for Carlos, she blushes all over and breaks out into a sweat. She "begin[s] praying frantically. 'Oh, Mary! Oh, Mary! Queen Mother of mercy!' while deep underneath her words her thoughts were rushing along in a kind of trance: Oh, dear God, that's my secret; that's a secret between You and me. I should die if anybody knew." At another point, her feelings of jealousy of her sister and of desire for Carlos still surging, she thinks of clasping "her hands over her heart tightly, to quell the slow, burning ache. It felt like a little jar filled with flames, which she could not smother down" (CS, 26, 27).

When later Carlos, alone with Violeta, flirts with her, taking her hand and kissing her, thus fulfilling her wildest dreams, Violeta cannot respond. In the place of romance, Violeta sees in Carlos only lust. When she peers up at him, she expects to share a state of warmth and gentleness. Rather, the narrator reports, "she felt suddenly, sharply hurt, as if she had collided with a chair in the dark. His eyes were bright and shallow, almost like the eyes of Pepe, the macaw. His pale, fluffy eyebrows were arched; his mouth smiled tightly." Her shock and discomfort in large part derive from the Church morality that still shapes her perceptions: "A sick thumping began in the pit of her stomach, as it always did when she was called up to explain things to Mother Superior. Something was terribly wrong. Her heart pounded until she seemed about to smother" (CS, 29). Shortly thereafter Violeta breaks into hysteria, the wrenching tensions between her Catholic morality, her now-shattered romantic dreams, and her perception of a threatening dimension to her instinctual life too severe to control.

After her recovery, Violeta is thoroughly changed. She now understands that both her Catholicism and her youthful romanticism are illusory. Her religious faith represses her inner life while her romantic dreams idealize it. She protests against returning to the convent, declaring that there is "nothing to be learned there." Instead of daydreaming happily about Carlos and future romances, as she used to, she now gloomily ponders the nature of life and love, gripped by a disturbing unhappiness "because she could not settle the questions brooding in her mind" (CS, 32). Whatever structure she had once had for understanding and accepting her feelings has been destroyed by the explosive forces of her inner self: "Everything she could remember in her whole life seemed to have melted together in a confusion and misery that could not be explained because it was all changed and uncertain" (CS, 31).

Despite her disillusionment and unhappiness, Violeta at the end of the story has in some ways made a significant step toward achieving growth and understanding. She has recognized the distortions of her Catholic faith and her sentimental romanticism and has a fuller, if not totally satisfying, understanding of the complexity and depth of her inner life. But unlike María Concepción, whose deep emotional life shatters the structures meant to confine it, Violeta achieves neither reconciliation nor happiness. She lacks an enriching community that accepts rather than denies the threatening forces of the self's abyss, and without this community Violeta lives without the means to channel her destructive elements into fruitful and satisfying endeavor.

"Virgin Violeta" thus points to a growing awareness by Porter of the potential complexities and problems of simply embracing a primitivist vision to comprehend self and world, particularly in modern society. While still using primitivism as a reference point to judge and analyze, Porter at the same time points to its limits. For if the thrust of "Virgin Violeta" is the embracing of a clear vision of the self, there is at the end no obvious celebration of this vision. The forces of the self here appear more harrowing than nourishing and seem in need of some sort of controlling order. After her crisis with Carlos, Violeta lacks this control and thus remains unhappy and unsatisfied. For her to achieve wholeness, the story seems to suggest, she must incorporate the insights of primitivism into a larger vision of things acceptable both to the modern world and to the rational mind.

In Porter's other Mexican story from this period, "The Martyr" (1923), the primitivist ideal is present only in its absence. That is, in this slight story of romantic disillusionment and blindness, characters live shallow and empty lives, denying the blood knowledge of the inner self and never reaching, as María Concepción and Violeta do, an awareness of the distortions by which they live. No one, as a result, lives richly or deeply in this story, and if the primitivist ideal is not explicitly present, it nonetheless looms large as the standard for evaluating the empty lives of those who live without it. Of particular interest here is that "The Martyr" focuses on the plight of an artist and on his failed art and thus on one level expresses Porter's ideas on the artistic imagination and the failings to which it is prone.

The martyr in the story is the artist Rubén, described as "the most illustrious painter in Mexico" (*CS,* 33). As Darlene Unrue has persuasively shown, Rubén is almost certainly based on Diego Rivera, a fact that by itself speaks significantly of the implied primitivism of the story.[14] The most prominent Mexican muralist of his time, Rivera drew upon the power of Mexican folk culture in his attempt to portray Mexico and its revolutionary spirit. But in Porter's story, Rubén is entirely out of touch with his country's folk traditions. His imagination instead wallows in dreams of romantic love. When Isabel, the model with whom he is smitten, leaves him for another artist, Rubén is so overwhelmed that he spends all his time stuffing himself with food and lamenting his lost love. To the dismay of his friends, who knew Isabel as "the lean she-devil," Rubén remains transfixed by his image of her as an unblemished paragon that he cannot do without, despite the fact that, as he says, "she used to kick my shins black and blue" (*CS,* 34). Lost to his romantic dreams, Rubén no longer paints, and eventually he eats himself to death.

Although Catholicism does not stand opposed to the implied primitivist ideal of the story, as it frequently does in Porter's other early work, Rubén's romantic vision nonetheless echoes what Porter elsewhere portrays as the destructiveness of the Catholic faith, and indeed it is described as a type of religious delusion. As Catholicism is "a deathly dream" for the Indians in "The Fiesta of Guadalupe," Rubén's romanticism is likewise deadly for him, literally. Rubén resembles the Indians who travel to the shrine at Guadalupe looking for succor in the image of Mary, "the adored Lady," the worship of whom draws them away from "the good earth which should fill them, to the vast and empty sky" (*CE,* 397, 398). He too looks blindly to an idealized image of a woman, Isabel, his "angelic" being. Inspired by her rather than the life about him, Rubén falls prey to false dreams that draw him away from the here and now and destroy his creativity. He continually grovels before Isabel's image, at least in his mind, much as the Indians literally do before Mary's image at the Guadalupe shrine. His eating binge grotesquely parodies holy communion. As Minrose Gwin remarks, Rubén's eating himself to death portrays a disruption of the natural rhythms

14. Unrue, *Truth and Vision,* 107–15.

of life, similar to the disruption of traditional Indian life wreaked by Catholicism in Porter's other early works on Mexico.[15] His final eating binge stands in sharp contrast with the restoration of natural rhythms in "María Concepción," where after spurning her Catholic faith by murdering María Rosa, María Concepción shares a meal with Juan and feeds Juan's baby, now hers also, with milk just drawn from their goat. Their meal represents communion with nature and traditional life. Rubén's eating is unnatural gluttony that destroys rather than nourishes.

Rubén is not the only person who suffers from a destructive blindness in "The Martyr." Indeed, no one in the Mexican community seems in touch with the forces of life. Everyone appears focused on pursuits of ingratiation, most particularly Rubén's artist friends. Although not as obviously blindly romantic as Rubén, his friends nevertheless wallow as he did in inflated dreams of self-worth and high art. Ramon's proposed biography of Rubén typifies their distorted vision. He makes clear that his biography will canonize Rubén. "Trust me faithfully to preserve for the future every smallest detail in the life and character of this great genius," he says to the café owner after declaring that the café "shall be a shrine for artists." "Each episode," he continues, "has its own sacred, its precious and peculiar interest" (*CS,* 38). Ramon's and his friends' worship of Rubén will be as false and destructive as Rubén's worship of Isabel, grounded in empty dreams rather than in reality. Appropriately and ironically, Rubén thus emerges as a fitting image of his followers' reverence: his false romanticism will be idealized every bit as falsely by theirs.

With no characters fulfilled or whole, "The Martyr" emerges as a bleak portrait of modern Mexico, particularly of its artistic community. Porter's criticism of the artists derives from a primitivist perspective: Rubén and his friends have cut themselves off not only from Mexican folk culture but also, even more destructively, from the blood knowledge of the primitive self. One senses here and in "Virgin Violeta," both of which are set in modern rather than in traditional Mexico, less a concern for Mexican folkways themselves—the traditional life as seen in "María Concepción" and "Chil-

15. Minrose Gwin, "Mentioning the Tamales: Food and Drink in Katherine Anne Porter's *Flowering Judas and Other Stories,*" *Mississippi Quarterly,* XXXVIII (1984–85), 50–51.

dren of Xochitl"—than for the knowledge of self and world that a primitivist vision represents. A central problem emerges: How does a person break through the constraints of modern society that inhibit an honest recognition of self, particularly of its dark and unflattering aspects, and integrate into his or her life the nourishing forces of nature and self without simply abandoning modern identity and embracing primitivism?

In this early period of Porter's career, then, her imaginative vision underwent a significant shift. Her initial enthusiastic celebration of primitive Indian culture, using the rich, instinctual life of the Indians as a reference point to order her thoughts and perspective, gave way to a more searching, cautious appraisal, particularly of primitive culture's relevance to those who live in modern society. Porter's interest in primitivism became less cultural, less focused on the structures and expressions of primitive society, and more psychological, exploring the depths of internal life, the emotions and needs that shape our lives no matter what restraints we try to impose on them.

Evidence of Porter's skepticism about primitive culture's relevance to the modern experience can be found even in the very early work from this period, where occasional details end up working against the overall thrust of the work's otherwise enthusiastic portrayals of the Indians' primitive ways. In "Children of Xochitl," for instance, the narrator praises one of the Indian women for her serenity and inner repose, describing her appearance this way: "There is a trance like quality in her motions, an unconsciousness in her sharpened profile, as if she never awakened from the prenatal dream" (McKeldin). Whatever repose the woman possesses, these words suggest, comes at a dear cost, at least by the standards of modern civilization. Her life is entirely instinctual, devoid of the intellect. Even the title "Children of Xochitl" implies this ambivalence: on the one hand the Indians are celebrated for their continued ties with Aztec culture, while on the other they are depicted as merely children, immature and naïve. Struggling to be a modern artist, Porter knew perfectly well that living as a child was not conducive to creating great art or developing intellectual maturity. Porter said as much in a surviving fragment from one of her early letters, apparently written in 1921, in which she attacked those people who unthinkingly embraced primitivist ideals. "I am simply not a palpitating savage," Porter wrote, arguing that her zest for life did not make her one, "and I think it would be rather snobbish to pretend to be one simply because that is a fashionable attitude, especially as I pretend so badly. . . . Really my emotions are rather lyric than otherwise, and I do love the mind quite as much as I do the emotions. . . . I know the fad of the moment is to pretend one doesn't think, but I do think, and like it" (McKeldin).

Porter's attitude toward primitivism was thus ambivalent and complex, even in her work that apparently suggested otherwise. With its emphasis on traditional Indian culture, primitivism gave Porter an initial reference point for structuring her thinking and her art, but eventually that foundation, under pressure from her increasing skepticism, gave way to what one might call a primitivism of the self, the mysterious realm of our inner life. Eventually this turn inward, as we shall see, led Porter to explore the realm of memory, a realm encompassing both instinctual, and thus primitive, desires and intellectual constructs of order and meaning.

# 3

# A RETURN VISIT TO MEXICO

In her 1926 review of *The Plumed Serpent,* "Quetzalcoatl," Katherine Anne Porter judged the novel as evidence for what she saw as Lawrence's failed quest both to understand the primitive mysteries of Indian life and to invigorate his own life with these mysteries. Porter wrote, "It seems only incidentally a novel, in spite of the perfection of its form; it is a record of a pilgrimage that was, that must have been, a devastating experience." Porter went on to describe Lawrence's pilgrimage, writing that he "went to Mexico in the hope of finding there, among alien people and their mysterious cult, what he had failed to find in his own race or within himself: a center and a meaning to life. He went to the Indians with the hope of clinching once for all his argument that blood-nodality is the source of communion between man and man, and between man and the implacable gods. He desired to share this nodality, to wring from it the secret of the 'second strength' which gives magic powers to a man." Lawrence failed in his efforts, Porter argued, because he was too much a man of modern society. Citing an observation made by Kate Leslie, a character in the novel, that the psychological distance between the Indians and the whites "left a wide space of neutral territory" (*CE,* 421), Porter said that it was precisely this neutral territory that Lawrence could never cross, despite the tenacity of his will and the richness of his poetic imagination. He turned away from modern society and its neuroses and looked instead to Indian ways for his soul's sustenance. Porter cites Kate's cry as an expression of Lawrence's own quest: "'Give me the mystery and let the world live again for me,' Kate cried in her own soul. 'And deliver me from man's automatism'" (*CE*, 422). Lawrence could not see that the despairs and problems of modern people were also his own. Lawrence, Porter said, could not "touch the darkly burning Indian mystery" because "he is too involved in preconceptions and simple human prejudice. His artificial Western mysticism came in collision with the truly occult mind of the Indian, and he suffered an extraordinary shock." For all his efforts to achieve an enriching communion with the Indians, Lawrence in the end "remains a stranger gazing at a mystery he cannot share, but still hopes to ravish, and his fancy dilates it to monstrous proportions" (*CE*, 422).

Porter's interpretation of *The Plumed Serpent* and Lawrence's feelings toward Mexico can also be read as a striking evaluation by Porter of her own interest in and involvement with Mexico. Although her quest to understand and draw from Mexican folk culture may not have been as consciously conceived or endowed with as much as mystical import as Lawrence's, nonetheless, like Lawrence, she looked to the primitivism of the Indians as a means to shape her understanding of the world. Her critique of Lawrence's failure to cross the "neutral territory" separating him from the Indians is, by this reading, also a statement of her own failure to do so. Despite her continued interest in Mexican folk culture as an expression of life's depths and mysteries, as a counterforce to the abstractions and mystifications of modernity, Porter focused her analysis on the difficulty, if not the impossibility, facing Lawrence—and by extension all people of modern society—of ever experiencing fully the primitive earth. Like Lawrence, Porter appears to be saying, modern people carry with them too much social and cultural baggage that separates them on a fundamental level from Indian culture. Rather than knowing Indian culture—that is, of crossing the neutral territory separating modern and traditional cultures—moderns merely create their own vision of the Indians to fulfill their own needs. Such manipulation in representing primitive culture is precisely what Marianna Torgovnick finds endemic in the twentieth century's confrontation with premodern societies:

> Those who study or write about the primitive usually begin by defin-
> ing it as different from (usually opposite to) the present. After that, reac-

tions to the present take over. Is the present too materialistic? Primitive life is not—it is a precapitalist utopia in which only use value, never exchange value, prevails. Is the present sexually repressed? Not primitive life—primitives live life whole, without fear of the body. Is the present promiscuous and undiscriminating sexually? Then primitives teach us the inevitable limits and controls placed on sexuality and the proper sub-ordination of sexuality to the needs of child rearing. Does the present see itself as righteously Christian? Then primitives become heathens, mired in false beliefs. Does the present include vigorous business expansion? Then primitives cease to be thought of as human and become a resource for industry, able to work mines and supply natural wealth. In each case, the needs of the present determine the value and nature of the primitive. The primitive does what we ask it to do. Voiceless, it lets us speak for it. It is our ventriloquist's dummy—or so we like to think.[1]

Lawrence's downfall, says Porter, and I think her words speak more generally to the modern experience with primitive culture, is that "he turned soothsayer, and began to interpret by a formula: the result is a fresh myth of the Indian, a deeply emotional conception, but a myth none the less, and a debased one." Lawrence's Indians, she says later in the review, "are merely what the Indians might be if they were all D. H. Lawrences" (CE, 422–23, 425).

"Quetzalcoatl" thus expresses the growing complexity of Porter's attitude toward primitive Mexican culture, an attitude that by the mid-twenties was both celebrating Indian culture and questioning its relevance to the modern experience. Porter's questionings only intensified with time, so that by the late twenties and early thirties, and particularly after her return visit in 1930, her writings on Mexico—letters, reviews, and fiction—reveal her progressive disenchantment with the country and more generally with primitivism and its vitalizing potential. By the early thirties, as revealed in a letter dated November 11, 1931, to Eugene Pressly, Porter had thoroughly revised her perspective on the value of folk culture and art to the modern mind. Whereas she had once seen primitive culture as a reference point—

1. Marianna Torgovnick, *Gone Primitive: Savage Intellects, Modern Lives* (Chicago, 1990), 8–9.

what Clifford Geertz calls a "conceptual center-point around which a comprehensive system of analysis can be built"—she now found such a perspective false, a posture, chicanery.[2] Describing to Pressly a critical survey of modern Mexican art on which she was then working, Porter wrote that the work was to be a "critical re-estimate" and "a firm but I hope gentle remonstrance against the fashionable adoration of peasant and 'primitive' art, which I believe is a sign of debased judgement and pernicious esthetic anemia." After acknowledging that much peasant art possesses beauty and value ("it exists in its own right and some of it has a wonderful quality"), she roundly attacks those artists who attempt to be "primitive," that is, those who draw from and imitate peasant art even though that tradition is alien to the modern mind that first and foremost has shaped the artists' sensibilities. She scornfully dismisses "the easy and indiscriminate hurrah for everything peasant and primitive; the imitation, the attempt to impose as a dogma, the standards, the state of mind, that went into these things." She concludes that "it is impossible and highly undesirable" for modern people to recover the primitive understanding of reality. "To be primitive it is necessary to think and feel that way; all imitation is bad, all attempts to put on a state of mind, a tradition foreign to our souls, is just fakery. . . . This will lead to my protest against the whole present Mexican snobbism and artifical simplicity, from Diego on" (McKeldin).

Porter never published this essay, but in a 1929 review of Anita Brenner's book on Mexican art and artists, *Idols Behind Altars,* she critiqued the Mexican artistic renascence, focusing on, as she later put it in her letter to Pressly, its "snobbism and artificial simplicity." Porter pointed out in this review that none of the Mexican artists who profoundly shaped the direction of the renascence of Indian art were true-blooded Indians. Indeed "the great renascence of Indian art was a movement of mestizos and foreigners," almost all of whom had been educated in Europe and had returned to Mexico "with years of training and experience, saturated with theories and methods, bent on fresh discoveries" (*BR,* 86). Their situation was very close to what Porter saw as D. H. Lawrence's. The artists looked to the Indians

2. Clifford Geertz, "Thick Description: Toward an Interpretive Theory of Culture," in Geertz, *The Interpretation of Cultures* (New York, 1973), 3.

for inspiration and in so doing "adopted habits of thought, and adapted methods of working, and went, in the process, very consciously 'primitive,' imitating the Indian miracle paintings, delving among ruins, searching in the archives, attending Indian fiestas, using the native earths for their colors" (*BR,* 85). And yet they failed to see that their understanding of Indian life and the primitive ways they emulated had less to do with the dynamics of Indian culture than with their own desires as manifested in their theories, and thus their imaginations were never touched deeply by the Indians. Indeed so strong were the intellectual pretensions of the artists— pretensions they incorrectly presumed to have discarded in order to embrace "the darker, profounder current of instinct" (*BR,* 86)—that the Indians were effectively silenced by the very movement that was hailing them. "The non-Indians made the experiments and did the explaining," Porter wrote, noting that in their utter domination of the movement the artists in effect "shouted for [the Indians'] silence at the top of their lungs" (*BR,* 86). Rather than actively engaging the Indians, the artists "talked among themselves, compared findings, defending each his own point of view, and ended, evidently, in confirming one another's discoveries in all essentials" (*BR,* 85). Thus their movement was not a flowering, returning to Porter's observation to Pressly, but instead merely "snobbism and artificial simplicity." In part an attack on the artists' blindness and naïveté, Porter's review also questioned seriously the significance of primitivism itself, suggesting that primitive folk culture may finally have little, if anything, to offer the modern person.

Porter's reoriented perspective on the primitive Mexican culture she had earlier so enthusiastically celebrated drastically altered the shape and thrust of her fiction. As several critics have noted, Porter's stories on Mexico written after 1928 are much darker and forbidding than her earlier work, with Mexico less the place of simple truth and beauty than the battleground of death and destruction.[3] Gone completely are the prelapsarian world of

3. The authoritative work on Porter and Mexico is Walsh, *Katherine Ann Porter and Mexico.* For other discussions, see particularly Drewey Wayne Gunn, *American and British Writers in Mexico, 1556–1973* (Austin, Texas, 1974); Hendrick and Hendrick, *Katherine Anne Porter;* William L. Nance, "Katherine Anne Porter and Mexico," *Southwest Review,* LV (1970), 143–53; Colin Partridge, "My Familiar Country: An Image of Mexico in the Work of Katherine Anne Porter," *Studies in Short Fiction,* VII (1970), 597–614; Titus, "The 'Booby

"Children of Xochitl" and the affirmation of traditional culture found in "María Concepción." Porter's subject also shifts from Mexicans and the tensions within their own culture with which they struggled to expatriates, outsiders to Mexican culture, and their attempts to "know" the mysteries of Mexico. None of these expatriates succeeds in the quest for understanding, a fact that suggests both Porter's awareness of the difficulties involved in such endeavor (one's perceptions being shaped by one's desires and preconceptions) and her disenchantment with the relevance of traditional Mexican culture to the modern experience.

Perhaps the most damning portrait of Mexico comes in "Hacienda" (1932, revised in 1934), a story Porter wrote after her 1931 visit to Hacienda Tetlapayac, where she witnessed Sergei Eisenstein filming *Que Viva Mexico!* Whereas in the early twenties Porter had depicted Catholicism as "a deathly dream," standing opposed to the nourishing forces of the land and Mexican folk culture, she now portrayed Mexico itself as a life-sapping illusion. One of the titles Porter considered for the story was, appropriately enough, "False Hopes."[4] Late in the story, the narrator refuses an offer to stay an extra day at the hacienda, admitting her difficulty in merely enduring the "wait for tomorrow in this deathly air" (*CS,* 170). This oppressive atmosphere of sickness rather than of health, the story makes clear, encloses not merely the hacienda but all of Mexico.

The opening scene on the train points to a significant reason for Mexico's malaise: the failure of the revolution to improve the status and condition of the Indian peasantry. The revolution has wrought changes in name only: the basic class structure and inequities have remained intact. And so, as the narrator informs us, even though the revolutionary government has done away with third-class train fares, there are still three fares: Pullman, first class, and second class. Merely the designations, not the conditions, have changed, suggesting that manipulations of language rather than of reality distinguish postrevolutionary Mexico. "Now that the true revolution

Trap' of Love," 617–34; Unrue, *Truth and Vision;* Thomas F. Walsh, "The Making of 'Flowering Judas,'" *Journal of Modern Literature,* XII (1985), 109–30; and Walsh, "Xochitl: Katherine Anne Porter's Changing Goddess," *American Literature,* LII (1980), 183–93.

4. Walsh, "Xochitl," 189.

of blessed memory has come and gone in Mexico," the narrator writes, "the names of many things are changed, nearly always with the view to an appearance of heightened well-being for all creatures" (CS, 135).

The revolution has also failed to transform the political situation. Once again the changes are in name only. The names of rulers are different but not the despotism. Revolutionists, like Velarde, now wield great power, but it is clear they act less from revolutionary fervor than from the desire for personal wealth and influence. Described as "the most powerful and successful revolutionist in Mexico" (CS, 156), Velarde possesses an impressive list of holdings, his power and sway stretching into just about every sector of Mexican life, allowing him to manipulate prices, the courts, even the president of the republic. The narrator writes:

> He owned two pulque haciendas which had fallen to his share when the great repartition of land had taken place. He operated also the largest dairy farm in the country, furnishing milk and butter and cheese to every charitable institution, orphans' home, insane asylum, reform school and workhouse in the country and getting just twice the prices for them that any other dairy farm would have asked. He also owned a great aquacate hacienda; he controlled the army; he controlled a powerful bank; the president of the Republic made no appointments to any office without his advice. He fought counter-revolution and political corruption, daily upon the front pages of twenty newspapers he had bought for that very purpose. He employed thousands of peons. (CS, 156)

Powerless, as always, stand the Indians, treated as little more than beasts of burden by those above them. "They are animals. Nothing means anything to them," doña Julia says at one point. At another, speaking of her hacienda, she observes: "It is hopeless to try keeping the place up. The Indians destroy everything with neglect" (CS, 169, 152).

Even though the revolution has not changed the basic structure of Mexican society, within that structure a breakdown of sorts of the traditional order has occurred. Andreyev's comment that "everything is pretty mixed up, and it's going to be worse" (CS, 146) speaks not only to the disorder of the film company but also to that of the hacienda and more generally to that of Mexico. At the hacienda, for instance, traditional family bonds have broken, wreaking havoc and disenchantment. Don Genaro takes a mistress, only to find, after being discovered by his wife, doña Julia, that doña Julia is having a liaison with the same woman. Even more dramatic, Justino shoots his sister, Rosalita, under mysterious circumstances, perhaps because of an incestuous relationship. On a larger scale, the everyday political life of the nation is in utter disarray. Before the film crew arrives from California every sort of wild rumor precedes them: they are supported by the government; they are underwritten by antigovernment forces; Uspensky is a Communist agent; Uspensky is a German spy. With no control of the situation, "the government officials themselves did not seem to know what was going on. They took all sides at once" (CS, 145). One group of officials arrests the movie crew upon their arrival, while another promptly lets them go with profuse apologies.

The traditional life of Mexico, both that of the aristocracy and that of the folk, possesses no vitalizing force to stem the chaos. At one extreme stands don Genaro's grandfather, characterized as a "gentleman of the very oldest school" (CS, 153), whose rigid outlook falters powerlessly before the energy of those coming after him, most particularly don Genaro and doña Julia. Once the head of a patriarchal community and the arbiter of taste and fashion, the grandfather now wields no influence and lives in self-imposed exile in one corner of the hacienda. "He did not understand the boy and he did not waste time trying," the narrator writes, speaking of the grandfather's relationship with don Genaro. "He had moved his furniture and his keepsakes and his person away, to the very farthest patio in the old garden, above the terraces to the south, where he lived in bleak dignity and loneliness, without hope and without philosophy, perhaps contemptuous of both, joining his family only at mealtimes" (CS, 153).

Likewise, at the other extreme, traditional Indian culture is powerless before the confusion of modernism. Absent here is the vital folk culture that Porter celebrated in her earlier Mexican writings, as is the pastoral structure that set the chaotic life of modernity in dynamic opposition to the simpler life of the countryside. Rather than standing against modernity, traditional folk culture has fallen victim to it, incorporated into the all-encompassing malaise that enshrouds Mexico. As Thomas F. Walsh has shown, the goddess Xochitl, the embodiment of the nourishing forces of folk traditions in

"Children of Xochitl," has become in "Hacienda" a goddess of destruction and death.[5] The wisdom of Indian culture no longer speaks vitally: even though the mural in the hacienda's distillery relates the legend of Xochitl, its state of disrepair suggests that the Mexican folk no longer worship the goddess as a great provider. "The walls were covered with a faded fresco relating the legend of pulque," the narrator writes, "how a young Indian girl discovered this divine liquor, and brought it to the emperor, who rewarded her well; and after her death she became a half-goddess. An old legend: maybe the oldest: something to do with man's confused veneration for, and tenor of, the fertility of women and vegetation" (CS, 165). To the narrator, Xochitl's story is merely anthropological trivia, another version of a fertility legend. Her response, although that of an outsider, in all likelihood also indicates the trivialization of Aztec myth by educated Mexicans, the transformation of a living faith into a textbook entry.

Also undergoing profound transformation is the drink of Xochitl, pulque, once the divine liquor of legend but in modern Mexico merely a rancid intoxicant. The smell of the drink pervades the hacienda's grounds, and when the narrator visits the vat room she is almost overwhelmed by the odor, which "rose in a thick vapor through the heavy drone of flies, sour, stale, like rotting milk and blood" (CS, 161). Later the narrator comes to see the drink as a fitting image for the deathlike malaise that grips Mexico, particularly Indian culture, and its production and distribution as the embodiment of the corrupt political and economic system that controls all endeavor. "The white flood of pulque flowed without pause," she writes. "All over Mexico the Indians would drink the corpse-white liquor, swallow forgetfulness and ease by the riverful, and the money would flow silver-white into the government treasury; don Genaro and his fellow-hacendados would fret and curse, the Agrarians would raid, and ambitious politicians in the capital would be stealing right and left enough to buy such haciendas for themselves. It was all arranged" (CS, 168). Noteworthy here is the forgetfulness of the Indians. Whereas Porter in the early twenties had described Indians as "forgetting" personal memory and embracing primitive racial memory, here the Indians are shown forgetting both realms, out of

5. *Ibid.*, 183–93.

touch with themselves and their traditional culture. Despite the ugliness of her prejudice, doña Julia is probably close to the truth when she observes that Justino will be essentially the same man despite his killing of his sister, given the plight of the Indians. "He will forget everything, the minute it is over . . . his sister, everything," she says (CS, 169).

In an effort to deny the deathly atmosphere that enfolds the country, Mexican authorities do their best to put forth a wondrous description of their homeland, both to justify the revolution and to promote the romantic mystery associated with Mexican culture—the type of mystery that has long attracted artists and other seekers to the countryside. The government authorities see Uspensky's film as perfect for this promotion, and so they make sure that the movie depicts Mexico as they want it seen. The narrator describes their efforts at assisting the film crew, evidence, Andreyev naïvely believes, of their devotion to art:

> They wanted to improve this opportunity to film a glorious history of Mexico, her wrongs and sufferings and her final triumph through the latest revolution; and the Russians found themselves surrounded and insulated from their material by the entire staff of professional propagandists, which had been put at their disposal for the duration of their visit. Dozens of helpful observers, art experts, photographers, literary talents, and travel guides swarmed about them to lead them aright, and to show them all the most beautiful, significant, and characteristic things in the national life and soul; if by chance anything not beautiful got in the way of the camera, there was a very instructed and sharp-eyed committee of censors whose duty it was to see that the scandal went no further than the cutting room. (CS, 146)

Lost in the cutting room is of course a view of Mexico based on actual conditions instead of on the rhetoric of the revolution and the legend of primitive culture embraced by civilized outsiders.

Although several members of the film crew have rather cynical views on the state of affairs in Mexico and the idealization of the Indian, the movie they make will be every bit as romantic as the vision of the Mexican censors. The film will show that the suffering of the Indians—suffering the film crew witnesses in real life every day—has been, in Andreyev's words, "swept away by the revolution" (*CS,* 145), existing now merely in memories of prerevolutionary days. Clearly this cinematic version of Mexican history imposes a rigid interpretative structure that not only distorts but also overlooks much of Mexican life. Echoing Porter's criticism of Lawrence, one could say that the Russians' vision of Mexico is merely what the country might be if it were peopled by the revolutionary proletariat they celebrate.

If the foreign visitors fail in understanding Mexico—blinded to its true reality either because, like Kennerly, they reject everything Mexican or because, like Uspensky, they idealize everything—so too do Mexican intellectuals and artists flounder in their efforts to create. Adrift in a world lacking a vitalizing traditional culture, these figures remain uninspired and uninspiring, without an honest commitment to artistic and intellectual endeavor. Betancourt, for example, while not entirely forsaking his Mexican heritage, refuses to confront the tensions arising from his Mexican traditionalism and his modernism, tensions that in the hands of a master might lead to great art. Instead of firing his imagination, these tensions enervate: "Betancourt, Mexican by birth, French-Spanish by blood, French by education, was completely at the mercy of an ideal of elegance and detachment perpetually at war with a kind of Mexican nationalism which afflicted him like an inherited weakness of the nervous system." Part of Betancourt's problem is that his "Mexican nationalism" derives not from faith in traditional Mexican life but from blind idealization of the country. Because of this, he easily resolves whatever tensions arise between his Mexican and modernist loyalties merely by holding fast to an unreal image of Mexico. As the narrator writes, "his ambiguous situation seemed to trouble him not at all," and he enjoys his job of making sure "that nothing hurtful to the national dignity got in the way of the foreign cameras." The limits of Betancourt's narrow vision, dominated by his ideal of elegance, can be seen in his brushing aside all those who do not fit into his imagined Mexican landscape. "Beggars, the poor, the deformed, the old and ugly, trust Betancourt to wave them away," says the narrator. "'I am sorry for everything,' he said, lifting a narrow pontifical hand, waving away vulgar human pity which always threatened, buzzing like a fly at the edges of his mind" (*CS,* 152).

Even more revealing of Betancourt's lack of a vital relationship with his Mexican heritage is his philosophy of Universal Harmony. As the narrator informs us, Betancourt's mysticism derives more from European, American, and oriental thought than from Mexican:

> Betancourt had spent his youth unlocking the stubborn secrets of Universal Harmony by means of numerology, astronomy, astrology, a formula of thought-transference and deep breathing, the practice of will-to-power combined with the latest American theories of personality development; certain complicated magical ceremonies; and a careful choice of doctrines from the several schools of Oriental philosophies which are, from time to time, so successfully introduced into California. From this material he had constructed a Way of Life which could be taught to anyone, and once learned led the initiate quietly and surely toward Success: success without pain, almost without effort except of a pleasurable kind, success accompanied by moral and esthetic beauty, as well as the most desirable material reward. Wealth, naturally, could not be an end in itself: alone, it was not Success. But it was the unobtrusive companion of all true Success. (*CS,* 158–59)

Notably absent from Betancourt's philosophy are any influences from traditional Mexican life. His is a universal dream, not so much for harmony but for success and its rewards, material wealth and power.

The poet and songwriter Carlos is another Mexican adrift. Once the most popular songwriter in Mexico, Carlos has lost his inspiration and, according to Betancourt, "does almost nothing now" (*CS,* 158). A Mexican counterpart of the American artists of the lost generation, Carlos suffers from the same woes that Porter saw plaguing these writers. In some of her notes, cited previously, Porter wrote that those of the lost generation "lacked richness because they had cut away from themselve[s] all that traditionally gave meaning to human sorrow, to love, to all experience. They had no point of reference except their own unsupported emotions." Without a meaningful context and perspective to shed light on their endeavors, the artists remained firmly centered in the self, their dominant emotion self-pity. "How sorry they were for themselves," Porter added, "each one for himself and no one else" (McKeldin). Carlos clearly lacks this larger context and perspective, his songwriting consisting of slight dabblings instead of deeply felt expressions. His song about Justino's killing of his sister, in which he caters to the audience's emotions by manipulating facts, represents his failed art. Carlos himself shows little concern for the death and suffering. He sees the entire incident merely as a welcome break from his monotonous life. The narrator underscores Carlos' insensitivity to any suffering other than his own when she describes him roaring with laughter as three dogs torment a pig in the barnyard.

Whereas Porter discovered inspiration in Mexico during the early twenties, the narrator of "Hacienda" finds nothing in her visit that uplifts or nourishes. She portrays Mexico less as an invigorating contrast to the travails of modern life, providing a means for understanding modernism in light of a meaningful primitivism, than as a descent into the modern malaise itself. Thus at the end of the story she looks forward to leaving, knowing that the life at the hacienda is oppressive and monotonous, its tedium broken only by the occasional excitement of a shooting or some other unexpected intrigue. The narrator comes to see, further, that for both expatriate and native artists and intellectuals, Mexico deceives with dreams of primitivist and revolutionary splendor, dreams that blind rather than inspire, turning people away from the tortuous struggle necessary to discover deep truths of self and existence.

The lure of Mexico, particularly in its legend as a land of primitive naturalness and unrestraint standing opposed to puritanical Western culture, is central to another of Porter's Mexican stories, "That Tree" (1934). Here two American expatriates, a journalist and his wife, Miriam, look to Mexico for succor and fulfillment. They hope that, immersed in what they see as Mexico's freedom, they will find liberation from their repressed and stunted bourgeois lives. Rather than emerging unencumbered and whole, however, both merely succumb to the romance of their naïve desires. While they come to see the falsity of their dreams, they nonetheless continue to strive after them.

For the journalist, Mexico is the appropriate place for fulfilling his dream of becoming a poet, or at least of living the life of a poet. Mexico represents for him an escape from the dreariness of modernity, particularly the middle-class life of getting and spending to which he feels he would be shackled were it not for his artistic dreams. Naïve and romantic, he envisions poetic endeavor merely as the abandoning of everyday responsibilities to give free reign to emotions. There is no real work involved: poetry for the journalist comes freely and easily. "He had really wanted to be a cheerful bum lying under a tree, in a good climate, writing poetry," the narrator reports of the journalist's early efforts at poetry. "He wrote bushel basketsful of poetry and it was all no good and he knew it, even while he was writing it. Knowing his poetry was no good did not take away much from his pleasure in it. He would have enjoyed just that kind of life: no respectability, no responsibility, no money to speak of, wearing worn-out sandals and a becoming, if probably ragged, blue shirt, lying under a tree writing poetry. That was why he had come to Mexico in the first place" (*CS,* 66). Here is another manifestation of an artist of the lost generation wallowing in unanchored emotion. As the narrator makes clear, the journalist's aspirations have as much to do with life-style as with poetry. His artistic failure is anything but surprising.

The romance of Mexico also entices Miriam. Like the journalist, she envisions Mexico as a haven from the puritanical constraints of modern American society. During the three years before she went to Mexico, she wrote to the journalist about "how dull and dreadful and commonplace her life was, how sick and tired she was of petty little conversations and amusements, how narrow-minded everybody around her was, how she longed to live in a beautiful dangerous place among interesting people who painted and wrote poetry, and how his letters came into her stuffy little world like a breath of free mountain air, and all that" (*CS,* 73–74). But as quickly becomes evident upon her arrival in Mexico, Miriam has no intention to live out her desires for romance and intrigue. She instead embraces middle-class stability and security, precisely the values from which she professes to be fleeing. The life-style she wants to maintain is embodied in the huge trunk with which she arrives, packed full of linen and silk underwear. It also lies behind the terrified look she gives upon seeing the journalist's home, empty of the stylish furniture and conveniences she had expected. By her middle-class vision, Miriam sees in Mexico's primitive conditions not romance but waste and poverty and, even worse, savagery.

Little wonder that the journalist comes to hate Miriam. Her vision of things undermines the world he has constructed around his romantic visions of Mexico and poetic endeavor, forcing him to question his artistic ideals and to confront that part of him that he has attempted to repress. To Miriam there is nothing romantic about artists who wear dirty clothes and have no money. "Why didn't they go to work and make a living?" the journalist characterizes her argument, adding that "it was no good trying to explain to her his Franciscan notions of holy Poverty as being the natural companion for the artist." Miriam argues, over the journalist's objections, that his artist friends have not deliberately chosen poverty ("Nobody but you would be such a fool," she tells him) but are merely biding their time for something better. To the journalist's dismay, he eventually sees that she is right. The journalist admits to his guest that he "lived to see Jaime take up with a rich old woman, and Ricardo decide to turn film actor, and Carlos sitting easy with a government job, painting revolutionary frescoes to order, and I asked myself, Why shouldn't a man survive in any way he can?" (CS, 76). The journalist's question here, an attempt to excuse his friends' actions, indicates both the severity of Miriam's challenge and his resistance to it.

Undermining the journalist's resistance to Miriam is the disturbing emergence of his own middle-class voice that sympathizes with her, the voice he had sought to silence by coming to Mexico. "His old-fashioned respectable middle-class hard-working American ancestry and training rose up in him and fought on Miriam's side," the narrator reports. "He felt he had broken about every bone in him to get away from them and live them down, and here he had been overtaken at last and beaten into resignation that had nothing to do with his mind or heart. It was as if his blood stream had betrayed him." Eventually the journalist gives in to Miriam's, and now his own, challenge: "When it came to a showdown, he hadn't a single argument in favor of his way of life that would hold water. He had been trying to live and think in a way that he hoped would end by making a poet of him, but it hadn't worked" (CS, 77). Despite his anger at Miriam for forcing him to see the truth about himself, he grudgingly admits that her criticism of him, culminating when she walks out on him to return to the United States, saved him from wallowing in his dreams and jarred him into seeking, and achieving, a respectable career as a journalist. His success with journalism is of quite a different order than his earlier attempts with verse: "He had made the kind of success you can clip out of newspapers and paste in a book, you can count it and put it in the bank, you can eat and drink and wear it, you can see it in other people's eyes at tea and dinner parties" (CS, 78).

As the journalist recounts his life story to an unnamed guest at a café, he at first glance appears to be a fitting representative of Porter's vision of the artist as seeker of truth through the exploration of memory. Porter by the thirties saw artistic creation as first and foremost an activity exploring the depths of memory, an activity that she once characterized as "endless remembering" (CE, 468). Despite the fact that the journalist creates his narrative from his memories, he is anything but a mature artist. Rather than actively searching out his memory, bringing the voices of the past into interplay with those of the present so that the perspectives of each shed light on the other and thereby create fuller perspectives for both, the journalist calls forth his memories merely to insert them into a preconceived narrative frame. Nowhere in his story to the guest does the journalist deeply explore his past. Instead he merely constructs what he hopes will be an entertaining story—one with a surprise ending—that will at the same time justify him. Near the end of the story, the journalist prepares to spring the two big surprises: Miriam's letter asking him to let her return and their impending reunification. "He smoothed out the letter he had been turning in his hands and stroked it as if it were a cat," the narrator writes. "He said, 'I've been working up to the climax all this time. You know, good old surprise technique. Now then, get ready'" (CS, 78). Here and in the rest of his story, the journalist manipulates his past for narrative suspense, pigeonholing rather than opening himself up to the insights and challenges of memory. Entertainment for his guest, his story is also flattering self-appraisal, an attempt to structure his life into a pattern of progressive enlightenment and growth that ends with his and Miriam's new life together.

The journalist's efforts to convince himself of his impending fulfilled life, however, in the end collapse. The silence of his guest, now described as the journalist's "shadow opposite," accuses the journalist of what he knew all along but has done his best to deny: that his impending life with Miriam will be as disappointing as it was before, another cycle of hope ending in despair. He says to his guest that he imagines that she thinks he does not know what he is doing this time but adds, "Don't deceive yourself. This time, I know." But of course it is the journalist who deceives himself, as the narrator's comment after his words underscores: "He seemed to be admonishing himself before a mirror" (CS, 79). The journalist has sought to plot his life by a narrative model celebrating growth and fulfillment when actually it is better represented by a cyclic repetition of hopeful dreams and painful frustrations. As the story ends, it is clear that despite the silent rebuke of the guest—embodying the journalist's own deep-seated criticism of the story he tells—the journalist still strives to deny everything that calls into question the fictional shape he has given his life. He thus remains a romantic dreamer, spinning out narratives every bit as false as his earlier verse.

Self-delusion is also central to "Flowering Judas," Porter's finest story set in Mexico. Looking at "Flowering Judas" is an apt way to conclude this chapter, for the story brings together most of the ideas already identified in Porter's writing about Mexico and points to issues and problems Porter explored in her fiction set in the American South, the subject of the following two chapters. The richness and depth of "Flowering Judas" derive from the complexity of its central character, Laura, a young American woman living in Mexico. Although it is not absolutely clear why Laura originally came to Mexico—"Uninvited she has promised herself to this place" is all the narrator says (CS, 93)—it seems apparent that on one level at least her journey represents her desire to free herself from her past. In all likelihood she was drawn to Mexico by preconceived notions of the romance and mystery of the country and its revolution. Laura's present unhappiness derives in part from the shattering of her romantic illusions. Symbolizing her general disillusionment is the revolutionary leader Braggioni, who is fat and cynical rather than, as she had imagined such figures to be, "lean, animated by heroic faith, [and] a vessel of abstract virtues" (CS, 91). Even more disturbing for Laura, however, is her failure to live free from her past. Her earlier life still haunts her, keeping her so firmly in its grip that she actively embraces it while at the same time seeking to repudiate it. "She has encased herself in a set of principles derived from her early training," the narrator writes, "leaving no detail of gesture or of personal taste untouched" (CS, 92).

For this reason, Laura wears only handmade lace, despite the fact that to her revolutionary comrades such preference smacks of counterrevolutionary elitism.

The dominant shaping force of Laura's upbringing is her Catholicism. Although she is no longer an active participant in the Church and espouses revolutionary loyalties—loyalties that see the Catholic church as the enemy of revolutionary change—Laura nonetheless still feels the pull of the Church. Risking scandal, she frequently ducks into Catholic churches to kneel and say a Hail Mary on the rosary she carries with her. But appeals to the Virgin fail to fulfill her needs ("It is no good," the narrator says of Laura's response to her prayers [CS, 92]), and Laura concludes her visits not as a consoled believer but as a detached observer, noting the beauty of the objects on the altar but not feeling their spiritual power. That Laura repeatedly returns to the churches underscores both her desire for faith (together with the structure and order that religious belief would give her) and her resistance to abandoning her previous beliefs, something her fellow revolutionaries call for in their enthusiasm for building a new future. "Everything must be torn from its accustomed place where it has rotted for centuries, hurled skyward and distributed, cast down again clean as rain, without separate identity," Braggioni tells Laura. He goes on to describe the elect who will survive and rule society, concluding: "Pistols are good, I love them, cannon are even better, but in the end I pin my faith to good dynamite" (CS, 100). Laura remains unimpressed by Braggioni's bluster.

Even if Laura cannot bring herself to embrace the spiritual dimensions of Catholic faith, she nonetheless enthusiastically adopts aspects of Church tradition, stripped of their spiritual dimensions, to structure her everyday life. Most obvious and important is her rigid asceticism, a manifestation of cenobitic monasticism, whereby the faithful, as Geoffrey Galt Harpham says in *The Ascetic Imperative in Culture and Criticism,* "submitted themselves to extraordinary regulation, discipline, and obedience, living under a Superior in strict adherence to a Rule which prescribed their conduct, their attitudes, their food, and even their thoughts." Cenobitism, argues Harpham, ultimately entails the renunciation of self, in that the cenobite "tries to live a life without content, without events," and seeks "not to be led into temptation so that the self would grow indistinct in its outlines, and would, ideally, simply cease to be."[6]

Laura, of course, does not live in a religious community, but she does live by a rigid discipline of renunciation that, as Jane Krause DeMouy has pointed out, resembles the "abstemious life of an anchoress." Janis P. Stout attributes Laura's disciplined reticence and withdrawal to a need for ethical and physical self-preservation in a threatening world.[7] Such a strategy, however, also closes her off from the enriching human community. Thus, even though she actively interacts with other people as a teacher and a revolutionary collaborator, she always resists becoming deeply involved with anyone and thus remains an outsider. The narrator describes her situation:

> She is not at home in the world. Every day she teaches children who remain strangers to her, though she loves their tender round hands and their charming opportunist savagery. She knocks at unfamiliar doors not knowing whether a friend or a stranger shall answer, and even if a known face emerges from the sour gloom of that unknown interior, still it is the face of a stranger. No matter what this stranger says to her, nor what her message to him, the very cells of her flesh reject knowledge and kinship in one monotonous word. No. No. No. She draws her strength from this one holy talismanic word which does not suffer her to be led into evil. Denying everything, she may walk anywhere in safety, she looks at everything without amazement. (*CS,* 97)

Laura's rejection of others is matched by her rejection of her ample body, which she hides under thick and heavy clothes. When courted by Braggioni, Laura sits primly and rigidly, a posture that speaks of the discipline that shields her body and its virginity. The narrator writes that with Braggioni she acts "like a good child who understands the rules of behavior. Her knees

6. Geoffrey Galt Harpham, *The Ascetic Imperative in Culture and Criticism* (Chicago, 1987), 21, 29, 28.

7. DeMouy, *Katherine Anne Porter's Women,* 82; Janis P. Stout, *Strategies of Reticence: Silence and Meaning in the Works of Jane Austen, Willa Cather, Katherine Anne Porter, and Joan Didion* (Charlottesville, Va., 1990), 130.

cling together under sound blue serge, and her round white collar is not purposely nun-like. She wears the uniform of an idea, and has renounced vanities" (CS, 92).

Laura's asceticism pits her in direct opposition to Braggioni, who is driven by momentous self-love and self-esteem. As the narrator writes, "Braggioni loves himself with such tenderness and amplitude and eternal charity that his followers . . . warm themselves in the reflected glow" (CS, 91). If Braggioni was once driven by sincere commitment to revolutionary ideology calling for a more just world, he now focuses his energies, acting with cold calculation, on maintaining his power and on fulfilling his worldly desires. "He has the malice, the cleverness, the wickedness, the sharpness of wit, the hardness of heart, stipulated for loving the world profitably," the narrator writes, and that profit is always his own, not others' (CS, 98). Braggioni relishes the trappings of power, and he indulges himself with free and easy abandon. Despite the grimness of the times, he always has plenty of food, drink, and women. "One woman is really as good as another for me, in the dark," he tells Laura. "I prefer them all" (CS, 99).

Braggioni's comment on women underscores his self-centeredness and his consequent lack of regard for other people, except in their capacity to serve him. When he is with the men whom he leads in the revolutionary struggle, Braggioni is always sympathetic and supportive, praising their efforts and promising them rewards, telling them that "they are closer to him than his own brothers, without them he can do nothing." To Laura he speaks of them quite differently: "They are stupid, they are lazy, they are treacherous, they would cut my throat for nothing" (CS, 98). Braggioni may be right about his men (it is not clear from the story), but in any case what is significant is that Braggioni has no true comrades, no one with whom he shares a bond not tainted with deceit and manipulation. This holds true even with his wife, from whom he demands fidelity and hero worship, despite his own amorous entanglements with other women. Braggioni's abuse of his wife derives not merely from the double standard toward sexuality that typifies relationships in patriarchal societies but even more crucially from the self-centeredness and selfishness that fundamentally shape Braggioni's character and direct his actions.

In their manipulation of others and their commitment to noncommitment, Braggioni and Laura share a great deal, despite the fact that opposing drives propel their lives—self-denial for Laura and self-indulgence for Braggioni. Ultimately both Laura's and Braggioni's actions embody a renunciation of human community, of the self in a world of others, and perhaps even of the world itself, since both place all value squarely within their isolated consciousnesses, thus emptying the world of value and significance in their quests to satisfy personal desires. Both Laura and Braggioni, in spite of their differences, sense that they share this fundamental identity. After telling Laura that he suffers from painful disappointment in his life, Braggioni says that she too will so suffer. "We are more alike than you realize in some things," he tells her. "Wait and see." Braggioni's words sting her, and she sees their truth: "It may be true I am corrupt, in another way, as Braggioni," she thinks, "as callous, as incomplete" (CS, 93).

Eugenio's death severely tests both Braggioni's and Laura's ideologies of noncommitment. Braggioni scorns Eugenio in death and refuses to accept any responsibility for his suicide. He strives to maintain his disinterest and to deny any resemblance between his life and the prisoner's. Accepting such a resemblance would severely undermine Braggioni's celebration of self, for Eugenio's separation in prison from a vital human community and his discovery of the emptiness of life when focused merely on self-indulgence suggest similar failings in Braggioni. Eugenio's suicide points to the logical conclusion of a life directed totally toward pleasure when pleasure no longer fulfills. Adding to the pressure upon Braggioni is Laura's guilt about Eugenio's death. Her feelings suggest a commitment to and a concern for others that transcend narrow loyalties to the self and that underscore what is missing in Braggioni's manipulative relationships. Laura knows that his relationship with her is of just this sort, and she taunts him by mocking his revolutionary zeal and his destructive interaction with others. "Put that on," she tells him, speaking of his pistol belt (his pistol is a charged image of the domination, sexual and otherwise, he seeks over others), "and go kill somebody in Morelia, and you will be happier" (CS, 100).

Shaken by his encounter with Laura, Braggioni does not follow through on her derisive challenge but instead returns home to his wife, from whom he has been living apart because he had found her not subservient enough. Braggioni's return to his wife and his tender treatment of her—

"You are so good, please don't cry any more, you dear good creature," he says upon first seeing her—suggest that he now seeks a relationship shaped not by selfish self-love but by generous love for another. After his wife washes his feet, Braggioni is so thoroughly humbled that he breaks down in tears and invites her to join him in a meal to celebrate their love. Rather than crying tears of jealous anger, tears that Braggioni had earlier found so disturbing, his wife now cries tears of joy that soothe and comfort and suggest the beginning of a sustaining and giving relationship.

Eugenio's suicide likewise deeply stuns Laura, severely pressuring her ascetic life. Several forces impinge upon her. To begin with, feelings of responsibility for Eugenio's death haunt Laura (she carried Eugenio the drugs with which he killed himself, and she did not call the prison doctor to save him), thoroughly disrupting her attempt to characterize all the people she knows as strangers, no matter how well she is acquainted with them. Ironically, only with Eugenio's death does he become alive to her—as a human being whose presence is entangled deeply with hers, rather than a faceless revolutionary with whom she has merely transacted business and for whom she has no genuine concern. Moreover, Eugenio's suicide speaks crucially to Laura's predicament, as it did to Braggioni's, offering a disturbing representation of her own suicidal turn inward into the prison of the isolated consciousness.

Not surprisingly, Laura is torn by conflicting feelings of guilt and denial. Despite her words to Braggioni suggesting their complicity in the suicide, Laura does her best, after Braggioni leaves and she rests alone, to repress all thoughts of her guilt. She is almost certainly aware of the disturbing implications to which her suspicions of guilt speak, implications that if openly accepted would dismantle the structure of her asceticism. Not unexpectedly, she looks to her ascetic discipline to maintain her stability. When she lies down to sleep, the narrator writes, "numbers tick in her brain like little clocks, soundless doors close of themselves around her." Despite her efforts to close off the self from itself, Laura nonetheless fears sleep, for she knows her dreams are outside her conscious control. She admonishes herself not to remember anything if she sleeps and thinks ahead to the coming day in school rather than back on the day's events. Her efforts fail her. The schoolchildren remind her of Eugenio ("poor prisoners who come every day bringing flowers to their jailor"), and her attempt to count away her thoughts, one-two-three-four-five, collapses in disorder, the binary oppositions that structure her thought dissolving before Eugenio's image: "It is monstrous to confuse love with revolution, night with day, life with death—ah, Eugenio!" (*CS*, 101).

The dream that follows works out her worst suspicions, looking backward to her complicity in Eugenio's death and forward to her own, with her departing with Eugenio on the journey to the other side of life. In an echo of the Last Supper quite different from that in the reconciliation of Braggioni and his wife (when she washes his feet), Eugenio offers Laura flowers from a Judas tree to eat, and then he becomes the very tree from which the flowers are stripped: "She saw that his hand was fleshless, a cluster of small white petrified branches, and his eye sockets were without light, but she ate the flowers greedily for they satisfied both hunger and thirst." "Murderer!" Eugenio accuses her, "and Cannibal! This is my body and my blood." Laura cries out, "No!" and awakes in terror, fearful now of returning to sleep (*CS*, 102).

Eugenio's stinging rebuke of Laura accuses her of betrayal, a betrayal not only of Eugenio but also of Laura herself. Her interaction—or, better, her lack of interaction—with Eugenio is merely one manifestation of the life of denial she has so greedily embraced. Laura now comes to understand that her asceticism, bolstered by her stoic resolve, fails to nourish in the ways she thought it would. Earlier, after a rash act that she refuses to regret, Laura, the narrator writes, "persuades herself that her negation of all external events as they occur is a sign that she is gradually perfecting herself in the stoicism she strives to cultivate against the disaster she fears, though she cannot name it" (*CS*, 97). Now, however, she sees that her process of denial is the means less to perfect herself than to destroy herself, and also those about her. In her drastic turn inward that devalues the external world and her relationships with other people, Laura thus becomes precisely what Eugenio accuses her of being—a murderer and a cannibal, a person who sees other people merely as objects (thus "murdering" their selves, their humanity) to be manipulated in whatever way that will nourish her own desires (she thus "cannibalizes" them). Further, Laura's asceticism speaks to her own death and cannibalization. Her isolation of herself entirely within her self is ultimately a life that feeds horrifyingly on itself.

As the narrator's words on Laura's "stoicism" suggest, Laura in part lives her ascetic life as a defense against an envisioned violent catastrophe that haunts her consciousness. But as she may understand upon waking from her nightmare at the end of the story (it is, finally, unclear precisely what Laura comes to accept about herself), the disaster she fears comes not with her death, but with Eugenio's. Eugenio's death, as we have noted, points to the catastrophe that Laura has carried with her all along, her destructive life of denial. In this Laura is not unlike John Marcher in Henry James's "The Beast in the Jungle" (Porter held a deep admiration for James), a man who commits his life to waiting for the disaster he foresees. This disaster, he tells May Bartram, will "suddenly break out in my life; possibly destroying all further consciousness, possibly annihilating me." The catastrophe, of course, is the waiting itself, because Marcher all the while closes himself from any deep commitment to other people. With the death of May, the woman who had offered him love and thus the escape from his self-imposed exile from others but who had received from him merely a detached regard formed "in the chill of his egotism and the light of her use," Marcher comes to see that the beast he has feared has been within himself all along and that his life has already fallen prey to it.[8] He collapses onto May's grave at the end of the story, his rigidly restrained life, like Laura's at the end of "Flowering Judas," completely undone.

Laura's asceticism, as was suggested earlier, in large part derives from her inability to resolve the searching tension between her Catholic upbringing and her revolutionary present. Rather than bringing these two powerful forces into a constructive dialogue within her consciousness whereby the two ideologies challenge and provoke each other and so become deepened and enriched, Laura instead brings them together for a destructive battle for utter domination. The tension thus lacerates rather than nourishes, driving Laura into inaction as she fluctuates between the two ideologies. She

8. Henry James, "The Beast in the Jungle," in *The New York Edition of the Novels and Tales of Henry James* (New York, 1909), XVII, 72, 126.

remains a traitor to both causes, unable to give full commitment to either. In the end, she falls victim to her own inaction and denial, as corrupt as the country in which she lives.

At one point in his wooing of Laura, Braggioni speaks of the upcoming violent disturbances in Morelia, where on May Day the Catholics and Socialists hold competing festivals. "There will be two independent processions," he tells Laura, "starting from either end of town, and they will march until they meet, and the rest depends . . ." (CS, 99). Braggioni does not finish his story (or at least the narrator does not report it), but the ending is clear: a violent conclusion to the day of festivities looms. Such violence arising from ideological conflict also rages within Laura, and the violence at Morelia also signifies the disruptions that rage throughout all of Mexico, at least the Mexico of Porter's fiction of the late twenties and early thirties—a land torn to pieces by an internal war of competing ideologies, a land once of hope but now of destruction, a land run by people, revolutionists or not, whose only commitment is to themselves and their welfare as individuals. Laura's confusion, despair, and suffering are Mexico's. The Edenic paradise of "Children of Xochitl" and "María Concepción" has become the wasteland, a land that has betrayed itself, a land of the flowering Judas.

# 4
## SELF AND VISION

In the early thirties, Katherine Anne Porter worked on the plans for a sweeping novel of a southern family—clearly based on her own—undergoing transformation and change through different eras. Tentatively entitling her proposed novel "Many Redeemers," Porter in some notes from this period divided the novel into three books: "Introduction to Death: The Beginning," "Midway of This Mortal Life," and "Beginning Again: The End." As she planned it, the first book was to be a "history of the rise and break-up of an American family up to the Great War, or a little before." The second book would follow one character, maybe more, from the first book through the traumatic twenties, "that season in hell which any being who can think or feel must pass through at least once." She wrote additionally of this section: "The Mexican interval, which is a tangent for Miranda, the complete negation of all she has known, a derailment." The final book would depict the breakup of the family: "The present scene, the sick and crumbling society with some of the cures offered by diverse Saviours. The various roads by which the characters separate and go to their several ends" (McKeldin).

Of particular interest to Porter's own career is her comment on the second book about Miranda's experience in Mexico (Miranda is of course the semiautobiographical character who appears in a number of Porter's works and who, of all of Porter's characters, is generally considered the one most crucially embodying the struggles Porter herself underwent), an experience, as Porter says, of "the complete negation of all she has known, a derailment." Porter's words here also speak to her own experience in Mexico in the early twenties, when, as a result of her initial enthusiasm for the country and its people, she embraced for a time a primitivist vision and a hopeful revolutionary agenda that represented a new structure for ordering self and world. Her early years in Mexico forced her to rethink and revise her views on ethics, politics, and art. This is nowhere more apparent than in her perceptions of Roman Catholicism, a faith to which early on she was converted but which during her first excursion to Mexico she had come to see as both a corrupt political institution and the purveyor of a deathly dream that drew people away from the nourishing forces of life. Her time in Mexico disrupted her intellectual continuity and security, but this disruption also proved to be the catalyst for her literary career.

As we saw in the previous chapter, Porter's return to Mexico in the late twenties was not such an iconoclastic experience as her earlier visit had been. By this time Porter's enthusiasm for the country had cooled dramatically, particularly her admiration for primitive Indian culture and her hopes for improvements brought about by the revolution. In a 1929 review of Anita Brenner's *Idols Behind Altars,* Porter wrote that despite its enchantment "Mexico is a disturbing country" where "the contradictions are too violent" (*BR,* 83). Her own frustration with Mexico and with what she saw as its failure to achieve its revolutionary dreams most certainly lies behind the comments of Herr Lutz in *Ship of Fools:* "In 1920 there was revolution. Likewise in 1921, 1922; then counterrevolution in 1923 and '24: and so, revolution again, and so on, until now" (*SF,* 102). It is repetition rather than progress. Mexico, in other words, was no safe harbor for artists, no refuge from modernity's ills. Indeed, the Mexico Porter portrayed in the thirties and then later in *Ship of Fools* was every bit the wasteland that she had come to see modern civilization as being.

Porter's revised views on Mexico represent not merely a change in her understanding of that country but, even more significant, a change in her imaginative vision and perspective. By the late twenties Porter's vision had grown markedly more rich, complex, and ironic. Irony was the keystone of her mature imaginative life. Certainly the most forceful and eloquent statement of Porter's ironic vision comes in Robert Penn Warren's seminal essay "Irony with a Center: Katherine Anne Porter." In his close readings of the themes and structures of Porter's fiction, Warren repeatedly finds examples of what he identifies as "tissue[s] of contradictions" and "intricate tissue[s] of paradox," attributes of Porter's ironic vision that Warren claims is her "central intuition." To those who find in Porter's irony merely a destructive skepticism that negates all positive values, Warren answers that "her irony is an irony with a center, never an irony for irony's sake. It simply implies, I think, a refusal to accept the formula, the ready-made solution, the hand-me-down morality, the word for the spirit. It affirms, rather, the constant need for exercising discrimination, the arduous obligation of the intellect in the face of conflicting dogmas, the need for a dialectical approach to matters of definition, the need for exercising as much of the human faculty as possible."[1]

As Warren's comments suggest, the center of Porter's vision—the standard from which she established values and perspective—lay not in any predetermined truth but in the ongoing quest for meaning and understanding. By not centering her vision on a single unassailable and monolithic view, Porter thus aligned herself with what she saw as the tradition of inquiry and dissent typified by Thomas Hardy. Unlike T. S. Eliot, who from his orthodox theological position found Hardy "diabolic" because his work derived from "a powerful personality uncurbed by any institutional attachment or by submission to any objective beliefs" (CE, 4), Porter found Hardy's refusal to accept orthodox positions merely because they were orthodox invigorating and even heroic. Porter wrote that Hardy was not a "Believer," a person whose ideology was unchallenged and unchallengeable, but an "Inquirer," a person whose views were always undergoing constant challenge and revision in the search for meaning. As Porter wrote, "the yawning abyss between question and answer" haunted Hardy and defined his quest. With many others, he belonged to a tradition of dissent

1. Robert Penn Warren, "Irony with a Center: Katherine Anne Porter," in *Katherine Anne Porter: A Critical Symposium,* ed. Lodwick Hartley and George Core (Athens, Ga., 1969), 55, 56, 65, 66, originally published as "Katherine Anne Porter (Irony with a Center)," *Yale Review,* XXXII (1942), 29–42. Warren gives another reading of Porter's tensions and ambiguities in "Uncorrupted Consciousness: The Stories of Katherine Anne Porter," *Yale Review,* LV (1965), 280–90.

that was "persistent, obdurate, a kind of church itself, with its leaders, teachers, saints, martyrs, heroes" (*CE,* 6).

There can be little doubt that by the late twenties Porter had come to see herself as an artist within this dissenting tradition. In a January 30, 1932, letter to her sister Gay, speaking of herself and her brother and two sisters, Porter wrote that "there's a streak of Lone Wolf in all of us, a streak of something misanthropic, solitary and non-conformist" (McKeldin). Porter's observation here revealingly identifies not only the central psychological attributes she saw within herself and her family but also what she had come to see as the significant traits of the artist. The artist is a "Lone Wolf," a solitary person whose integrity and imaginative life derive from a commitment to individual visions and desires, a commitment close to misanthropy in its focus on detachment rather than involvement, irony rather than sympathy.

Throughout her letters and notes Porter stressed the pressing necessity she felt as an artist for privacy, for maintaining strict boundaries between her inner self and the world at large that always threatened to intrude and to scatter her energies. So distracting were these threats that Porter came to see artistic endeavor as requiring withdrawal from life and rigid ascetic discipline. To Janice and Ford Madox Ford, Porter wrote on January 25, 1936, that she had finally realized after a great deal of frustration with her writing that "unless I am severe with myself, and then with everything and everybody, my time and my life will go on being completely wasted and pointless, as it seems to me to have been until now" (McKeldin). If her husband Eugene Pressly came before her and her work, she told the Fords, she would not hesitate to divorce him: she was that desperate and that committed to her writing. In an earlier undated letter from 1931 to Pressly, Porter spoke of what she saw as her progressive withdrawal from society and into self. After declaring that she would be an individualist until she died, Porter wrote: "More and more I look upon life as something for my personal use and contentment, I feel very little call to explain myself or conform in any way to anybody else's set of rules. Less and less I am disposed to keep open house in my heart or mind. . . . I like fewer and fewer persons. . . . I need less and less human society." She admitted that "some of this clearing away might be taken for a kind of death to many things" but said that she had "such an extraordinary feeling of being slowly re-born, as if new life were taking root painfully in the wreck of the old" (McKeldin).

If Porter equated the asceticism of the artist with rebirth, the inner self emerging anew from the death of the social self, she also knew that the artist's disciplined life was a terrible burden, particularly for a person like herself whose fundamental personality was anything but ascetic (as her numerous husbands and lovers, together with her flashy and flamboyant lifestyle, attest). For this reason, as she wrote on December 14, 1931, to Caroline Gordon, writing was "now just a horrible grim burden" that brought merely occasional "little bursts of joy at times. . . . I wouldn't do it if I were not morally engaged to do it" (McKeldin). Porter's comment here that she is "morally engaged" to her writing underscores the ethical imperative that she believed all artists must follow: they must never cater to tastes and judgments other than their own and particularly never to those of the marketplace or to those of some cause—political, religious, or otherwise. "He had better follow the bent of his own mind, whether it is for the moment fashionable or not," Porter said in a 1934 lecture to the American Women's Club in Paris, speaking of the artist (*CE,* 438). In this same speech she elaborated on the necessity of the artist's independence:

> We don't need any more types. We need individuals. We always did need them. The value of a writer can be measured best, probably, by his capacity to express what he feels, knows, is, has been, has seen, and experienced, by means of this paraphrase which is art, this process of taking his own material and making what he wants to make of it. He cannot do this, indeed he is not an artist, if he allows himself to be hampered by any set of conventions outside of the severe laws and limitations of his own medium. No one else can tell him what life is like to him, in what colors he sees the world. He cannot sit down and say, Go to, I will be a writer because it's an interesting career! Even less can he say, I must be an American writer; or French, or whatever. He has already been born one kind of person or another, and taking thought about it cannot change much. He cannot even worry about whether the publishers are going to accept his work or not; if he does, he is as good as done for: he may as well never have begun. He may be interpreter, critic, rebel, prophet, conformist, devil, or angel, or he may be all of these things in turn, or all of them a

little at once; but he can be none of these things to order: nobody's order, not even his own. (*CE,* 438–39)

Porter saw her toil as an artist, as she wrote in some comments on writing in 1939, as a search for the "clearest and most arresting way to tell the things I wished to tell" (*CE,* 453). To adapt one's vision to the mold of a political or religious cause, in contrast, was to betray one's calling. In committing such a betrayal, Porter wrote in her introduction to Eudora Welty's *A Curtain of Green,* "the artist dehumanizes himself, unfits himself for the practice of any art" (*CE,* 287). Great artists, Porter argues here and elsewhere, are never propagandists; great stories are never tracts.

Living by one's artistic calling—and Porter saw art as a calling, a vocation—and maintaining one's independence, however, could take a drastic toll on the writer, particularly financially. Porter herself so suffered almost her entire career and particularly during the twenties. (Not until the publication of *Ship of Fools* did Porter achieve complete financial stability.) "One must have freedom of mind, or freedom from worry about money," she wrote in an undated 1931 letter to Eugene Pressly, "and these two things are so mixed it is almost impossible to untangle them." She then described her own sufferings: "For years upon years I have exhausted myself utterly in the fight to live without compromise—the surrender of the mind, the spirit—there was almost no way in which I could earn a living that I did not truly despise the means, yes, and the ends, too. . . . Well, what happened? I was almost utterly crippled by poverty, by hunger, by the horrible necessity of borrowing from friends, by a perpetual gnawing worry about tomorrow. . . . I lost my health and my nerves broke under it" (McKeldin). In another letter to Pressly dated May 28, 1932, she wrote that from the beginning of her career she had always felt "that anything was better than to spoil what I had by rushing into print, by writing just anything in order to make a living," and that her artistic honesty had kept her in poverty and hardship. "I never said I liked being poor," she went on. "I never did like it. I need not have been, either. I really had a choice. I never felt poor, if you can understand that point of view: that is, morally and mentally I never felt hampered by it, even when I wasn't certain where my next meal would show up. But I find that one thing happened: poverty can become a habit, and it can stigmatize you in the eyes of those very persons who should prevent your poverty by paying a decent price for your wares, instead of exploiting you: and it is easier to borrow money on your gifts and prospects than it is to earn your living by the very work which your gifts produce.... This is a fatal, a vicious circle" (McKeldin).

Poverty was not the only threat facing the artist. Besides enduring material deprivations, together with the many problems that these deprivations engendered, the artist also had to struggle with potentially paralyzing psychological problems arising from the withdrawal into the self. This turn inward always threatened to become a debilitating solipsism in which all meaning and value were located in the isolated self. At its extreme, such isolation cut the writer off from the richness of life's diversity: the world outside the self, by the very fact that it lay outside the self, was devalued and emptied of significance. In *Poets of Reality: Six Twentieth-Century Writers,* J. Hillis Miller characterizes this radical subjectification of reality as "nihilism"—"the nothingness of consciousness when consciousness becomes the foundation of everything"—and he describes the radical consequences to the self in its placement in and relationship to the world: "The ego has put everything in doubt, and has defined all outside itself as the object of its thinking power. Cogito ergo sum: the absolute certainty about the self reached by Descartes' hyperbolic doubt leads to the assumption that things exist, for me at least, only because I think them. When everything exists only as reflected in the ego, then man has drunk up the sea. If man is defined as subject, everything else turns into object." For the imaginative writer, the credibility of whose work in large part depends upon the creation of a believable world and believable characters, subjectifying reality has potentially disastrous effects. Flannery O'Connor's comment on the alienated hero of modern fiction—"the borders of his country are the sides of his skull"—also applies to the subjectivist modern writer, a person out of touch and out of place with the world. Allen Tate's telling remark on modernist poetry of the twenties suggests the extremes to which imaginative writing could—and did—go as a result of writers' glorification of consciousness at the expense of all else: "The external world is a permanent possibility of sign-posts upon which the poet may hang his attitudes, his sensibility. Not the world, but consciousness; hence, his difficult abstractness." Tate added elsewhere in this 1924 essay that for the modern poet the "only possible themes are the manifold projections and tangents of his own perception. It is the age of the Sophist." [2]

The artist's turning inward also threatened to isolate his or her imaginative vision from the challenges and pressures of other views and perspectives. Without such challenges from contending viewpoints, the self languished in what it saw as its own superiority, retreating ever deeper into itself, since from its isolated and inviolate perspective nothing outside the self had any significance. Rather than engaging in procreative dialogue with other consciousnesses, with the self opening itself to other voices, the single-minded artist sought to dictate and prescribe truth, smothering other voices into silence. Mikhail Bakhtin called such monolithic thinking "monologism," writing of it in some notes for his revised version of *Problems of Dostoevsky's Poetics:*

> Monologism, at its extreme, denies the existence outside itself of another consciousness with equal rights and equal responsibilities, another *I* with equal rights (*thou*). With a monologic approach (in its extreme or pure form) *another person* remains wholly and merely an *object* of consciousness, and not another consciousness. No response is expected from it that could change everything in the world of my consciousness. Monologue is finalized and deaf to the other's response, does not expect it and does not acknowledge in it any *decisive* force. Monologue manages without the other, and therefore to some degree materializes all reality. Monologue pretends to be the *ultimate word*. It closes down the represented world and represented persons. [3]

In dialogue, the self continually remakes and redefines itself in response to the ever-changing world and self's context within it; in monologue, the self hardens into stone, isolated from the world and unchallenged by it.

2. J. Hillis Miller, *Poets of Reality: Six Twentieth-Century Writers* (Cambridge, Mass., 1965), 3; Flannery O'Connor, "The Catholic Novelist in the Protestant South," in O'Connor, *Mystery and Manners: Occasional Prose,* ed. Sally Fitzgerald and Robert Fitzgerald (New York, 1969), 200; Allen Tate, "One Escape from the Dilemma," *Fugitive,* III (April, 1924), 35.

3. Bakhtin, *Problems of Dostoevsky's Poetics,* 292–93.

Porter clearly felt the threat of the artist's physical and intellectual seclusion, despite the fact that she understood the need for such a withdrawal in order to marshal the forces of the self for insight and creation. She knew that taken to its extreme, the artist's withdrawal from active engagement with life was finally destructive. In an unpublished personal essay, dated February 27, 1928, Porter discusses the problems with her life and art. She begins the essay by laying the blame for her abortive relationships and her failures at completing much of her writing squarely on her father and others (unnamed) who raised her. She says that as a child she was "romantic and egoistic" and so "took naturally to the examples of laziness, inefficiency and arrogance I saw about me." These traits were crucial in her later "failure to train myself in habits of concentration and of finishing one job before I undertook another." This failure, she adds, "has destroyed my health, my nervous system, and almost destroyed my vital contacts with reality" (McKeldin). Withdrawal into the self clearly is one antidote for these shortcomings.

The refuge of the isolated consciousness was for Porter not entirely fulfilling, however, since it often led to cynicism and despair. Porter goes on in her essay to say that in her withdrawal from long-term relationships, she has "taken refuge in skepticism" and that she now "seem[s] unable to believe in anything, and certainly my doubt of human beings and their motives is founded in a fear of their power over me." Robert Penn Warren, we remember, found Porter's skepticism one of her enduring strengths, but the skepticism of which Porter speaks here is less the healthy open-endedness identified by Warren than the destructive cynicism or nihilism discussed by J. Hillis Miller, "the nothingness of consciousness when consciousness becomes the foundation of everything." Elsewhere, in some undated notes, Porter observed that cynicism "is often used as a synonym for worldly wisdom, or disillusionment, or bitterness. Perhaps in certain temperaments cynicism might be the end result of all these states of mind. But it is more than any sum of them. . . . I consider it to be the gravest accusation which can be made against anybody, or any motive, either personal or professional" (McKeldin). For the isolated artist who locates all value within the consciousness, cynicism transforms the open-endedness of skepticism into the disillusionment of despair.

Porter's comment that her "doubt of human beings and their motives is founded in a fear of their power over me" speaks not only of her cynicism (an outlook with which she had to struggle her entire career) but also of her retreat from intimate relationships. In large part because of the demands of the artistic calling, Porter feared that close relationships, particularly with men, distracted her from her work. Her lovers, she invariably found, demanded that she place relationships with them before her vocation. This was something Porter could not do, at least for long. Whether founded or not, Porter's fear of intrusion and domination by others had drastic consequences in her personal life: she was torn by desire for and repulsion from the intimacy of close relationships. In her notes for her essay "Marriage Is Belonging," Porter struggled to discover the secret of a successful marriage (something that had escaped her in her marriages), finally settling on the paradox "to belong without possessing." If such was the ideal that Porter sought—to share a life with another person without having one's inner self intruded upon—she also knew that she had never found it in her relationships. Her life as a writer was less one of belonging than of being alone, and in these same notes she made a telling comment that almost certainly speaks of her own suffering: "The most terrible loneliness in the world must be that of the self-alienated, the one who cannot give himself away for fear of being possessed" (McKeldin).

When she wrote her 1928 essay on her personal and artistic problems, as she noted in marginal commentary written in 1960, Porter was in Salem, Massachusetts, working at the Essex Institute preparing materials for her planned biography of Cotton Mather. Porter undoubtedly saw her stay in Salem as an attempt to marshal her creative energies in solitude in order to get her work done, but at the same time she saw her isolation as temporary, a respite that would last only as long as it took for her to finish the Mather project. As much as she enjoyed being hidden away to work, she looked forward to returning to the wider world and her life within it. "I here and now, today, take myself in hand," she vowed. "I will finish this job and leave my seclusion and face the world as I did before." Confronting the world successfully meant overcoming what she identified as her "egotistic desire to be right always, and the fear of criticism"—the monologic temptation—and her failure in stopping people from "trespass[ing] on my human rights because I was too timid to fight for them, and to[o] lazy and indifferent to put up the battle that I knew was necessary to hold my proper ground." She defined a meaningful life as one in which a person grows individually not by retreating from the world but by coming to terms with it. "A successful life," she wrote, "consists of developing your own potentialities without running from your environment or denying realities, or being blind about people" (McKeldin). This is no easy task, for Porter or anyone else.

Given her own personal and artistic struggles, it comes as no surprise that in much of her writing from the mid- to late twenties up through the mid-thirties (and arguably through her later writings as well, including *Ship of Fools*) Porter explored the temptations and diversions—"running from your environment or denying realities, or being blind about people"—to which people fell prey, knowingly or through indifference, thereby stunting their development. Her unfinished biography of Cotton Mather, several chapters of which were published individually, is one striking example. Joan Givner, in her biography of Porter, argues that Porter's fascination with Mather "was the natural outgrowth of preoccupations rooted in her southern childhood," specifically the religious frenzy of southern fundamentalists and their theology that underscored humanity's depravity, guilt, and damnation.[4] Whatever the connections between Mather and Porter's childhood memories of southern fundamentalism, I think Porter's desire to research and write about Mather derived more crucially from her interest in the consequences, both for the individual and for those about him or her, of the obsessive solipsistic withdrawal of the self within the self. Porter found Mather guilty of precisely this psychological isolation, and she explores in her biography the origins and consequences of his monomaniac consciousness. In "A Goat for Azazel (A.D. 1688)," for instance, she describes Mather as so driven by his "obsessional self-concentration" (*CE,* 340) that he remains completely out of touch with the everyday affairs going on about him. Mather's obsessiveness, Porter suggests in "Affectation of Praehiminincies (A.D. 1663–1675)," began early

4. Givner, *Katherine Anne Porter: A Life,* 184–85.

in his childhood and derived primarily from his family, who almost from the moment of his birth began preparing him for greatness by making him understand that he was someone special—one of God's chosen. "Shielded, flattered, and adored by his family and friends," Mather quickly picked up on his appointed—and anointed—role. "In his fifth year he resolved to be great," Porter wrote, adding that "this inflated self-importance of the infant Cotton was a reflection of the family feeling. He was surrounded by every possible attitude of moral grandeur, a tallness and solemnity of manner utterly unrelieved by any sense of proportion. He played saint in imitation of his elders" (*CE,* 315). As he grew older, his identification as saint evolved from play to all-consuming obsession. "Cotton pursued his apostolic labors among his classmates and devoured knowledge with an inhuman persistency that would be quite incredible if all the records of his later life did not bear witness to his unwearying pursuit of a single idea," Porter wrote. "This idea took on monstrous shapes and sizes, it sprouted in a thousand variations, but it remained essentially unaltered: the single aspiration of Cotton Mather to identify publicly and unmistakably his personal interests and ambitions with the will of God" (*CE,* 317). For Porter, Mather emerges as a terrifying example of the deformed shape the self can take when driven by arrogance and a monolithic idea of itself, two attributes that feed upon each other, driving the self further and further in upon itself so that it alone becomes the seat of all power and virtue.

In "A Goat for Azazel (A.D. 1688)" and "A Bright Particular Faith (A.D. 1700)," Porter describes in detail the havoc wreaked upon those unlucky enough to have had any doings with Mather. "A Goat for Azazel (A.D. 1688)," which focuses on the Salem witch trials, describes Mather as a Machiavellian power broker obsessed with consolidating his prestige and authority. Crucial to this effort is the assumption that only he possesses the power to interpret the divine significance of the events taking place. Mather wants to pronounce judgment with unquestioned authority. Because he has determined in his mind beforehand the nature of witchcraft and possession, what Mather finds in Salem merely confirms what he already believes: he sees what he wants to see rather than what is there, interpreting everything, as Porter writes, "by a formula" (*CE,* 339). Tzvetan Todorov calls such a strategy of interpretation "finalist," the desire not for "seeking the truth but [for] finding confirmations of a truth known in advance."[5] His comments in *The Conquest of America: The Question of the Other* on Christopher Columbus as interpreter of the New World as the earthly paradise speak tellingly of the "finalism" Porter finds in Mather:

> Columbus performs a "finalist" strategy of interpretation, in the same manner in which the Church Fathers interpreted the Bible: the ultimate meaning is given from the start (this is Christian doctrine); what is sought is the path linking the initial meaning (the apparent signification of the words of the biblical text) with this ultimate meaning. There is nothing of the modern empiricist about Columbus: the decisive argument is an argument of authority, not of experience. He knows in advance what he will find; the concrete experience is there to illustrate a truth already possessed, not to be interrogated according to preestablished rules in order to seek the truth.[6]

As Columbus integrates his experiences in the New World into his preconceived design, so too does Mather manipulate the happenings at Salem, with disastrous results. Blind to any interpretations of Salem's bizarre events other than his own—for instance, that the accusers may have been deceitful or that the witnesses may have been led to say what they think is expected of them—Mather plays an active role in what Porter clearly sees as misguided hysteria, hysteria that regrettably leads to the execution of some and the psychological destruction of many others.

Mather's finalism, a crucial aspect of his monologic vision rooted in his worship of self, also severely undermines the bonds of his family. In "A Bright Particular Faith (A.D. 1700)," Porter describes Mather's interior struggles during his wife Abigail's protracted and finally mortal illness. Although Mather fasted and prayed for Abigail's recovery during her time of sickness, Porter makes clear that from her perspective at least his focus was fixed primarily on his own predicament and interests rather than on

5. Tzvetan Todorov, *The Conquest of America: The Question of the Other,* trans. Richard Howard (New York, 1984), 19.

6. *Ibid.,* 17.

Abigail's. When Abigail first fell ill, Mather set aside a day of spiritual devotion to pray for her recovery, only to discover he lacked all enthusiasm for the task. He reflected sadly "that a man cannot believe what he will, when he will," and he struggled to reassure himself of his love for his wife "by saying that he feared her death so terribly he could not pray for her life." What Mather feared, however, was less the loss of a loved one than the loss of a woman to raise his children and to satisfy his sexual appetite. Porter writes that "he brooded at length on the inconveniences of a mother-less family—five of their children had survived—the coming perils of his own wifeless state, and in his brooding he was buffeted with impure thoughts, his mind dwelling with persistent carnality on Abigail." Ashamed of his thoughts, Mather attempted to spiritualize the entire situation, a move that in a sense emptied Abigail of her physical presence. He declared another fast, a means he hoped "of cleansing the imagination of Abigail the woman before he should pray for Abigail the soul" (*CE,* 343). Mather could not pray for Abigail's physical well-being because he had never acknowl-edged her humanity, and even in this crisis he still did not ("a man cannot believe what he will, when he will"). His prayers for her soul, one can easily surmise, came more from priestly duty than any special devotion. Before long, the fate of Abigail seemed to become for Mather almost trivial in light of the spiritual struggles her illness engendered in his consciousness. "His wife's deathbed was transformed into a battlefield where Mather fought another of his distinguished engagements with God," Porter writes (*CE,* 344). Even with his wife suffering before his eyes, Mather remained in the grip of his "obsessional self-concentration" (*CE,* 340), his focus turned al-most entirely upon his own intellectual and spiritual problems.

After Abigail's death, Mather's single-minded focus on self con-tinued. Much of his thoughts on Abigail's illness and death were self-congratulatory, particularly of his own cheerful endurance during the ordeal and of his control of his sexual desires. Porter writes: "He reflected that his own health must have suffered if he had run the venture of sleeping with her; undoubtedly he would have gone into a consumption, and the children, thus deprived of their main parent, would have received bad edu-cations" (*CE,* 350). Mather now came to see that Abigail's death settled things for the best: not only was she freed from her sufferings, but so was he. He thought with relief that he would no longer have to endure her "melancholy temper" (*CE,* 351), and he knew, too, that he could rest easy since Abigail never discovered his deceit in keeping from her the knowledge of her favorite brother's death, apparently for fear that grief would undo her, and of the disgraces of another one of her brothers. Mather knew that had his deceit become known, his authoritative position in the household would have been severely undermined. "If she had lived to learn these things," Porter reports Mather thinking about what he had kept from Abigail, "manifestly his own position would have been insupportable." So convinced was Mather of the fortune he reaped with his wife's death that "he sat day after day with gathering thankfulness reviewing all the probabilities of his misfortune if Abigail had not died. The assured permanence of her absence was a blessing, even though tendered in such a disconcerting form" (*CE,* 351). Eventually, as a result of obsessiveness, Mather's thankfulness gave way to bitterness. Driven by his sense of release from Abigail, he now reinterpreted their marriage and her illness, coming to see her as an antagonist who had striven to dismantle the structure of his life and faith. "Little by little the idea grew within him that death and Abigail had been secretly, firmly allied against him," Porter writes. "He perceived with astonishment that he had not fought the will of God, but her will, in her death. She had defeated him, had overruled his prayers with her own." The marriage he now considered "dissolved," his bitterness and resentment both negating his marriage vows and severing his ties with Abigail's family. He pledged to marry again, and quickly. Further underscoring the destructiveness that Mather's monomania wreaks upon the family, "A Bright Particular Faith (A.D. 1700)" ends with a description of Mather's daughter Nancy, gravely ill, hearing her father praying for her speedy death and then, after her recovery, saying, "I heard my father give me away today, but I shall not die this time, for all that" (*CE,* 351).

In both the society at large (as seen in the witch trials) and the family, Mather's monomania threatens to undo the bonds that normally undergird relationships, even those of kinship. The value of personal and social relations becomes secondary before the desires and projections of Mather's consciousness, a consciousness that in its drastic turn inward defines everything only in its significance to that consciousness. All sense of perspective, outside that of the isolated self, thus disappears before the consciousness's monologism, as does the possibility of engaging in enriching interactions with other people.

Besides representing the dangers of the monologic self both to itself and to others, Mather also embodies the destructiveness that such monomania wreaks upon the artist. Mather, of course, was an extremely prolific writer, and as Porter makes clear, his writings were profoundly shaped—or misshaped—by his monologism. In "Affectation of Praehiminincies (A.D. 1663–1675)," Porter describes his daily writing routine, itself a fitting model for the monologic artist. Every day Mather retired to his study where he posed to himself some doctrinal question. Porter writes that he "considered the causes, the effects, the adjuncts, as well as the opposites and resemblances of his theme" (CE, 327). As much as he explored the question on a theological level, he clearly was interested less in satisfactorily confirming accepted doctrine than in confirming his own exalted vision of himself. "As his theme was invariably himself, his sinfulness," Porter writes, "the question how best he might repent and stand well in the sight of God, he arrived logically at a general examination of his conscience, which resolved inevitably into a minute consideration of concrete sins; in the course of events there followed a severe expostulation with himself, and at last a resolution, increasing in imaginative momentum, to repent on the strength of the grace offered with the new Covenant" (CE, 327–28). Mather would then break down, seeing himself before the blazing light of the revealed truth of the doctrine as utterly false and facing damnation. "The results were monotonously the same," Porter observes. After sobbing prostrate on the floor for a while, Mather "would rise, make himself tidy, for he was fastidious in his dress, and, seated at his desk, he would record his crisis in detail, with pride and self-congratulation in his achievement" (CE, 328).

Mather's monotonous ritual, ostensibly a serious effort at understanding and a self-abasement to break the stranglehold of the prideful self, is actually a predictable exercise of self-praise, a confirmation not of sinfulness but of saintliness. This exercise typifies for Porter not merely the activity of the monomaniac theologian but also the monologic artist who, like Mather, writes "with pride and self-congratulation." In his everyday retreats to his study where he clearly manipulates his feelings, thoughts, and actions for self-aggrandizement, Mather acts out the manipulations that he later commits when he records his activities in words. His writing, returning to Todorov's term, is finalist, not written to explore the truths of self and world but to confirm preconceived ideology. It is literature written to order and illustrates the pitfalls that art suffers (predictability and monotony, for instance) when artists collapse everything into themselves, confining their world, recalling Flannery O'Connor's observation about alienated heroes, to the space within the sides of their skulls.

Despite all of her efforts, including an extended stay in Bermuda in 1929 where she worked free from the distractions of her friends, Porter never finished her Mather biography. In a letter dated May 21, 1929, to Becky Crawford, Porter spoke of the difficulties she was having with the book, problems that would later reappear in her efforts to complete *Ship of Fools:* "I can't bear to read it, and wish I'd never started it, even now that it's finished [it was not] I can't get warmed up to it any more. It's taken too long, there have been too many breaks in it. My copying and editing have degenerated into a plastering job, trying to conceal the cracks. I should have written it red-hot in the mood I was in at first" (McKeldin). Seven years later the book was still unfinished, and Porter at this time called it quits (although in the sixties she still spoke of finishing it). To Alfred Harcourt, her new editor—the Mather book was originally contracted with Liveright—Porter wrote on March 28, 1936, that she found it was "impossible, for me, at present, to finish or indeed to work at all, on the Cotton Mather manuscript" and that she was now convinced that "no further act of will on my part is going to have any good effect on it." She explained to Harcourt: "I have deceived myself into believing that I could force myself into the state of mind necessary to work on a project that has too long been a burden on me, a burden that has become an obsession. It threatens to obstruct all my other plans, I cannot work at it, and yet I am so preoccupied and worried with it I cannot work at other things either" (McKeldin).

Several factors contributed to Porter's failure to complete the Mather book. One was the very size and scope of the project. As is well known, Porter wrote in energetic bursts, often completing stories with wondrous speed. Longer projects, however, weighed heavily upon her, and her comment to Crawford that she should have written the Mather book "red-hot in the mood I was in at first" testifies to her problem in maintaining over extended periods the passion and enthusiasm necessary for her to write. Her enthusiasm for the project was sapped not only by the passing of time but also by what she discovered in her researches. As Givner has pointed out, Porter from the beginning had prejudged Mather as an absolute villain and was determined to shape her book to expose his villainy. Inevitably Porter came to see Mather as richer and more complex than her preconceptions made him. This realization created a tension between Porter's initial feelings of utter distaste for Mather and her later, more sympathetic understanding of him. Givner argues that this tension became so severe that it drained Porter's energy and her will to write the book as she had originally planned it.[7] I feel certain, however, that even more crucial to Porter's inability to finish her project was the disturbing realization she must have reached that her position as biographer resembled Mather's as theologian and writer. To write a debunking biography as she had originally planned, her understanding of Mather complete even before she began her researches, was to commit the same type of intellectual and artistic error that Mather had—to fall prey to a monomaniac passion that distorted vision and judgment and isolated the artist in the limited world of one controlling idea.

Porter's problems in maintaining enthusiasm for the Mather biography, particularly in light of the ironic connections between herself and Mather, must have only been exacerbated by Bernard DeVoto's 1933 essay "The Skeptical Biographer," which Porter read and spoke highly of. In this essay DeVoto argues for a biography of fact rather than of interpretation. The biographer's job, he writes, "is not dramatic: it is only to discover evidence and to analyze it," and analyzing for DeVoto means merely making a judgment on the validity of the evidence collected and how it should be arranged. "In the end he can say," DeVoto writes, speaking of the ideal biographer and the ideal work, "*A* did this, and I think he did that, and for the rest I am ignorant and refuse to guess."[8] In the first section of his essay DeVoto elaborates on what he sees as the most telling errors committed by

7. Givner, *Katherine Anne Porter: A Life,* 188–89.

8. Bernard DeVoto, "The Skeptical Biographer," *Harper's,* CLXVI (January, 1933), 192.

biographers: guessing, omitting evidence, distorting evidence for heightened effect, shaping the biography not according to the facts but by some ulterior motive (to make a political statement, for instance).

Two types of biographies come under DeVoto's particularly harsh attack: those that are psychoanalytic and those that are deliberately debunking. DeVoto's analysis of both is blunt. "Psycho-analysis has no value whatever as a method of arriving at facts in biography," DeVoto asserts. "No psycho-analytical biography yet written can be taken seriously—as fact. The assertion holds true for the work of the master himself [Freud], whose study of Leonardo is absolute bilge uncontaminated by the slightest perceptible filtrate of reality, and for other biographies by professional analysts." Psychoanalytic biographies, to the dismay of DeVoto, disregard the external world to explore the subject's mind, a realm that the biographer can never know for certain. Biography thus becomes fantasy, the stuff of guesses, and, to make matters worse, fantasy shaped by preconceived models (Freud's different complexes, for instance) into which the subject's life is fitted. Deliberately debunking biographies are misguided because the author has intentions other than truthfully presenting the facts of a person's life. DeVoto writes that "the man who starts out to write a debunking biography has notified us that he is either a special pleader or a charlatan. He has something to prove. His purpose is not to find out and report the facts of history: it is to argue *ex parte*. He is not a judge. At best he is a prosecuting attorney; at a lower level, he is a kept detective; at the lowest level—one fairly common in recent years—he is a man who designs 'composographs' for a scandal sheet." Such work, DeVoto concludes, "has nothing to do with fact or integrity, and so it is not biography."[9]

All of DeVoto's criticisms here speak, in varying degrees, to Porter's biography of Mather, but none does more explicitly or crucially than a critique that DeVoto gives special pleading: that literary people are incapable of writing honest biographies. DeVoto argues that writers of imaginative literature thrive on invention rather than fidelity, and so their efforts at biography are doomed from the start. Speaking of the literary mind,

9. *Ibid.,* 185, 183.

DeVoto writes that it is "habitually, even professionally, inaccurate. Accuracy is not a criterion of fiction, drama, or poetry; to ask for it would be as absurd as to appraise music by its weight or painting by its smell. Hence the literary person is horribly inept at the practice of biography, whose first condition is absolute, unvarying, unremitted accuracy. He is subject to credulity—a reliance on intuition, on appearance, on rumor and conjecture and sheer imaginative creation." No doubt Porter would not have agreed with everything DeVoto wrote about the literary person, particularly his assertion that the artist is naïve and "has little experience of the great world and none at all of the world of action." Nonetheless, much of what DeVoto wrote about the artist surely struck home with Porter, and I doubt she would have disagreed with his claim that the literary mind "is effective when it is evolving a world out of its own inner necessities, when it is creating its own material and data." This fact, DeVoto goes on to say, explains why that mind "has worked so much stupidity in biography." While Porter did not see her work on Mather as exhibiting stupidity, DeVoto's criticisms certainly must have added to her own doubts of and troubles with the biography. DeVoto's assertion that "so many recent biographers have been novelists turned rancid" probably hit Porter especially hard, increasing her own fears that the biography of Mather was drawing her away from the writing that was most important to her and that she did best—her fiction.[10] In her 1936 letter to Alfred Harcourt, we recall, Porter made precisely this complaint, saying that the Mather book "threatens to obstruct all my other plans" and that her obsessive preoccupation with it was preventing her from working on her other writing projects.

Despite her claim to Harcourt, Porter was not so paralyzed by the Mather book that she was writing nothing else. Indeed much of her best fiction dates from the period 1927–1936, during which she struggled with the biography. Not surprisingly, a good deal of the fiction, particularly that from the mid- to late twenties, explores issues also central to the Mather book, most obviously the alienation of the isolated self and the dangers of monologic thinking—of the consciousness obsessed with a single idea or

10. *Ibid.,* 184, 185, 188.

ideology that (mis)shapes the self and its perception of the world. This idea was of course not entirely new to Porter. Her early critiques of Catholicism written during her first years in Mexico, for instance, on one level center on this idea, as can be seen most clearly in "María Concepción," where the title character becomes obsessed with her Catholic faith after her desertion by Juan and the death of her baby. She must break free of this obsession for growth and fulfillment. Rubén's all-consuming love for Isabel in "The Martyr" also speaks tellingly of the dangers of the obsessive self. If not exactly heavy-handed, Porter's early treatment of this theme is rather clear-cut and unambiguous, usually developed from a relatively simple opposition between honesty and dishonesty with one's inner feelings, openness to and closure from experience. In her later fiction, however, Porter explores this theme with greater depth and discrimination, creating the complex and ironic fiction celebrated by Robert Penn Warren that resists simple and easy patterns of interpretation. We have already seen evidence of Porter's more subtle handling in her portrayal in "Flowering Judas" of Laura's life of rejection and denial.

Much of Porter's richness and complexity derives from the development of her ironic narrative voice. Quietly and persistently, this voice embodies an attitude of unrelenting skepticism—of the questioning of and challenge to accepted "truths" and prevailing ideologies—and implicitly challenges the reader to approach the fiction with the same determined questioning. Perhaps nowhere is this ironic voice more forcefully at work than in "He," a story that explores the complex relationship of a mother with her retarded son. All aspects of the story's rhetorical technique, from the positioning of events to the structuring of sentences, point to the piercing skepticism Porter came to value so highly. Darlene Unrue points out that one of the narrative consciousness's most prevalent and effective techniques of ironic narration involves the immediate undercutting of statements that had, until the ironic commentary, appeared to be straightforward and uncomplicated. Unrue notes that the narrative consciousness routinely follows seemingly clear-cut statements "with a comment or modifier that undermines the accuracy of the statements and establishes a paradox, almost as if the first statements were paraphrases of what one of the characters, usually Mrs. Whipple, has said, and the follow-up comment a perspective by the all-wise author establishing balance."[11] An example of this technique comes early in the story in a sentence that at once establishes Mrs. Whipple's professed generosity of spirit and then straightaway undermines it: "Mrs. Whipple was all for taking what was sent and calling it good, anyhow when the neighbors were in earshot" (CS, 49). Such undercutting occurs time and again throughout the narration, particularly when Mrs. Whipple professes love for her retarded son. In another effective technique, again used primarily to examine Mrs. Whipple's commitment to her son, the narrative consciousness describes events that question, and sometimes thoroughly contradict, her stated love for him. Most disturbing in this regard are the life-threatening situations she casually puts him in, such as having him take a baby pig from its enraged sow (Mrs. Whipple's other son refuses to go after the pig, knowing better. "That sow'd rip my insides out all over the pen," he observes [CS, 52]) and having him lead a bull on a three-mile walk.

So complex is the ironic narration of "He," with statements continuously undercut by other statements and these in turn undercut by events, that getting a sure grasp on Mrs. Whipple's feelings toward her retarded son is a slippery, if not finally impossible, task. Critics still regularly contest Mrs. Whipple's motives. In paired essays in a 1982 issue of *Modern Fiction Studies*, Bruce W. Jorgensen and Debra A. Moddelmog come close to capturing the critical opposition that has followed the story almost from the beginning.[12] Jorgensen argues that the example of the probing ironic narrative consciousness compels the reader to make equally probing judgments that in effect preclude the possibility of the simple condemnation of Mrs. Whipple and instead invite an understanding of her complexity as both loving mother and burdened farm wife. This is an understanding, Jorgensen writes, "allowing the validity of Mrs. Whipple's natural motherly feelings but also insisting on the reality of her unadmitted guilt and hostility." Moddelmog, in contrast, finds nothing motherly in Mrs. Whipple.

11. Unrue, *Truth and Vision,* 71.

12. Bruce W. Jorgensen, " 'The Other Side of Silence': Katherine Anne Porter's 'He' as Tragedy," *Modern Fiction Studies,* XXVIII (1982), 395–404; Debra A. Moddelmog, "Narrative Irony and Hidden Motivations in Katherine Anne Porter's 'He,' " *Modern Fiction Studies,* XXVIII (1982), 405–13.

"In 'He,' Porter shows us not a weak but well-meaning mother of a retarded child, but rather one whose pride and hypocrisy make her a moral monster," Moddelmog writes. "To be swayed by Mrs. Whipple's self-serving rationalizations is to miss the point of the story." [13]

Whatever Mrs. Whipple's deep feelings toward her retarded son, she is best understood as a monomaniac person close to Porter's characterization of Cotton Mather. Like Mather, Mrs. Whipple seeks status and power and strives for both primarily through the effort to control others' interpretations and judgments of herself. Most obviously this desire for control can be seen in her angry rebuttals to all those who offer a contrary view of things, particularly an unflattering one. When a neighbor, for instance, suggests that she prohibit her retarded son from scampering about atop trees because he cannot properly understand the danger involved, Mrs. Whipple, her voice almost at a scream, fires back: "He *does* know what He's doing! He's as able as any other child!" (*CS,* 50). Mrs. Whipple's response here is typical: she refuses to acknowledge the value of any perspective outside her own; she wants to dominate, not engage, others. Whenever her husband disagrees with her, she exhorts him to keep quiet. "Don't never let anybody hear you say such things," she says to him at one point, after he has commented on He's lack of sense. Mrs. Whipple desires to silence all competing voices, a desire she forthrightly expresses to her husband: "I'm not going to have people say anything. I get sick of people coming around saying things all the time" (*CS,* 51).

Besides attempting to silence criticism, Mrs. Whipple also strives to manipulate appearances in order to influence the perceptions of others. This in itself is not necessarily a destructive activity. We all do it, as when our houses get wonderfully spick-and-span before the guests arrive. But Mrs. Whipple's manipulations are far from innocent, and indeed they at times bring suffering and hardship to those to whom she is closest. The most obvious example is her demand that one of the family's suckling pigs be served up to her brother's family when they come to visit. This is an extremely improvident act, given the family's precarious financial condition.

13. Jorgensen, " 'The Other Side of Silence,' " 401; Moddelmog, "Narrative Irony and Hidden Motivations," 413.

Despite the complaints of her husband, who knows full well how valuable the pig will be by the time of winter slaughter, Mrs. Whipple is adamant, valuing the appearance of prosperity before visitors above prosperity itself. "I'd hate for his wife to go back and say there wasn't a thing in the house to eat," she complains, speaking of the impending visit (CS, 52). Here and elsewhere Mrs. Whipple reveals her obsession with maintaining a façade of contentment: she is willing to do just about anything to convince neighbors and visitors of the family's well-being. "Don't ever let a soul hear us complain," she continually tells Mr. Whipple in an effort to keep the façade intact. Behind much of this compulsion is Mrs. Whipple's hatred and fear of being pitied, a deep-seated compulsion that leads her to vow that no matter what financial burden the family might come to bear, she will make sure that "nobody's going to get a chance to look down on us" (CS, 49).

Mrs. Whipple's obsession with being pitied profoundly affects not only the family's financial fortunes but also her troubled relationship with He. That Mrs. Whipple wants others to view He as essentially a normal child apparently derives less from what she believes about her son than what she desires others to believe. She fears, and her fears are founded, that the neighbors see He as a blot on the family, a sign of retribution for previous sins in the family line. "There's bad blood and bad doings somewhere, you can bet on that," the neighbors agree, and they bluntly assert, "A Lord's pure mercy if He should die" (CS, 49–50). Such comments Mrs. Whipple cannot bear, and in response to them she attempts to deny her son's mental handicap by not giving him any special care (indeed in some cases He receives even less care than her other children) and by putting him in situations fairly commonplace for farm children but life-threatening to a retarded child. In this way Mrs. Whipple implicitly answers those who offer her pity, refuting their interpretation of the boy's handicap and at the same time acting out her own unacknowledged death wish for the boy (one part of her believes, most certainly, that He *is* a stain on the family). Significant here is how much Mrs. Whipple's obsession with status and image determines the family structure, if not entirely displacing then at least severely undercutting the bonds between husband and wife and parent and child. Her prayer as she watches He lead the bull speaks crucially of her attempts to manipulate events to protect her own image while disregarding the emotional and physical consequences of these manipulations upon others. In the midst of what she rightly perceives as the danger facing He, her prayer seems an appeal to safeguard her image rather than the life of her son: "Lord, don't let anything happen to Him. Lord, you *know* people will say we oughtn't to have sent Him. You *know* they'll say we didn't take care of Him. Oh, get Him home, safe home, safe home, and I'll look out for Him better! Amen" (*CS,* 56). One recalls here Cotton Mather's prayers during Abigail's extended illness, prayers that, in single-mindedly focusing on the struggles of the one doing the praying instead of the one in true crisis, devalue everything outside the monologic self.

Although Mrs. Whipple never struggles to write down her feelings and her interpretation of events, her manipulation of her family to project and protect her self-image calls to mind Mather's manipulations of deeds and words as monologic artist. In his glorification of himself in his writing, Mather, as we have seen, established a simple and monotonous narrative pattern that had him always emerging victorious over trial and tribulation. Mrs. Whipple time and again structures her life into a similar pattern, and it is just as monotonous and self-serving, with Mrs. Whipple always arising vindicated before her own self-doubts and the carpings of others. In this narrative, Mrs. Whipple seeks as monologic artist to fit her family's lives into a neat structure always under her control. For her, the "characters" in her story—her family—are objects to manipulate rather than subjects with autonomous lives of their own. She thus trivializes their concerns, interests, and perspectives, in effect silencing their voices, voices that if recognized as valid and significant would severely challenge the monolithic power of her own. Mrs. Whipple's control as all-powerful author is particularly true in her treatment of He, who cannot speak and whom Mrs. Whipple repeatedly places in situations of her own choosing, without regard for his feelings or needs.

Significantly, however, Mrs. Whipple at the end loses control of her "story" when she and He journey to the mental hospital. Here He for a moment steps free from the identity established for him by his mother, emerging as a person with deep feelings that lie beyond Mrs. Whipple's control. His bellow and his tears forcefully challenge Mrs. Whipple to see him as a complex and sensitive individual who perhaps has known all along how Mrs. Whipple was using—and abusing—him. Instead of her pawn, He now stands as a disturbing challenge to Mrs. Whipple's monologism. In the face of this challenge her power and self-control come undone:

> Mrs. Whipple kept saying, "Oh, honey, you don't feel so bad, do you? You don't feel so bad, do you?" for He seemed to be accusing her of something. Maybe He remembered that time she boxed His ears, maybe He had been scared that day with the bull, maybe He had slept cold and couldn't tell her about it; maybe He knew they were sending Him away for good and all because they were too poor to keep Him. Whatever it was, Mrs. Whipple couldn't bear to think of it. She began to cry, frightfully, and wrapped her arms tight around Him. His head rolled on her shoulder: she had loved Him as much as she possibly could, there were Adna and Emly who had to be thought of too, there was nothing she could do to make up to Him for His life. Oh, what a mortal pity He was ever born. (*CS,* 58)

Shattered, Mrs. Whipple now embraces her long-repressed feelings for He and acknowledges that her situation is indeed pitiable. As the story ends, it is not clear if Mrs. Whipple has been markedly changed by this experience, ready now to abandon her monomania and open herself honestly and caringly to those about her. She may instead quickly reassert her monologic authority, closing herself off once again within the confines of the isolated self. But it is clear that at least momentarily the hard shell of Mrs. Whipple's monologism has been cracked wide open, transforming for that short time her relationship with others.

Porter explores in other fiction from the late twenties to the mid-thirties the dangers of the isolated self turned inward, with particular focus on the illusions people construct and retreat into that distort their visions. As in "He," these stories frequently end with a shattering moment that opens characters to an understanding, if only momentary, of the limits of their isolated lives. A strong admirer of James Joyce's work, particularly *Dubliners,* Porter often fixed the fulcrum of her stories in these epiphanic moments. We have already seen, for instance, Laura's shattering realization in "Flowering Judas" of the destructiveness of her life of denial in her nightmare at the end after Eugenio's suicide. This narrative structure also underlies another of Porter's significant works from the period, "Theft" (1928).

"Theft" portrays another of Porter's women protagonists who suddenly gain insight about the emptiness of their lives of denial and negation. Like Laura in "Flowering Judas," the main character here (she remains unnamed) has withdrawn so far into her interior world that she lives essentially without will, allowing others to manipulate and control her life. She trivializes everything outside the self—possessions, friends, relationships. The narrative consciousness characterizes the governing force of the protagonist's life as a "principle of rejection," writing at one point of this character's thoughts: "She remembered how she had never locked a door in her life, on some principle of rejection in her that made her uncomfortable in the ownership of things, and her paradoxical boast before the warnings of her friends, that she had never lost a penny by theft; and she had been pleased with the bleak humility of this concrete example designed to illustrate and justify a certain fixed, otherwise baseless and general faith which ordered the movements of her life without regard to her will in the matter" (CS, 64). Her disarming passivity, like Laura's, represents another debilitating danger of the isolated self, quite different from the monomanic power exercised by the mother in "He" and by Cotton Mather: the danger of not taking responsibility for either one's own life or those of others, thus inviting and permitting domination and abuse by others not so withdrawn and submissive. Although not as spectacularly destructive as the monomaniacs, these passive individuals wreak pain and hardship on others through their apathy, as we have seen in Laura's complicity with Eugenio's suicide. In "Theft," the protagonist casually, even callously, dismisses her lover. Despite the deep feelings he voices in his letter to her—"thinking about you more than I mean to . . . yes, I even talk about you . . . why were you so anxious to destroy . . . even if I could see you now I would not . . . not worth all this abominable . . . the end" (CS, 63)—the protagonist remains unmoved, tearing up the letter with mechanical exactitude and then burning it.

The protagonist's crisis of identity comes after a maid steals her gold purse. When the woman confronts the maid about the missing handbag, the maid admits taking it, claiming that her niece needs it more than the protagonist does. The maid says that the protagonist has already had her chance at love and beauty (her words suggesting that she has come away with neither) but that her youthful niece still has a chance for fulfillment. The purse, she argues, should go to her, a woman still vibrant and hopeful. The maid's words completely disrupt the stability of the protagonist's sheltered life, bringing her to understand that she has lost a deeply felt emotional life shared with others by living entombed in her private world of self. The story ends with the protagonist's crushing realization that she herself is the most terrifying thief of all: "I was right not to be afraid of any thief but myself, who will end by leaving me nothing" (CS, 65).

Not all of Porter's stories from the mid-twenties to the mid-thirties focus exclusively on the terrors of the monologic self, the self conceived as sufficient and complete in its isolation. Porter was also well aware of the dangers to the individual in a controlled and constricted society, and in "Holiday," she explores this problem, depicting the struggles of another young woman given to withdrawal (as in "Theft") and of a family trying to come to grips with a disabled child (as in "He").[14] The family in "Holiday," however, is quite different from that in "He": rather than being controlled by an individual whose monologic power wreaks havoc on the family fortunes and the life of the disturbed child, the Müller family works as a cohesive unit, with each family member subsuming his or her individual identity into the larger group identity. Both in the home and in the fields, the family operates with precision and efficiency, but its success comes at a high cost. The Müllers' strengths and drawbacks emerge most clearly in the contrast between the life-styles of the family and the young woman who comes to visit and in the family's treatment of the misshapen daughter, Ottilie.

"Holiday" is the narrative of a woman recounting an episode from her younger days when she had fled to the countryside for temporary respite from her troubles. "It no longer can matter what kind of troubles they were, or what finally became of them," she writes. "It seemed to me then there was nothing to do but run away from them, though all my tradition, background, and training had taught me unanswerably that no one except a

14. Porter completed a first draft of "Holiday" in 1924. She put the manuscript aside and then worked on it again in the early thirties and again in the late fifties. The story was first published in 1960. Porter claimed that the published version was very close to her original draft.

coward ever runs from anything" (CS, 407). The narrator seeks precisely what Porter herself said time and again was necessary for her mental health: a period of withdrawal to collect thoughts and to gather energies, free from the pressures of everyday living and the demands of other people. Life at the Müllers' home suits her immensely. Off by herself in her room, she enjoys hearing the family speaking German in the rooms below. Not knowing the language, and thus not concerned with what they are saying, she takes comfort in the sounds and rhythms of "the thick warm voices," happily aware, as she writes, that "they were not talking to me and did not expect an answer." The silences she finds even more enriching. "I loved that silence which means freedom from the constant pressure of other minds and other opinions and other feelings," she observes, "that freedom to fold up in quiet and go back to my own center, to find out again, for it is always a rediscovery, what kind of creature it is that rules me finally, makes all the decisions no matter who thinks they make them, even I; who little by little takes everything away except the one thing I cannot live without, and who will one day say, 'Now I am all you have left—take me' " (CS, 413).

The narrator initially marvels at the Müllers' organization and efficiency, so different is the family's structured life from her less-ordered one. Watching and listening to one of the family's animated conversations, she notes that despite the apparent cacophony ("it sounded like a pitched battle," the narrator observes) the family members "were united in their tribal scepticisms, as in everything else. I got a powerful impression that they were all, even the sons-in-law, one human being divided into several separate appearances" (CS, 417). Mixed with her wonder, however, is a realization of the potential cost to identity that such demands for conformity entail. She notes that the only truly autonomous individual in the family is Ottilie, whom at this point she knows only as the servant girl. But autonomy means being outside the charmed circle of the family, and so Ottilie "belonged nowhere" (CS, 417). Indeed for most of the story we only see her at work, stumbling between kitchen and table, never at rest or settled. Her distance from the family's world is always apparent: as Ottilie scampers about unsteadily, the narrator observes that "no one moved aside for her, or spoke to her, or even glanced after her when she vanished into the kitchen" (CS, 415).

The tension in the narrator's feelings about the family only increases when she discovers that Ottilie is actually one of the Müllers' daughters. Aghast at the family's treatment of the girl, the narrator nonetheless attempts to reason out—the verb is hers—the Müllers' actions. She begins by observing that given the family's emphasis on efficiency and productivity, there was no place in their lives for what Ottilie represented to them: past pain and suffering. Their ignoring of her, the narrator suggests, is merely "simple forgetfulness," a forgetfulness that means Ottilie "moved among them as invisible to their imaginations as a ghost. Ottilie their sister was something painful that had happened long ago and now was past and done for; they could not live with that memory or its visible reminder—they forgot her in pure self-defense." The narrator continues to work through what she conjectures is the Müllers' thinking in their treatment of Ottilie, moving progressively toward a sympathetic understanding of their situation:

> The Müllers, what else could they have done with Ottilie? By a physical accident in her childhood she had been stripped of everything but her mere existence. It was not a society or a class that pampered its invalids and the unfit. So long as one lived, one did one's share. This was her place, in this family she had been born and must die; did she suffer? No one asked, no one looked to see. Suffering went with life, suffering and labor. While one lived one worked, that was all, and without complaints, for no one had time to listen, and everyone had his own troubles. So, what else could they have done with Ottilie? (*CS*, 427)

Finally, if somewhat begrudgingly, the narrator comes to accept the Müller family's structure and Ottilie's place within it. She finds the family's refusal to pity themselves and their determination to make do come whatever disaster particularly compelling. She concludes that the Müllers "with a deep right instinct had learned to live with her disaster on its own terms, and hers; they had accepted and then made use of what was for them only one more painful event in a world full of troubles, many of them worse than this. So, a step at a time, I followed the Müllers as nearly as I could in their acceptance of Ottilie, and the use they made of her life, for in some way that I could not quite explain to myself, I found great virtue and courage in their steadiness and refusal to feel sorry for anybody, least of all for themselves" (*CS,* 428). The narrator's admiration of the Müllers in large part derives from her knowing that they possess the fortitude to confront their problems that she herself sorely lacks, although she does not say so here. As she admitted at the outset of the story, her need to flee her problems precipitated her holiday excursion.

Despite her assertion of the Müllers' rightness in their dealings with Ottilie, the narrator does not sit entirely easy with her own conclusion, primarily because she has been deeply touched by the girl's humanity, the humanity that she knows that the Müllers do not recognize. The Müllers essentially ignore Ottilie, but the narrator does not, and perhaps the most telling thing she notices about her are the signs of anxiety in her actions and her gazes. The narrator is particularly fascinated with Ottilie's eyes, which she describes at one point as "troubled," at another as "wide and dazed," and at another, speaking particularly of her pupils, as "very large and strained with the anxiety of one peering into a darkness full of danger" (*CS,* 421, 425, 420). The depth and feeling that she notices in Ottilie's eyes suggest to the narrator that the servant girl is not the unfeeling automaton to which the Müllers' system reduces her, but an individual who suffers under subjugation. She suffers alone, unnoticed and uncared for, except for provisions for her basic physical needs. Ottilie's anxious eyes mirror the narrator's own unspoken uneasiness with the Müllers.

Further undermining her confidence in the Müllers is the intense connection the narrator feels with Ottilie. The narrator experiences a stunning shock of recognition after Ottilie, pointing to a picture of herself as a child, brings the narrator to realize that she is a member of the family. Her and Ottilie's lives suddenly intertwine: "The bit of cardboard [mounting Ottilie's photograph] connected her at once somehow to the world of human beings I knew; for an instant some filament lighter than cobweb spun itself out between that living center in her and in me, a filament from some center that held us all bound to our unescapable common source, so that her life and mine were kin, even a part of each other, and the painfulness and strangeness of her vanished." Although the mysterious moment of connection passes, with Ottilie retreating back into her secret existence from which she views everyone as a stranger, including the narrator, the narrator observes that "she was no stranger to me, and could not be again" (CS, 426).

The bond the narrator feels with Ottilie deepens during their ride together in the country on the day of Mrs. Müller's funeral. Shaken by Ottilie's howls as the funeral procession passes by the window, the narrator decides to take Ottilie to the ceremony, and the two of them ride out in a wagon in pursuit of the procession. As she had when Ottilie had showed her her photograph, the narrator experiences an overpowering sense of connection with the servant girl, this time so profound that on some deep level she enters Ottilie's world, gripped by a compulsion to let out a fierce howl—Ottilie's method at communication—to voice her rage at the Müllers' injustice and her and Ottilie's isolation. "My sense of her realness, her humanity, this shattered being that was a woman," the narrator writes, "was so shocking to me that a howl as doglike and despairing as her own rose in me unuttered and died again, to be a perpetual ghost. Ottilie slanted her eyes and peered at me, and I gazed back" (CS, 434).

The narrator's perceived interconnection with Ottilie quickly comes undone when the girl unexpectedly laughs aloud and claps her hands for joy, not because she is on the way to the funeral or because she has been touched deeply by the narrator's gaze, but from something much simpler, the warmth of the sun perhaps, or the lurching of the wagon. The narrator immediately realizes her mistake in thinking that she had broken through to the young woman, seeing that "she was beyond my reach as well as any other human reach." Nonetheless, she also understands that her time with Ottilie has not been without significance for either of them. "Had I not come nearer to her than I had to anyone else in my attempt to deny and bridge the distance between us, or rather, her distance from me?" she asks. "Well, we were both equally the fools of life, equally fellow fugitives from death. We had escaped for one day more at least. We would celebrate our good luck, we would have a little stolen holiday, a breath of spring air and freedom on this lovely festive afternoon" (CS, 434–35). Here the narrator affirms the separateness that divides all people but also the value of striving to overcome that separateness, a finally impossible but nonetheless meaningful task since our humanity emerges most fully in our struggles. This is the struggle the Müllers refuse to make, living instead to maintain and protect their design, the family order, thereby in a sense "forgetting" both their humanity as well as Ottilie's. As outsiders, both Ottilie and the narrator are, as the narrator suggests, "fools"—not dupes, but "fools of life," individuals who are piercingly aware of the enriching springs of their humanity and of the simple joys possible in an otherwise harsh and forbidding existence. The narrator achieves her insight through her interactions with Ottilie and preserves her knowledge, as Ottilie does, with a commitment never to forget. Ottilie, as we saw in the incident with her photograph, maintains her integrity by never forgetting her past and by attempting to communicate it to others. Likewise the narrator, the story suggests, overcomes her spiritual barrenness by never forgetting her brief life with Ottilie, a victory heralded by her retelling of her story, "Holiday."

Quite different is the narrator's achievement in "Holiday" from the monomania of Cotton Mather or the utter insularity of the protagonist in "Theft." Unlike these other two individuals, the narrator of "Holiday" breaks the stranglehold of solipsism that threatened to smother her life into silence. So too does she resist the finally dehumanizing life of the Müllers, a dehumanizing existence of assembly-line efficiency, each person confined to his or her place in the rigid order. The narrator's ongoing efforts to achieve insight and fulfillment, as she realizes, demand courage and honesty both in her life with others and in her explorations of the teeming depths of her memory.

# 5

# The Southern Heritage

Most writers now associated with the southern literary renascence did not begin their careers seeing themselves as southern writers. In fact many went out of their way to avoid any type of regional identification. Even the editors of the *Fugitive,* the literary journal whose short run from 1922 to 1925 many mark as the beginning of the renascence (though clearly Kate Chopin, James Branch Cabell, and Ellen Glasgow, among others, had already been preparing the way), began the initial issue by forthrightly announcing both the demise of southern literature and the journal's distance from the region's literary heritage. "Official exception having been taken by the sovereign people to the mint julep," they wrote, "a literary phase known rather euphemistically as Southern Literature has expired, like any other stream whose source is stopped up. The demise was not untimely: among other advantages, THE FUGITIVE is enabled to come to birth in Nashville, Tennessee, under a star not entirely unsympathetic. THE FUGITIVE flees from nothing faster than from the high-caste Brahmins of the Old South."[1] This came from a group of writers, many of whom, including Allen Tate, John Crowe Ransom, and Donald Davidson, were soon to be committed southern chauvinists, literary and otherwise.

Many southern writers of the twenties and thirties did not embrace a regional identity until after they had left the region and lived elsewhere.

1. "Foreword," *Fugitive,* I (April, 1922), 2.

The turnabout in literary allegiance of Allen Tate, a writer not much in favor these days but who nonetheless stands as a crucial figure in southern writing during much of the twentieth century, is not atypical, even in its extremity. While at Vanderbilt University as an active member of the Fugitive group, Tate enthusiastically espoused his modernist—but not his southern—allegiances. Not long after moving to New York in 1924, however, Tate began a profound reevaluation of his southern roots and identity. As Louis D. Rubin, Jr., has remarked, with Tate's "predictable experience of provincial unease in the metropolis, the awareness of his southern origins and attitudes became much more important to him. In Nashville he could confidently identify himself with modernism and cosmopolitan sophistication, for the value of the southern identity went unquestioned and unremarked; but in New York it was another matter." It was another matter indeed: in fact, so encompassing was the pressure of New York intellectual life upon Tate—"his whole background, his whole being, was under challenge," Radcliffe Squires observes—that in response Tate not only reassessed his own "southernness" but also looked to the South's history and tradition for perspective, order, and stability. He even went so far as to become an expert on the Civil War (besides immersing himself in partisan reading, Tate also traveled to battlefields and studied intricate battle tactics) and to write biographies of Stonewall Jackson and Jefferson Davis. He began but did not complete one on Robert E. Lee. "I think if I'd stayed in the South, I might have become anti-Southern," Tate commented years later, "but I became a Southerner again by going East."[2]

At about the same time that Tate was reevaluating his southern heritage and identity, Katherine Anne Porter, who was a friend of Tate's and other southerners living in New York, began going through a similar, if less openly political and chauvinist, reappraisal of her Texas roots and her relationship with the South. Before this time, Porter could have been called a rebel only in the sense of being scornful of tradition and authority. Quite simply there was nothing unreconstructed about her. After leaving her first

2. Louis D. Rubin, Jr., *The Wary Fugitives: Four Poets and the South* (Baton Rouge, 1978), 92; Radcliffe Squires, *Allen Tate: A Literary Biography* (New York, 1971), 60; Tate quoted in Irv Broughton, "An Interview with Allen Tate," *Western Humanities Review*, XXXII (1978), 329.

husband, John Henry Koontz, in 1916, Porter lived a freewheeling (if not completely happy) life that ran roughshod over her traditional upbringing and that boldly stamped her as an independent woman, a social activist, and a writer—three roles antithetical to the subservience customarily demanded of southern women. As we have seen, by the early twenties Porter had centered her life in two places that aptly embodied her deep disregard of restraint: Greenwich Village, America's hotbed of artistic and political dissent, and Mexico, a land troubled by the throes of violent social revolution. Porter felt inspired and energized by both places, at least initially. The traditional heritage of her Texas upbringing and more generally of the South, on the other hand, had little or no place during this time in her thinking and her art.

That situation changed rather dramatically in the mid- to late twenties, when Porter began looking to Texas and the South for inspiration and identity. Her exploration of the world of her upbringing largely derived from her growing interest in the significance of memory in the creation of self and art. As we saw in the first chapter, Porter during this period began to look to memory as the means to resolve the conflicting pulls she felt between living as fully as possible—and thus dispersing her creative energies—and withdrawing into solitude to collect those energies—and thus living emptily, without what Porter called "adventures" that later could become, through the hard work of recollection and reflection, experiences. Memory was also a powerful weapon to resist what she now was seeing as the crushing dislocation and chaos marking modern civilization. By the early thirties, engaging the depths of memory clearly had become for Porter the primary creative process for forging a meaningful understanding of self and a rich and vibrant art. This creative process stood in stark contrast with that embraced by those writers, identified by Hayden White as modernist, who attempted to obliterate history and memory in their celebration of the fecundity of the present moment.

For Porter the engagement with memory was ideally dialogic, with one's present self freely interacting with—neither dominating nor being dominated by—the secret inner self that teemed with the mysterious meanings of one's memories. In this dialogic encounter, the conscious and secret selves were brought under challenge, each vulnerable to the other, each finally remade in the light of the other in an ongoing process of decentering and displacement. Rarely easy or painless, such regeneration was a means to enlarge the consciousness by shattering the everyday self's sense of wholeness, thereby opening it to a more expansive and enriched perspective of reality and self. Such growth, Porter believed, should be, and came to be for her, the driving force behind all human and, most particularly, artistic endeavor. The tensions involved in Porter's own dialogue between her conscious self and memory characteristically took the shape of a charged interplay between the modernism of her adult life and what she came to see as the southern traditionalism of her childhood. In her essay "Henry Green: Novelist of the Imagination," Eudora Welty argues that all writers, through their extended creative struggles, evolve distinctive fictional patterns—orderings of experience, embodied in the shape of their fiction, that recur again and again and reveal how the writers interpret, in Welty's words, "what life is up to."[3] In Porter's mature fiction, particularly that of the South, the interplay between self and memory is arguably her fictional pattern.

By the late twenties evidence of Porter's new interest in southern traditionalism began to surface just about everywhere in her life. In a stunning turnabout, given the bitterness that consumed her when she had years earlier moved away from Texas and the literal and psychological distance that she had maintained from the region, Porter in 1929 gave serious consideration to moving to Dixie, specifically Virginia, the citadel of the southern aristocratic tradition. (This was long before the state's tourist bureau heralded the slogan "Virginia Is for Lovers." Porter no doubt would have relished that.) Sparking her interest in returning was her close relationship with Allen Tate and Caroline Gordon. Tate and Gordon were at this time looking into the possibility of buying some family land in Virginia. They hoped to move there and to convince other southern writers to settle there too, forming a southern artists' colony. Porter was offered five acres, and she was excited. In a letter dated July 5, 1929, to Becky and John Crawford, she wrote enthusiastically of the project, saying forthrightly that "if I don't live in New York—and certainly I can't say I have ever really lived there,

3. Eudora Welty, "Henry Green: Novelist of the Imagination," in *The Eye of the Story: Selected Essays and Reviews* (New York, 1978), 26.

it[']s been such a bloody struggle—then I choose Virginia, of all places in this country." She invited the Crawfords to consider moving to Virginia too and wrote warmly of the community life she envisioned there: "After all, John's people were Virginians, mine were, Carolyn [Caroline Gordon], Red Warren, Andrew Lytle; all had grandfathers or fathers or as in my case, my mother, from that state: and I think it would be noble to get up a migration back to the Old Dominion. John ought to be able to work there, right in amongst the scenes of his ancestry, as twere. And each one of us would be within shouting distance of a sympathetic neighbor, yet separate enough to set up our little establishments independent like, and do our own tradin'" (McKeldin).

Porter's vision of life in Virginia is striking, describing what she had come to see as the ideal life-style of the writer: to work in seclusion but to live within a community of soul mates. Noteworthy, too, is that Porter's envisioned community is absolutely southern, located in the South and peopled by southerners. This southern orientation demonstrates the powerful pull of a southern identity, in her imaginative if not always her everyday life, that was now haunting Porter. It was a pull that profoundly affected Porter's imaginative vision and fiction, arguably the shaping force of most of her best fiction. Porter ended up not moving to Virginia because, upon their return from Europe, Tate and Gordon gave up their plans and instead moved to Tennessee. But even had her two friends followed through with their Virginia move, Porter probably would not have joined them. Whatever apparently unquestioned enthusiasm for the South Porter at times expressed, she nonetheless had deeply conflicting feelings about the region, torn as she was by the ongoing tension between her traditionalist and modernist sensibilities. Porter clearly was more interested in exploring the nature of her newly adopted southern identity, and in using that identity as a means of understanding herself and the world, than she was in living the everyday life of a southerner in the South. Her customary sensibilities and desires were primarily those of the sophisticated and fashionable of New York, and so it was much easier and more desirable for Porter to be a "southerner" while living outside the region. There she could imaginatively explore her "southernness" without having to live as a traditional southerner among traditional southerners—a life that never appealed to her.

(The envisioned writers' colony in Virginia was of course far from traditional southern life.) Moreover, because Porter's interest in the South and
southern identity derived far less from contemporary happenings in the
South than from the workings of her consciousness (most particularly those
within the realm of memory), being away from the South allowed for a
freer play of thought and imaginative construction, a vision truer to the
mind and heart of the creator than necessarily to the reality of Dixie.

That Porter spent very little of her adult life living in the South—
except for relatively brief stays in Texas and Louisiana in the late thirties,
when she was involved with and then married to Albert Erskine—points
to her resistance to embracing wholeheartedly an unadulterated southern
identity. Even in her letter to the Crawfords, singing the praises of life in
Virginia, she still foregrounds life in the cosmopolitan North ("if I don't
live in New York"), suggesting the pull northward, with all that it entailed
for perspective and vision, that always gripped her. This tension between
her modernist and traditionalist sympathies became even more apparent
by the early thirties, a time when a number of Porter's southern writer
friends—Allen Tate, Andrew Lytle, and Robert Penn Warren, for example—were deeply involved in the Agrarian movement. Unlike them,
Porter never took her stand. Despite expressing sympathy for agrarianism
in her correspondence, Porter kept her distance from active involvement in
the movement, a choice similar to her response to the South in general.[4] In
a revealing letter to her father on June 26, 1931, Porter discussed her conflicting sympathies for the communism of the Soviet Union and the tradi-

4. Mary Titus has argued that much of Porter's fiction of the South can be understood
as a "gender-inflected response to the Agrarian pursuit. . . . a cultural myth she found both
appealing and repressive." See Titus, "Katherine Anne Porter's Miranda: The Agrarian
Myth and Southern Womanhood," in *Gender and Genre in Literature: Redefining Autobiography in Twentieth-Century Women's Fiction,* ed. Janice Morgan and Colette T. Hall (New
York, 1991), 193–208. Porter's early dabbling into radical politics certainly had an impact on
her views of her homeland. She claimed that at age fourteen she saw Eugene Debs speak
and was favorably impressed; and there is no doubt she was painfully aware of the plight of
small farmers and sharecroppers. For a discussion of Porter's early politics, see Walsh, *Katherine Anne Porter and Mexico,* 1–4.

tionalism of the South (as celebrated by the Agrarians), an opposition that in itself reveals how far she stood from her Agrarian friends, several of whom had wanted *I'll Take My Stand* to be entitled "Tracts Against Communism." Saying that she was planning to travel to Europe to get a good look at Germany and Russia, "the two most promising and hard-driven countries in Europe," she adds: "I have, and have had for twelve years a sympathy for Russia, but I want to see for myself what is really going on there. I doubt if ever I can be a real communist, but am what Trotsky defined as a 'Fellowtraveller.'" Porter then recommends that her father read Andrew Lytle's *Bedford Forrest and His Critter Company,* calling it "a very grand new book out by a good friend of mine." Of Lytle she writes: "Andrew is a throw-back, and whoops her up for the Old South. I told him I'd heard of the war being fought over again at intervals in those parts, and had even listened to some of it in my time, but I never saw it fit [*sic*] over round by round, charge by charge, volley by volley, until I read his Bedford Forrest" (McKeldin).

Porter identifies Lytle in this letter to her father as one of the "Southern Agrarian Crowd" who had recently brought out *I'll Take My Stand,* and she notes, in a statement indicating both her affinities with the group and her desire to impress her father, that "of the twelve contributors, six are friends of mine." Whatever ties she held with the Agrarians, Porter goes on in her letter to make it clear that she is no flag-waving supporter of the cause. In a revealing comment, suggesting the far-from-serious attitude with which she regarded the Agrarians, she says that of all the essays in the symposium, Lytle's "The Hind Tit: A Defense of the Plain People" "was the most amusing." Given the scope of Porter's modernist allegiances, her casual dismissal of Lytle's essay, and more generally of the entire Agrarian symposium, is anything but surprising. Porter's singling out of Lytle's essay no doubt owes to the literalism of his Agrarian vision. As Louis D. Rubin, Jr., has pointed out, the contributors to *I'll Take My Stand* had very different ideas about the nature of agrarianism, some seeing the basic ideas as expressed in John Crowe Ransom's "Introduction: A Statement of Principles" as primarily a perspective for understanding the South and more generally Western society and history, others seeing them as the basis for a concrete program of social and political action.[5] With "The Hind Tit," Lytle clearly fell in with the latter, and with this group Porter had particularly little sympathy, other than perhaps sharing a nostalgia for the southern myth of the simple life in bygone days.

For Lytle, however, the southern legend of happy life on the farm was anything but legendary, and in "The Hind Tit" he makes a forthright call for a society based on self-sufficient small farmers. Lytle argues that life on the traditional small farms untainted by newfangled inventions (like tractors) and economic concerns (like money) is whole and wholesome, and in the essay's long second section he describes one day in the life of a yeoman farm family, from early morning rising and chores to evening folk singings and get-togethers. During the day everyone labors happily, secure in his or her role and responsibilities. Leisure is equally enriching, as healthy as the family meals and as joyful as the communal sing-alongs. The archfiend of this Eden is the "pizen snake" of modernism that has ever since the fall of the Confederacy been slithering into the southern countryside, wreaking havoc not only upon the rural economic system but upon the entire culture that that system supports and indeed embodies (a process of disintegration that Lytle describes in excruciating detail in the essay's third section). The conflict between traditionalism and modernism on the farm is nothing short of Miltonic: "It is a war to the death between technology and the ordinary human functions of living," Lytle declares.[6] Lytle's answer to the destructiveness of industrialism is quite simple: people should turn their backs on all inroads of modernity (including the very roads themselves—Lytle has a good deal to say about the instability to the traditional countryside ushered in by good roads projects) and make do on their small plots of land. Lytle's call to the small farmer approaches the outrageous in its hopefulness and simplicity:

> Until he and the agrarian West and all the conservative communities throughout the United States can unite on some common political action, he must deny himself the articles the industrialists offer for sale. It is not

5. Rubin, *The Wary Fugitives,* 187–250.
6. Andrew Lytle, "The Hind Tit," in Twelve Southerners, *I'll Take My Stand: The South and the Agrarian Tradition* (1930; rpr, New York, 1962), 202.

so impossible as it may seem at first, for, after all, the necessities they machine-facture were once manufactured on the land, and as for the bric-à-brac, let it rot on their hands. Do what we did after the war and the Reconstruction: return to our looms, our handcrafts, our reproducing stock. Throw out the radio and take down the fiddle from the wall. Forsake the movies for the play-parties and the square dances. And turn away from the liberal capons who fill the pulpits as preachers. Seek a priesthood that may manifest the will and intelligence to renounce science and search out the Word in the authorities.[7]

Even if, as some have argued, Lytle exaggerates here for shock effect (a proposition far from conclusive, as his statement is perfectly consistent in the context of the entire essay), his words suggest the intensity with which he rejects the modern spirit and what he sees as its industrial culture.

Certainly it is this blanket disavowal of modern society that Porter found so amusing in Lytle's essay. If Porter felt the attraction of the simple life on the farm, she never saw her feelings constituting an utter rejection of her modern identity or its culture. Had she moved to Virginia with Tate and Gordon, she would have been a writer (and not one of Civil War biographies and romances), not a farmer, and no doubt would have listened to the radio, kept food in a refrigerator, and read and written by electric light. Amusing, too, Porter must have found Lytle's comment on the danger to the settled mind that a knowledge of the North, specifically New York City, could bring. Commenting on the amazement of a traveler to the South named Olmstead about the ignorance he had found in young southern farmers (some of whom thought New York lay south of Tennessee), Lytle counters that "although [Olmstead] could never know it, it was the tragedy of these people that they ever learned where New York lay, for such knowledge has taken them from a place where they knew little geography but knew it well, to places where they see much and know nothing."[8] Although no rabid defender of New York, Porter also knew that the social and intellectual freedom she found there offered her a much richer opportunity for reaching full artistic and personal achievement than did the roles desig-

7. *Ibid*, 244.
8. Lytle, "The Hind Tit," in Twelve Southerners, *I'll Take My Stand,* 211.

nated to women on small farms. And she knew, too, that a number of the best writers from the South were then or had been living in New York, and not in, say, Opelika, Alabama, or Cairo, Georgia. (Lytle of course had for a time lived in New York, but in 1929 he returned to permanent residence in the South.) Unlike Lytle, who recognized modernism only to dismiss it before his beloved traditionalism, Porter came to see the two as ideologies poised in an unresolved opposition that fostered healthy resistance and dialogue rather than the silencing of one by the other. Both sides had their say; both sides were privileged. In this same letter to her father Porter spoke of her own conflicting feelings toward the South and agrarianism, poising them against her sympathies for the Soviet Union, at that time the embodiment for Porter of the most modern of societies. Of Lytle's enthusiasm for the South, Porter wrote: "I have a deep sentimental feeling about it all,—near communist that I am—and am torn between a feeling that it[']s all perfectly useless and a wish that it were not. Between the Old South, or even the New One, and Russia there's a long, long way to go. Let's see whether or not I make it" (McKeldin).

During the thirties Porter's enthusiasm for the Soviet Union cooled while her feelings for the South intensified. Even so, during this time of eager interest in the South, Porter, unlike Lytle and some of the other Agrarians, continued to resist the temptation to embrace with unquestioning zeal the ideal of "southernness" and instead strove to maintain in her consciousness and her fiction what she saw as the procreative dialogue between southern traditionalism and northern modernism. Porter saw this dialogue as incomplete and ongoing, the most potent expression of the interplay between her social self (associated with the present, particularly her sophisticated life as modern artist) and her memories (the past, particularly her Texas upbringing). In many regards the presence of this dialogue in Porter's thinking marks the maturation of her imaginative vision, the resistance and tension between the two voices providing her with perspective and insight for critical understanding and judgment. Flannery O'Connor, in a letter dated September 15, 1955, to Andrew Lytle, described a similar tension in her consciousness, commenting that the interplay between her Catholic and southern sensibilities crucially defined her vision. "To my way of thinking," O'Connor wrote, "the only thing that keeps me from being a regional writer is being a Catholic and the only thing that keeps me from being a Catholic writer (in the narrow sense) is being a Southerner."[9] For O'Connor the opposition between her conflicting sensibilities (an opposition she embraced) kept her from being limited by the single perspective of either. Indeed, one could argue, as her words here suggest, that the foundation of O'Connor's imaginative vision lies somewhere in the murky frontier between her southernness and her Catholicism. Similarly, the interplay between Porter's modernism and traditionalism enlarged and invigorated her vision. Like O'Connor's, Porter's fiction was thus a "frontier" art, fiction arising from the interactions of opposing views that did not resolve themselves in neat dialectical syntheses but rather remained interlocked in active and ongoing engagement.

By the mid-thirties Porter's interest in the South had become so prominent that she was now seeing herself as a southern writer. Because being Southern did not mean to her that she had to silence her modernist voice—as it did to, say, Andrew Lytle and Donald Davidson—Porter saw herself as a southern writer with a difference. "I don't have to be Stark Young to be southern, thank God," she wrote on March 14, 1938, to Albert Erskine, and she discussed her relationship to the southern literary tradition:

> It[']s true that I feel rather generally and amply southern, rather than "regional" whatever that may mean, and I see no reason why I should not write about any kind of person or any part of the world I know enough to write about, nor why I should adopt any attitudes or sets of beliefs because some southerners have so adopted them, and in the long run I mean to think[,] feel and write as I please, and say what I believe, the same as I have from the beginning. I am not in the least afraid of not being southern, since I am, born, bred, and for a hundred fifty years. If I am not quite according to pattern, still it remains and no one can change it that I am one kind of product of the south. . . . So in this matter at least I am very serene and fixed and unassailable. (McKeldin)

9. Flannery O'Connor, *The Habit of Being: Letters,* ed. Sally Fitzgerald (New York, 1979), 104.

In another letter to Erskine dated October 16, 1940, Porter discussed her complicated feelings toward her southern readership, an audience that she felt both far from and close to. "I have had several letters from extremely old people from the south," Porter wrote, "and it is strange how touching they are to me: I feel so far away, and I could not live in their company, or share their beliefs or thoughts, I fairly tore myself by the roots out of that way of life, and yet it makes me very tender to know they approve of me, and feel that I am really theirs; they produced me, after all, and are proud of me" (McKeldin). Porter's ambivalence here is of course a manifestation of her uneasy relationship with the region in general.

Given the charged dynamics of the interplay between her traditionalism and modernism, together with her fickleness, Porter not surprisingly wavered in her professed allegiances to her southern and modern identities, even if on one level she strove to keep them in balance. While neither voice was ever entirely silenced, Porter from the late twenties through the thirties passed through periods in which she distinctly favored one voice over the other, although never for long and never with unchallenged authority. At times Porter came close to identifying herself fully as a down-home southerner, as in her May 3, 1933, letter to Ford Madox Ford in which she distanced herself from the Agrarians not because of her modernism but because of her closeness to rural life, a claim that no doubt would have surprised the Agrarians as it most certainly must have Ford. Porter wrote Ford: "As an agrarian—I mean a real one, not one of those literary fellows who plants all his potatoes on paper—I was fascinated with the experiments in making a new kind of potatoe, and I wish I might have particulars of your way of raising corn" (McKeldin). Even more revealing than her words here to Ford of what we might call Porter's southern chauvinism are her frequent defenses of the region in her letters to friends. Porter was particularly riled by those critics who she believed unfairly attacked, for personal or political reasons, the South's settled way of life and the traditions that underpinned the region's identity and community structure.

Porter's comments on James Agee's poem "Dixie Doodle," published in the February, 1938, issue of *Partisan Review,* are representative of these defenses. "Dixie Doodle," reproduced here in full, bitterly attacks what the poet sees as the destructive provincialism and racism undergirding southern gentility and honor:

> In the region of the Tee Vee Aye,
> Of the cedars and the sick red clay,
> We've discovered a solution
> Neither hearstian nor rooshian
> In the embers of a burnt-out day.
>
> When the world swings back to sense
> (But the world is *so* damned dense)
> An indisputably aryan
> Jeffersonian Agrarian
> Will be settn awn the Ole Rail Fence,
>
> Swaying lightly with a hot cawn bun,
> Quoting Horace and the late Jawn Donne,
> He will keep the annual figgers
> Safe away from the eyes of niggers,
> And back his Culture up with whip and gun:
>
> And in every single solitary region
> We'll each frame our millenium
> In a native-hewn proscenium
> Unbedunged by any nonindigenous pigeon.[10]

Porter voiced her fury with Agee's poem in a February 22, 1938, letter to Erskine, calling it "nasty," adding that Agee "knows better, the little bastard." Especially loathsome to Porter was what she saw as Agee's pretentiousness, a stance she believed Agee took to impress both ignorant poor whites and educated northerners, two prominent threats to the southern status quo, particularly when galvanized by radical ideology. For Porter, coming to terms with the South and one's relationship to its traditions was a complex and convoluted enterprise, involving the deepest depths of

10. James Agee, "Dixie Doodle," *Partisan Review,* IV (February, 1938), 8.

KATHERINE ANNE PORTER'S ARTISTIC DEVELOPMENT

memory and identity. Although she did not say so explicitly in her letter to Erskine, she apparently interpreted Agee's attack on the region as a refusal to wrestle with these problems on the deep level she saw as necessary for achieving fullness in both personal development and artistic creation. Rather than trying to fathom both the virtues and the evils of the South—for Porter they were interconnected, each interpenetrated by the other—Porter saw Agee simplifying merely for poetic and political effect, his manipulation of southern dialect indicative of his overall distortion of southern life. Noting Agee's depiction of the southern gentleman and then expanding her criticism to the entire poem, Porter wrote:

> Here is one Aryan Jeffersonian Agrarian who is going to get a rail fence to perch on, bake corn pone (shame on him, saying *bun* for the sake of rhyme)[,] quote Horace and Donne if my memory serves me; and think it is the good life. As for the rest of his poem, it is fustian and he knows it. All of it is, for that matter. But he has no doubt made a marvellous effect in certain ineducable circles; but they really say these things better, and he should leave it all to them. . . . that sort of thing, to be said really well, needs a background of ignorance such as Agee cannot pretend to, though it would be better for him if he could. (McKeldin)

Clearly Porter saw Agee in "Dixie Doodle" as wearing a mask false to self and vision. By her standards he possessed little, if any, artistic integrity.

That Agee was a southerner only increased Porter's anger. As she commented, he should have known better. But Porter's ire toward outside critics of the South could be just as fierce, particularly if they happened to be from the North, those damn Yankees! When she was awash in her southern chauvinism, her attitude toward Yankees, as she put it in an undated letter to Gay Holloway (probably written in 1933, according to Porter's later marginal comment), was quite simple: "I'd rather *see* than *be* one" (McKeldin). Porter saw northerners as not only askew in their understanding and judgment of the South but also in large part responsible for the region's problems. To Malcolm Cowley, Porter wrote on October 2, 1942, that the South was under the grip of what she called the "New Carpetbaggers," wealthy northerners who had moved to Dixie to ape southern gentility and/or to exploit the working class. "The New Carpetbaggers have got the place really," she wrote Cowley, speaking of the region as a whole, "and if you want to see a negro mistreated, you should see the feudal establishments set up by the Yankees who come down and buy up places and pretend they are old southern aristocrats with slaves; and go through the Yankee owned factories established there explicitly to exploit cheap labor." Porter ended her discussion with a blunt analysis of Yankee imperialism: "The south as it stands is the work of the north and the north must be made to admit it. Anything else is just bloody lying nonsense. It is a colonial province exploited in much the same way as colonies are exploited anywhere" (McKeldin).

If Porter at times staunchly defended the South, sounding if not like a loyal Daughter of the Confederacy ("I am the grandchild of a lost War, and I have blood-knowledge of what life can be in a defeated country on the bare bones of privation," she begins her 1944 essay "Portrait: Old South" [*CE*, 160]) then at least like a Nashville Agrarian, she also at other times severely criticized the region and its traditions, particularly the Agrarian ideal of small-farm life. Her commentary on the privations of rural living in part derived from her more aggressive sympathy with the aristocratic, patriarchal southern ideal, but even more crucially from her urban, modernist sensibility.[11] In some notes she made in 1937 at Allen Tate's and Caroline Gordon's farm, Benfolly, near Clarksville, Tennessee, Porter bemoaned the wretched lives of a farm laboring family, the Normans, who worked there. She idealized nothing here in her portrait of southern farm life. After describing a comic car trip taking the Normans to church (ten people crammed into a five-seater), Porter comments on the futility of the Normans' lives, beginning with a statement on the shouting tradition that highlights their intensely emotional religious service: "This awful hysteria, the only outlet they have. It takes the place of every good and human thing with them. They are inept in everything, cannot plant and keep a garden going, cannot use their hands expertly, cannot milk a cow so that she will give her milk properly, cannot wash and comb themselves so they will be

11. For discussions of how the yeoman and patriarchal ideals have shaped the southern imagination, see two works by Richard Gray: *The Literature of Memory* and *Writing the South: Ideas of an American Region* (Cambridge, Eng., 1986).

comfortable" (McKeldin). Porter's words here call to mind Tate's "The Mediterranean" (1932), wherein the poet depicts the South as less the inheritor of Western civilization (the ancient glories of which the poet, at a picnic on the Mediterranean, describes in the first part of the poem) than a wasteland that is fertile but untended, with crops rotting and lives languishing:

> Now, from the Gates of Hercules we flood
>
> Westward, westward till the barbarous brine
> Whelms us to the tired land where tasseling corn,
> Fat beans, grapes sweeter than muscadine
> Rot on the vine: in that land were we born.[12]

Similarly, Porter in her notes contrasts the languishing South with a more glorious Europe, although in her case she looks not to the Mediterranean and its ancient traditions but to the Black Forest with its efficient social and economic structure. She remembers the Black Forest as a region "with every foot of land under cultivation, with careful people taking thought of their affairs, each man making a garden spot, everyone living to the best of his ability every hour of every day." Far different is Porter's description of the idleness and despair at Benfolly, where the Normans fail to draw sustenance from the land and its traditions. In her depiction of Benfolly, Porter finds particularly striking the listless life of the Norman children, but her criticism quickly becomes more encompassing: "The children, just standing about all day long, doing not[h]ing, no love of life, nothing to look forward to, no interest in the present moment . . . sad, sickly teeth growing badly, no love of their land, no memory of tradition . . . idle and weary and hopeless. . . . Here are a hundred acres, beautiful woods, a good spring, a fine bottom land, two cows, everything neglected, nothing used properly; they live in misery and the Tates in a bitter, endless, futile anxiety. . . . WHY? There is something wrong with this country." What is wrong, Porter makes clear, is the hopelessness. "Any one can defeat these people,"

12. Allen Tate, "The Mediterranean," in Tate, *Collected Poems, 1919–1976* (New York, 1977), 67.

Porter writes of those living in rural South, "for they have already given up hope." The people of the Black Forest, in contrast, whom Porter says are vibrant with "the forces of life," are Germany's hope for the future (McKeldin). Porter goes so far as to suggest that it may be the people of the Black Forest who can still bring down Hitler.

Of particular interest in these notes is Porter's criticism of Tate and Gordon, two southern intellectuals who, not unlike herself, were at that time struggling to integrate their southern heritages into their identities as modern artists. Porter's critique suggests that she saw Tate and Gordon, in their returning to the South to live on a farm, as taking their struggles to seize hold of their southern traditions too literally. Near the end of "Remarks on the Southern Religion," Tate's contribution to *I'll Take My Stand,* Tate asks how modern southerners, adrift from their tradition, can reinvigorate their lives with the southern heritage and achieve fulfillment. Tate's famous answer is "by violence," and by this he does not mean that southerners should take up arms in social revolution but instead that they should will themselves to embrace their southernness. Such acts of psychological desire are violent in that they thoroughly disrupt the modern sensibilities by which southerners—those, at least, of Tate's persuasion—normally live. Tate never underestimated the difficulty, and indeed the possible futility, of such endeavor. "Remarks on the Southern Religion" ends not with southern jingoism but with hesitancy and reservation: "The Southerner is faced with the paradox: He must use an instrument, which is political, and so unrealistic and pretentious that he cannot believe in it, to re-establish a private, self-contained, and essentially spiritual life. I say that he must do this; but that remains to be seen."[13] Despite these reservations, Tate and, to a lesser extent, Gordon for a number of years sought to will themselves into a nourishing relationship with their heritage. Their move to Benfolly was in large part a statement of their commitment to their efforts and to the South.

No doubt on one level Porter sympathized with Tate's and Gordon's ordeals, for she too sought to ground her identity and vision thoroughly in

---

13. Allen Tate, "Remarks on the Southern Religion," in Twelve Southerners, *I'll Take My Stand,* 174, 175.

a southern past. And yet for Porter to embrace southern tradition did not entail a move to the South and the establishment of a southern social and political agenda. Her involvement with the South was less literal than it was psychological, and it called for a turn inward to engage the depths of memory in an ongoing quest for understanding. Flannery O'Connor liked to say that the descent into self was also a descent into region, since a person's imaginative life was shaped more by the world of his or her upbringing than by later learned beliefs. In "The Catholic Novelist in the Protestant South," O'Connor discussed how the deepest imaginative lives of southern Catholic writers are finally southern rather than Catholic. Her observations speak to the imaginations of all writers:

> The things we see, hear, smell, and touch affect us long before we believe anything at all, and the South impresses its image on us from the moment we are able to distinguish one sound from another. By the time we are able to use our imaginations for fiction, we find that our senses have responded irrevocably to a certain reality. This discovery of being bound through the senses to a particular society and a particular history, to particular sounds and a particular idiom, is for the writer the beginning of a recognition that first puts his work into real human perspective for him.[14]

Porter, I believe, made a similar discovery, seeing her imaginative life integrally bound up in her Texas upbringing and her recontextualized southern interpretation of it. But her discovery challenged rather than resolved: she knew that to understand southern traditionalism and its significance to her vision and fiction meant continuously bringing her feelings toward the region under close investigation and working them into the larger context of her entire life. These efforts in part explain Porter's inconsistencies about and uneasiness toward Texas and the South. While Porter understood that her imagination at its most fundamental was shaped by her upbringing, she also knew that that life as it existed within her memory was not fixed and final but was rather ever changing and fluid in scope and significance—as her southern interpretation of it bears witness. The world of memory, Por-

14. O'Connor, "The Catholic Novelist in the Protestant South," in O'Connor, *Mystery and Manners,* 197.

ter came to see, was always being reshaped and redefined in encounters with the conscious self, just as the conscious self was always being reformulated in response to one's memories.

Certainly by the mid-thirties Porter had come to see artistic creation as a deeply reflective endeavor, a process in which, to cite again a passage from "Three Statements about Writing," "memory, legend, personal experience, and acquired knowledge" come together and interact "in a constant process of re-creation" (*CE,* 451). While Porter believed that art and artistic order ultimately derived from experiences in the memory, she also understood that mere recall was not enough for heightened understanding and enriched imaginative creation. Memories had to be pressured and transformed by one's present perspective. In some undated notes, Porter wrote that "no memory is really faithful; it has too far to go through too changing a landscape of the mind and heart, to bear any sort of really trustwort[h]y witness except in part." "For the truth of art," she continued, "is got by working[,] by working over materials until the[y] make some new harmony, it is a long process of transformation, clarification, transfigur[a]tion, selection and arrangements in a word, in the new lig[h]t of the imagination" (McKeldin). In her many interviews in the sixties, after the success of *Ship of Fools,* Porter frequently discussed the great lengths of time that experiences rooted around in her mind before she came to understand their significance and could then, in a confluence of memory and imagination, write fiction derived from them. Art for her was not the immediate response to an event but the result of years of reflection, imaginative creation best understood less as a bolt of lightning than as the slow development of a seedling into a tree. "Surely, we understand very little of what is happening to us at any given moment," Porter told Barbara Thompson in a 1963 interview. "But by remembering, comparing, waiting to know the consequences, we can sometimes see what an event really meant, what it was trying to teach us." To Thompson's prompting that Porter once said that every story originates with an ending, Porter responded: "That is where the artist begins to work: with the consequences of acts, not the acts themselves. Or the events. The event is important only as it affects your life and the lives of those around you. The reverberations, you might say, the overtones: that is where the artist works. In that sense it has sometimes taken me ten years to understand even a little of some important event that had happened to me. Oh, I could have given a perfectly factual account of what had happened, but I didn't know what it meant until I knew the consequences" (*C,* 88).

In the late twenties Porter began writing fiction distinctly southern in emphasis, using scenes and characters resembling those from her childhood experiences. This shift in direction in her work illustrates Porter's increasing interest in the significance of memory for personal and artistic wholeness and the affirmation of a southern identity that this interest initiated. Not surprisingly, the central conflicts of many of the protagonists in this fiction focus on the same struggles Porter herself was undergoing at the time, most particularly the tension between the knowledge of self derived from one's memories and the knowledge of self constructed by one's conscious mind, often accomplished by the repression and deliberate distortion of memories. Porter knew it was far easier and much more comforting to close oneself off from the challenge of memory and to live instead entirely by one's own constructed image. Opening oneself up to the secret self of memory was potentially painful and tortuous, if ultimately enriching. In "'Noon Wine': The Sources" Porter wrote that an author's exploration of the origins of his or her work—origins that lay in the author's "blood and bones, the subterranean labyrinths of infancy and childhood, family histories, memories, visions, daydreams, and nightmares"—and the examination of the connection between them and the author's adult perspectives was "a little like attempting to tap one's spinal fluid." She added that "if that is a gruesome and painful comparison, be sure that I meant it to be" (*CE,* 468). Just as painful could be a person's explorations of his or her origins, a quest that always threatened to undo the stability of one's conception of oneself. For Porter, however, the undermining of a person's regnant view of self was a crucial step toward larger understanding—an understanding that was never complete, since dialogue between self and memory was unending.

Two of Porter's well-known stories, "The Jilting of Granny Weatherall" and "Noon Wine," focus on a character facing a crisis of identity centering upon the tension between memory and conscious self. Both stories speak crucially to Porter's conceptions of memory and artistic creation, for the two protagonists, Granny Weatherall and Mr. Thompson, are in a large sense failed artists struggling to create coherent narratives of their lives by repressing and manipulating memory. Rather than opening themselves to a dynamic interplay with their memories, Granny Weatherall and Mr. Thompson retreat into their valorized understandings of themselves, seeking to silence other voices from within and without their consciousnesses that challenge their self-conceptions. Neither of their narratives, however, can finally resist the pressures of memory, and both end up deconstructing, bringing Granny Weatherall and Mr. Thompson to a richer, if more disturbing and threatening, understanding of self and world. If their situations are more dramatic than Porter's, both Granny Weatherall and Mr. Thompson nonetheless exhibit through their struggles a deep kinship with Porter's own efforts at achieving knowledge and creating fiction and with her own temptation to deny the truths of memory.

"The Jilting of Granny Weatherall" (1929) follows the deathbed musings of Ellen (Granny) Weatherall as she thinks back on her life and attempts to structure a narrative of it as neat and tidy as the household she used to keep. "Things were finished somehow when the time came; thank God there was a little margin over for peace: then a person could spread out the plan of life and tuck in the edges orderly," she thinks early in the story, and she comforts herself with thoughts of the orderliness of her bedroom and pantry (CS, 81). Whatever disruptions occur in her life, as her words here suggest, Granny believes that there will always be time enough to set matters straight. In her narrative, that is, there will be time to erase and to revise. For this reason she likes to focus her attention on the future, a time when everything will be set in proper order. Even as she lies desperately ill and close to death, Granny continues to think about all the projects that she needs to begin working on tomorrow—presumably when she will be well. One such endeavor is the sorting out of her old love letters. In seeking to control the narrative of her life, both as others see it and as she remembers it, she will discard all the letters that suggest her to be anything other than the heroine she wants to portray herself as being

Granny Weatherall has structured her life story to make it wondrously rewarding and fulfilling. Setbacks and crises, by her later rendering, have in the end worked out entirely for the best. Even her devastating jilting by

George ("The whole bottom dropped out of the world, and there she was blind and sweating with nothing under her feet and the walls falling away," she remembers [CS, 87]) she later sees as a blessing in disguise, since it opened the way for her meeting her future husband. At one point she imagines herself telling her daughter to find George and let him know that she had forgotten him. "I want him to know I had my husband just the same and my children and my house like any other woman," she muses. "A good house too and a good husband that I loved and fine children out of him. Better than I hoped for even. Tell him I was given back everything he took away and more" (CS, 86). Of course, as her words indicate, Granny Weatherall has not forgotten George, try as she might to convince herself—and others—that she has.

Indeed, memories of George keep surfacing in Granny's thoughts, challenging her to recognize that on a deep emotional level she has never recovered from her jilting. After her imagined words to her daughter that her marriage to John had given her back everything and more that George in his betrayal had taken, a painful awareness of her true loss suddenly arises: "Oh, no, oh, God, no, there was something else besides the house and the man and the children. Oh, surely they were not all? What was it? Something not given back" (CS, 86). So disruptive are such thoughts that they become indistinguishable from the physical pain that wracks her body. Granny rallies herself after each painful episode, frequently calling upon a stoic inner strength to help her endure: "Wounded vanity, Ellen, said a sharp voice in the top of her mind. Don't let your wounded vanity get the upper hand of you. Plenty of girls get jilted. You were jilted, weren't you? Then stand up to it" (CS, 84).

Besides this stoic fortitude, Granny Weatherall relies upon her Catholic faith to attempt to hold her memories in check. Indeed, during the sixty years since her jilting, Granny's Catholic faith has apparently been her major source of strength for marshaling her will to overcome her sense of loss and to achieve the stability to "weather all." (In this act of denial, Granny Weatherall strongly resembles María Concepción from Porter's earlier story.) "For sixty years she had prayed against remembering him and against losing her soul in the deep pit of hell," she thinks at one point, and

at another she gives thanks to God for helping her stand down her memories and thereby complete what she claims has been her successful life:
"God, for all my life I thank Thee. Without Thee, my God, I could never
have done it. Hail, Mary, full of grace" (*CS*, 84). Not surprisingly, with her
physical strength now faltering, Granny turns her thoughts progressively
to her Catholicism for reassurance, so that by the end of the story she conceives her jilting as a fortunate fall not only because it led to her marriage
with John but also because it paved the way for an even more significant
betrothal—her marriage to Christ, an act she envisions being completed at
her death with her ascension into heaven.

In spite of her fortitude and religious faith, Granny slides toward death
fitfully and anxiously. Most disturbing to her peace is the shocking realization that her death may be imminent. To die now, she realizes, would leave
her life's narrative incomplete, because she knows that there is something
lacking, some plot that needs to be resolved. When she discovers death
lurking in her mind, feeling "clammy and unfamiliar" (*CS*, 82), she immediately recognizes its threat to undo her narrative, and she responds by
intensifying her efforts at creating her tale of harmony and fulfillment. But
the sharp glare of memory continually intrudes to illuminate everything
from which she seeks to hide. Light in this story is clearly associated with
memory, with Granny forever seeking ways to shield herself from various
luminations, external and internal. (In many of her works, Porter characterizes memory as a bright spot of light: in "'Noon Wine': The Sources,"
for instance, she describes one of her childhood memories as "a spot of clear
light and color and sound, of immense, mysterious illumination of feeling
against a horizon of total darkness" [*CE*, 475].) The glare from the bedside
lamp and the unshaded window, working upon her like the clear illumination of memory, continually keeps Granny from peaceful repose, forcing
her to lie awake and to recall the disturbing events from her life. Time and
again she complains of the light in the room and struggles to rest in shadow.
After one particularly uncomfortable recollection of her jilting, she strives
to keep herself in the dark, literally from the light from the window but on
a more significant level from the insights of her memories: "Her eyelids
wavered and she let in streamers of blue-gray light like tissue paper over

her eyes. She must get up and pull the shades down or she'd never sleep. She was in bed again and the shades were not down. How could that happen? Better turn over, hide from the light, sleeping in the light gave you nightmares" (CS, 84–85).

By the end of the story, the external lights merge into the internal light of Granny's hidden self, her memory. As she slides toward death, "the blue light from Cornelia's lampshade drew into a tiny point in the center of her brain, it flickered and winked like an eye, quietly it fluttered and dwindled. Granny lay curled down within herself, amazed and watchful, staring at the point of light that was herself; her body was now only a deeper mass of shadow in an endless darkness and this darkness would curl around the light and swallow it up" (CS, 89). Granny's memory, freed now from the shackles of her conscious mind, emerges unmistakably as her secret and deepest self. Nonetheless, she still struggles against memory's illumination, turning to her Catholic faith and asking God for a sign signifying both the delaying of her death and the forthcoming heavenly splendor that will overshadow her painful and frustrated emotional life. Death, she admits, has caught her by surprise, and she hates surprises. For her to die now, she claims, would leave her life—and her narrative of it—messy and undone, incomplete. She wants more time to tidy up her affairs and to shape them into a narrative of earthly happiness and Christian fulfillment. "God, give a sign," she entreats (CS, 89).

When no sign comes, Granny's Catholic faith, her last defense against recognizing her true feelings, collapses, undoing her narrative of fulfillment that has rested upon its foundation. Granny now stands exposed to her unchecked emotions and memories, and she fittingly conceives the absence of God's sign as a jilting, a repetition of George's earlier betrayal: "For the second time there was no sign. Again no bridegroom and the priest in the house" (CS, 89). Her second jilting destroys the systematic ordering of her life, as the first had done, but now, with her physical strength gone and her religious faith lost, she has no means to build anew. Her narrative has come completely unraveled: rather than a story of a life transfigured, her story has evolved into one of a life betrayed. As if she were a writer now finished working, she blows out the light—the light of consciousness and memory, the very light that Porter believed should guide all artists but that Granny Weatherall cannot bear.

Granny is as much a failed artist as a failed person. By repressing her memories she has, until the very end, "weathered all" and structured a coherent self-narrative, but such stability and coherence come at a dear price. As Granny apparently understands at the moment of her death, her earlier turning to Catholicism embodied a rejection of her inner self of memory and a closing off from deep emotional life. On one level, Porter's critique of Catholicism in "Granny Weatherall" strongly resembles that found in her earlier essays and stories on Mexico, with religious zeal depicted as an ideological structure that restrains memories and distorts feelings. In this later story, however, there is less emphasis on the Catholic church as an institution of social and political power. Indeed, "Granny Weatherall" appears to be less a critique of Catholic belief—its specific tenets and structurings of reality—than an exposé of Granny's misguided manipulations of her faith to escape her responsibilities to herself and others. Porter had little sympathy for people who looked single-mindedly to God rather to themselves for direction in their lives and for answers to perplexing existential problems. More than twenty years after the publication of "Granny Weatherall," Porter, in a letter dated January 28, 1951, to a Mr. McCoy, commented on the inefficacy of prayer, in words that I believe also speak crucially to the critique of Granny in Porter's story: "Prayer is a form of self-indulgence, a kind of day-dreaming, a device for side-stepping personal responsibility in the life here below, a magic formula to put the intelligence and moral nature to sleep, a way of evading thought and a facing of the bitter truths of human motives and the consequences of human acts" (McKeldin).

Although Porter believed that the mysteries of life ultimately were divine in origin, her interest in religion and faith centered most significantly on questions of ethics and human relationships. To her mind God was absent from the world, and so she believed that a person must structure a meaningful life by experience and conscience, and not by the fixed and unchallengeable tenets of an organized religion. In some notes entitled "The Love of God," dated November 24, 1932, Porter wrote that God did not mingle with human affairs and that she would never go begging for safety and assurance:

> The Unknowable, "the end of all things[,]" the impenetrable darkness without end or beginning. Of whom I ask nothing in my mortal extremity, because nothing in my mortality is of Him or from Him. There is nothing to be gained or given having to do with this world, and the sense of communication is not caused or changed or modified by any external thing. No human exaltation or grief, satisfactions or disappointments, have to do with Him. If I were between the teeth of a wild beast my God is as much present to me as when I am at the highest moment of my human joys. Between the teeth of the wild beast I shall not call upon Him for help, for he is not concerned with sparing this body of my death. And why praise Him for fleshly benefits He did not bestow, for this is not His work. They do not exist through Him nor He in them. (McKeldin)

In large part because she had come to see meaning arising from the ongoing interplay between self and memory, Porter resisted the restraints of rigid and authoritarian theology. Oddly enough, however, Porter by 1929 was identifying herself not only as a Catholic but (mistakenly) as a born Catholic. Even so, despite her attraction to Catholicism (probably in large part because she saw Church rituals preserving a sense of the mysterious and the eternal), her faith was actually closer to the dissenting belief she saw in Thomas Hardy. According to Porter, Hardy "rejected the conclusions though not the ethical discipline of organized religion (and he knew that its ethical system in essentials is older than Christianity)" and served no master but his conscience (*CE,* 7). "He went," Porter wrote, "perhaps not so much by choice as by compulsion of *belief,* with the Inquirers rather than the Believers," to the end resisting "the military police of orthodoxy" (*CE,* 6, 7). Porter, too, went her own way, despite the fact that she never formally left the Church. This step not taken suggests her commitment to memory: rather than "forgetting" her faith, she struggled to wrench meaning and significance from it just as she did by pressuring, interpreting, and revising other areas of her memory.

Porter attributes the creation of one of her best stories, "Noon Wine," to this willingness to grapple with the insights of memory. In "'Noon Wine':

The Sources" she develops her mature theory of artistic creation, describing the tortuous workings of memory and imagination that she says were at work during the story's composition. "By the time a writer has reached the end of a story," she begins her essay, "he has lived it at least three times over—first in the series of actual events that, directly or indirectly, have combined to set up that commotion in his mind and senses that causes him to write the story; second, in memory; and third, in recreation of this chaotic stuff" (*CE,* 467). Porter writes that in trying now to trace the origins of her work she is "confronted with my own life, the whole society in which I was born and brought up, and the facts of it. My aim is to find the truth in it, and to this end my imagination works and reworks its recollections in a constant search for meanings" (*CE,* 468). "Noon Wine," she says, was not merely a reporting of events from her upbringing but instead was a re-creation of a number of events and characters from her past that at that earlier time were unrelated. Later, when writing the story, she reconfigured them into new combinations and patterns and, out of the dynamic interplay of memory and imagination, forged a coherent narrative. Crucial to the artistic enterprise was the author's willingness to work openly and honestly with the depths of consciousness and not to impose a preconceived order upon it.

Mr. Thompson in "Noon Wine" has none of this honest openness to memory and experience, and so he fails in his efforts to structure a truthful narrative of his life. Perhaps Mr. Thompson's most telling flaw is his obsession with controlling meaning—a monopoly that allows him to criticize others for their failings but to see none in himself. Despite the fact that he knows the farm is deteriorating, his interpretation of its decline focuses on everything but his own responsibility:

Head erect, a prompt payer of taxes, yearly subscriber to the preacher's salary, land owner and father of a family, employer, a hearty good fellow among men, Mr. Thompson knew, without putting it into words, that he had been going steadily down hill. God amighty, it did look like somebody around the place might take a rake in hand now and then and clear up the clutter around the barn and the kitchen steps. The wagon shed was so full of broken-down machinery and ragged harness and old wagon wheels and battered milk pails and rotting lumber you could hardly drive in there any more. Not a soul on the place would raise a hand to it, and as for him, he had all he could do with his regular work. He would sometimes in the slack season sit for hours worrying about it, squirting tobacco on the ragweeds growing in a thicket against the wood pile, wondering what a fellow could do, handicapped as he was. (*CS,* 234)

Mr. Thompson's handicaps, as he sees them, include useless help, a sickly wife, and lazy sons. Faultless to his own eyes, he must bear the burden of all of them.

The key to transforming the farm successfully is of course hard work, precisely what Mr. Thompson will himself not do. So concerned is he with appearances—and particularly with the image he cuts according to his preconceived notions of how a man in his station should act—that he does not even consider performing the necessary but to his eyes unmanly chores. "Slopping hogs was hired man's work, in Mr. Thompson's opinion," the narrative consciousness reports him thinking. "Killing hogs was a job for the boss, but scraping them and cutting them up was for the hired man again; and again woman's proper work was dressing meat, smoking, pickling, and making lard and sausage. All his carefully limited fields of activity were related somehow to Mr. Thompson's feeling for the appearance of things, his own appearance in the sight of God and man. 'It don't *look* right,' was his final reason for not doing anything he did not wish to do" (*CS,* 233). Only with the arrival of Helton, a steady and industrious worker who cares not at all for appearances, does the farm eventually turn around.

Helton's industrious management of the farm soon makes him "the hope and prop of the family" (*CS,* 241), and most particularly of Mr. Thompson, who in his reputed role of provider finds the farm's profitability especially rewarding. Protecting appearances now no longer means for Mr. Thompson avoiding particular kinds of work (since Helton does them all) but safeguarding Helton. Mr. Thompson vehemently resists anything he sees as a threat to Helton's life-style, not wanting to disturb the stability brought about by the hired man. "Let him alone," Mr. Thompson tells his wife after she complains of Mr. Helton's reserve at the meal table, and he says the same thing when she later suggests that they invite Helton to attend church with them. "The way I look at it, his religion is every man's own business," he adds. "Besides he ain't got any Sunday clothes. He wouldn't want to go to church in them jeans and jumpers of his" (CS, 236–37). When he learns of Helton's fury over his sons' playing with Helton's harmonicas, Mr. Thompson erupts with equal fury, saying, among other things: "I'll take a calf rope to them if they don't look out," "I'll break every bone in 'em," "I ought to break your ribs," and "They're so mean. It's a wonder [Helton] don't just kill 'em off and be done with it" (CS, 239, 240, 241).

The greatest threat to Helton, and thus to the farm, is of course Homer T. Hatch, a bounty hunter who reveals that years earlier Helton had in a fit of passion killed his brother and later escaped from an insane asylum. Mr. Thompson struggles to downplay the significance of Hatch's revelation, looking for means to excuse Helton's actions and thereby to maintain the farm's status quo. "Well, circumstances alters cases, as the feller says," he tells Hatch at one point. "Now, what I know of Mr. Helton, he ain't dangerous, as I told you" (CS, 253). Hatch, however, is relentless and will have nothing to do with Mr. Thompson's vision of things. Mr. Thompson finds himself in utter turmoil when Hatch makes it clear that he means to capture Helton and return him to captivity. He knows that Hatch has the law behind him and that the neighbors would talk if they knew of Helton's past, but he also knows he cannot give Helton up if he is to maintain the farm and his elevated sense of himself that its success brings. He has no idea what to do: "Mr. Thompson tried to see his way out. It was a fact Mr. Helton might go loony again any minute, and now this fellow talking around the country would put Mr. Thompson in a fix. It was a terrible position. He couldn't think of any way out" (CS, 255). Shortly thereafter, amid a blinding hallucination that has Hatch sinking a bowie knife into Helton's stomach, Mr. Thompson brings his ax crashing down on the bounty hunter's head.

Mr. Thompson's killing of Hatch undoes the stability by which he has lived, both literally in his life at the farm (Helton is hunted down and caught by the sheriff's posse and dies soon thereafter) and psychologically in his perception of himself. He does everything he can to see himself as guiltless and upstanding, directing the blame for everything onto Hatch. While he lies awake at night, Mr. Thompson constructs an imaginary narrative with a much happier ending: "He tried to imagine how it might all have been, this very night even, if Mr. Helton were still safe and sound out in his shack playing his tune about feeling so good in the morning, drinking up all the wine so you'd feel even better; and Mr. Hatch safe in jail somewhere, mad as hops, maybe, but out of harm's way and ready to listen to reason and to repent his meanness, the dirty, yellow-livered hound coming around persecuting an innocent man and ruining a whole family that never harmed him" (CS, 266).

But Mr. Thompson, as much as he would like to, cannot keep the blame entirely fixed on Hatch. As easy as it was for him before Helton arrived to blame others for the farm's misfortunes, keeping the gaze from himself, Mr. Thompson finds himself inextricably bound up in Hatch's death. Although acquitted of murder in court, and so by society's eyes judged proper in his actions, Mr. Thompson nonetheless rests uneasily, haunted by a shattering and irrepressible awareness of his own personal guilt. Torn as he is, he strives to construct a narrative of Hatch's death that absolves him of any blame, while at the same time he deconstructs this narrative for what it is—a calculated manipulation of memory to impose a fixed, and false, meaning upon the events. After his trial and successful defense by his attorney, Mr. Burleigh, "Mr. Thompson kept saying to himself that he'd got off, all right, just as Mr. Burleigh had predicted, but, but—and it was right there that Mr. Thompson's mind stuck, squirming like an angleworm on a fishhook: he had killed Mr. Hatch, and he was a murderer. That was the truth about himself that Mr. Thompson couldn't grasp, even when he said the word to himself" (CS, 261). Publicly he proclaims his innocence, but privately he works and reworks his memories in an effort, finally unsuccessful, to justify his killing of Hatch: "Try as he might, Mr. Thompson's mind would not go anywhere that it had not already been, he could not see anything but what he had seen once, and he knew that was not right. If he had not seen straight that first time, then everything about his killing Mr. Hatch was wrong from start to finish, and there was nothing more to be done about it, he might just as well give up. It still seemed to him that he had done, maybe not the right thing, but the only thing he could do, that day, but had he? *Did he have to kill Mr. Hatch?*" (CS, 265).

In his probings of self, Mr. Thompson on one level is fuller and wiser

than he was before Hatch's death when he was so confident of himself and
his views. Like the artist Porter envisioned, he now engages his memory in
endless remembering, searching for meaning and understanding. Ultimately, however, Mr. Thompson resists the truth of memory: instead of
giving himself over to its insights, he still seeks to impose his preconceived
version of events. To the very end, even when he takes up a pencil and
writes his suicide note, Mr. Thompson points his finger straight at Hatch
("He caused all this trouble and he deserved to die," he writes [*CS,* 268])
and away from himself, expressing sorrow only that it was he who *had* to
kill Hatch. A failed storyteller and a failed man, Mr. Thompson revises his
memory not to get at the truth but to justify himself. Finally, however, he
can not control his memories. As it was for Granny Weatherall, the light of
consciousness and memory is too much to bear, and he takes his life rather
than living with its burden.

For Porter, living with, rather than escaping, the burden of memory
was the means for growth and fulfillment. Memory had to be engaged and
responded to freely and honestly. By the early thirties this burden had become central to her understanding of imaginative creation, and it became
the crucial inspiration and focus of almost all of her fiction. "Ah my memories!" Porter wrote in an incomplete manuscript entitled "The Lovely Legend." "Someday they will cease to rise cooly in me a perpetual fountain, I
shall be as dry as the basin of the Lost Child" (McKeldin).

# 6

# THE ACHIEVEMENT OF THE
# MIRANDA STORIES

Katherine Anne Porter's developing interest in memory and the southern tradition signaled a profound fascination with her upbringing and family, immediate and ancestral. Her relationship with her family, particularly with her father, had been and would always remain ambivalent and strained, with her feelings fluctuating wildly, from outright scorn to nostalgic affection. Even during the late teens and early twenties when Porter was portraying herself as a fashionable rebel who had freed herself from and turned her back on her family, she nonetheless frequently sent endearing letters back home. In a Christmas letter dated December 21, 1916, to her father, she wrote, referring to her life in Dallas: "And then, Youngun, you know all this would be dust and ashes in my mouth if it wasn't for knowing that my Darling Old Dad and Sissers and my one goat of a bruvver are all getting along so fat and fine, making money and keeping well. If it wasn't for that I would want to die" (McKeldin). More gushing was a letter to her sister Gay, written from Mexico on December 31, 1920, and apparently meant for her entire family. "Since I saw you," she wrote, "I have been working too hard, and living too hard, to make any sort of record of it. . . . , but I love all of you, I do love all of you terribly, and you are the very background and foundation of my life, which I cannot get away from, and which I would not get away from—if I lost any part of it, I would lose too much!" (McKeldin). At the other extreme, she frequently bitterly attacked members of her family and their treatment of her during her childhood, even during periods, particularly the thirties and forties, when she was elsewhere waxing nostalgic about the old ways of the sunny South and her upbringing. In a letter dated October 11, 1933, addressed to "Gay and the rest: specially Dad," she lashed out: "As for being a family to me, when were you ever? I should have been dead in a ditch years ago if I had depended on my family to exhibit any of the old-timey characteristics" (McKeldin). To her nephew Paul Porter, she wrote on November 8, 1951, some of her harshest words on her family: "Do you know, what is the most unhappy thing in my life? That I do not have one single good or gay or sweet memory connected with my family; it has just been one single long unbroken line of painfulness in one way or another" (McKeldin).

Despite this ongoing ambivalence about and fluctuating feelings toward her family, Porter by the late twenties was examining both her origins and the family's with a seriousness that she had not shown previously. Even if she had written to Gay in 1920 that the family was "the very background and foundation of my life," she was then and for years afterward living completely otherwise. In her fiction of the early twenties she showed little if any interest in exploring her familial identity and heritage. But in the late twenties, Porter's writing and interests shifted dramatically, and judging from this new gaze southward toward home, she had come to see that exploring and reworking her memories of her upbringing by the light of her modern artistic consciousness, bringing what she now understood as her "southernness" and modernity into continuous interplay, were central to her imaginative vision. This new focus on familial origins led to the creation of much of Porter's best work, including those stories about Miranda, a semiautobiographical character whose struggles with identity and vision mirror Porter's own.

Outside of the fiction itself, perhaps the most telling evidence of Porter's newfound interest in her origins and their relationship to her role as modern artist is her almost consuming passion for genealogy, a passion that began in the mid- to late twenties and continued for the rest of her life. As Joan Givner has established, Porter spent much time and energy seeking to reconstruct her family tree and to discover the exploits of her ancestors.[1] If

1. Givner, *Katherine Anne Porter: A Life,* Chapter 1.

not always reliable in her efforts, she was always enthusiastic. Early on she turned to her father for help. In a letter to him dated February 16, 1928, she explained her concern for the family's past: "I suppose my interest has some connection with my being so far away from my base, as it were, it is probably an obscure symptom of homesickness" (McKeldin). Porter's enthusiasm rapidly intensified, so that before long she was poring over genealogical guides and sourcebooks. Her efforts were now much more than a "symptom of homesickness": they were an integral part of her imaginative vision. In a letter dated January 21, 1933, written after her father had sent at her request a long letter of family lore, Porter enthusiastically wrote back asking him for more. "Couldn't you just take your time and tell what you remember of your childhood," she asked, "where you were born, what life was like, how we came to go to Louisiana and Texas—I remember something about a sugar mill in Louisiana, what you remember of conditions during and after the war, all the things that no one remembers now; it would be interesting." *Interesting* does not quite express her desire for family stories. Although she told her father that if what he wrote "were full enough, I might even edit it a little if it needed it and get it published somewhere," there is little doubt that what she had most in mind for his narrative was her own work. After commenting that she had "very little patience with people who try to live on their ancestors, and southerners here wear me out talking about their families," she added: "But I do have a little private interest of my own in family history," a private interest, she made clear, that she wanted to make an integral part of her fiction. "It would help me, too," she wrote, speaking of her father's commentary, "in a novel I mean to write after this one is finished" (*L,* 89, 88, 89).

The novel in progress Porter mentioned to her father would remain unfinished. Tentatively entitled "Historical Present," she had planned it to be linked stories focusing on various individuals in Mexico, broken up into two sections, one on men, the other on women. The novel that Porter was then considering and soon would be working on was equally ambitious in scope: calling it "Many Redeemers," Porter planned it to follow the fortunes of several generations of an American family (clearly based on Porter's own), ending up with the present time. In some undated notes on her plans for the novel, Porter outlined its three books. Book 1, entitled "Introduction to Death: The Beginning" (elsewhere Porter usually referred to this section as "Legend and Memory") was to follow "the rise and break-up of an American family up to the Great War, or a little before . . . say 1910." Book 2, "Midway of This Mortal Life," was to focus on one or more of the chief characters from Book 1, including Miranda, up through around 1930. Book 3, "Beginning Again: The End," was to examine "the present scene, the sick and crumbling society with some of the cures offered by diverse Saviours. The various roads by which the characters separate and go to their several ends" (McKeldin).

"Many Redeemers" also remained unfinished, although a number of the stories Porter originally planned to incorporate into the novel, including "The Old Order" sequence, "Old Mortality," and "Pale Horse, Pale Rider," were eventually published separately. Even unfinished, "Many Redeemers" remains significant, for its plan suggests the evolution of Porter's mature artistic vision: Porter now understood that the depths of memory were the source of her imaginative consciousness and that artistic creation demanded bringing memories and personal legends into interplay with her modernist imagination. Out of this interplay both the memories and the imagination were reshaped and redefined, understood now in a context expanded in depth and limits. Porter attempted in her fiction not strict autobiography but what might be called fictional autobiography, works that were true not to fact but to her understanding of experience—that is, true by the expanded understanding she had achieved in her efforts at evaluating her life. In a June 9, 1935, letter to Caroline Gordon, Porter commented that in writing "Legend and Memory" she wanted to keep faithful not to historical fact but to her consciousness. "I am not looking up any facts, nor consulting with any one, nor going back to check my sources—*nothing,*" she wrote. "I depend precisely on what I know in my blood, and in my memory, and on something that is *deeper than knowledge*" (*L,,* 127) At some point later during her work on "Legend and Memory," Porter apparently changed her method somewhat, deciding to bring fact and legend into dynamic interaction. In some undated notes (in her later marginal annotation Porter suggests that the notes probably were from a letter to Henry Allen Moe in 1937) Porter wrote: "The first part of my novel is called *Legend and Memory,* using these two legitimate sources of poetry and fiction. But I want badly to compare these legends, these memories, with the documentary evidence as I can lay hold on. Neither the truth nor the legend need suffer by this; the one throws new light on the other, and the artist needs both" (McKeldin). This interplay of fact and legend mirrors the dynamic between memory and imagination that Porter saw at the heart of the creative process.

Much of Porter's fiction and nonfiction from the thirties and forties derives from her profound reappraisal of her upbringing and family. Especially fascinating to those attempting to understand Porter's artistic consciousness are her sympathetic portrayals of her elders, particularly of her paternal grandmother, Catherine Anne Porter, whose name Porter, born Callie Russell, took as a young adult. Her frequent focus on her grandmother, I believe, provides an insightful means for grasping Porter's efforts to define herself as artist both by and against her family and the southern heritage that she had self-consciously embraced. Two works, her essay "Portrait: Old South" and her story sequence "The Old Order," are particularly noteworthy.

The very title of "Portrait: Old South," an essay praising Porter's paternal grandparents, particularly her grandmother, indicates Porter's choice to rewrite her Texas roots as Deep South tradition. After first establishing her own southern credentials—"I am the grandchild of a lost War, and I have blood-knowledge of what life can be in a defeated country on the bare bones of privation," the essay begins (*CE*, 160)—Porter speaks of the strength and fortitude that her elders exhibited during the hard times of the Civil War and Reconstruction. She then tells several yarns drawn from family lore and connects herself closely to her elders by saying that they "all remained nobly unreconstructed to their last moments, and my feet rest firmly on this rock of their strength to this day." Her mind, she says, brims with stories of her elders, and the few stories that she has told in the essay are "the merest surface ripples over limitless deeps of bitter memory" (*CE*, 161).

After describing her grandparents' lavish wedding and reception, Porter proceeds to the heart of the essay, the celebration of her grandmother. Porter depicts her grandmother as a strong-willed woman who knew exactly what she believed in and who never altered that belief, despite misfortune and hardship that shook the foundations of the life about her. Hers was the life, according to Porter, of the landed aristocracy, a formal life based on a rigid code of conduct and order passed on from one generation to the next. Everything had its place, and everyone had duties to perform and standards to live up to. In its strictness and completeness, the grandmother's code was not easily transgressed. Her grandmother's firm response to her grandchildren's quarrels embodied everything she believed in: "It was 'vulgar,' she said, and for her, that word connoted a peculiarly detestable form of immorality, that is to say, bad manners. Inappropriate conduct was bad manners, bad manners were bad morals, and bad morals led to bad manners, and there you were, ringed with fire, and no way out" (CE, 164). When the family fortunes ebbed and life became difficult, her grandmother remained rock-solid, maintaining her ideals throughout all. "Though we had no money, and no prospects of any, and were land-poor in the most typical way, we never really faced this fact as long as our grandmother lived because she would not hear of such a thing," Porter writes. "We had been a good old family of solid wealth and property in Kentucky, Louisiana and Virginia, and we remained that in Texas, even though due to a temporary decline for the most honorable reasons, appearances were entirely to the contrary." To the grandmother's eyes, the family's misfortunes, despite the fact that they dragged on and that she never lived to see them turn better, were merely "temporary, an unnatural interruption to her normal fate, which required simply firmness, a good deal of will-power and energy and the proper aims to re-establish finally once more" (CE, 163). Nonetheless, the severity of the times "tapped the bottomless reserves of her character." Her unbending resolve, courage, and rage for order led Porter to conclude that she was "truly heroic" (CE, 162), towering above the rest of the family as well as the general run of humanity. Porter ends the essay: "She left the lingering perfume and the airy shimmer of grace about her memory" (CE, 165).

The parallels between Porter's depiction of her grandmother and her views of the artist are striking. On one level, her grandmother was an artist in her own right: according to Porter's interpretation she saw her role as head of the family as a vocation and felt it her duty to forge a dignified family life that radiated decorum and order. The chaotic nature of life, with all its trials and tribulations, was her chief antagonist, as it was for the artist. She was worthy of the task: "Her bountiful hospitality represented only one of her victories of intelligence and feeling over the stubborn difficulties of life" (*CE*, 163). Like an artist, she based her efforts on diligence, discipline, and high standards, and she was closely in touch with memory and tradition. Although she did not actively probe her memory to achieve an understanding of life and its mysteries (as Porter believed the modern artist must do), this was because she lived as most moderns do not, in direct contact with her past and her heritage. Lewis P. Simpson has observed that "in the traditionalist society, memory is yet in the flesh and in the blood."[2] It is not, as it was for many modern southern writers, a deliberate and self-conscious means to resist the dehumanization of contemporary life. Porter's grandmother, in other words, was already in direct contact with her memory without having to make a deliberate choice to be.

Yet, particularly as seen in "The Old Order," Porter saw potential dangers in her grandmother's approach to life, dangers that, by our understanding of the grandmother, also threatened the modern artist. Porter clearly based Sophia Jane, the grandmother in this story sequence, on her own grandmother, and the portrayals of her reveal much about Porter's ideas of memory and art. Like Porter's grandmother in "Portrait: Old South," Sophia Jane possesses strength and fortitude, driven by a consuming rage for order. In "The Source," for instance, as soon as she arrives for a visit at her country house, she immediately begins overseeing the complete overhaul of the grounds, outbuildings, and main house. Nothing escapes her eye. At the main house, "the big secretaries were opened and shabby old sets of Dickens, Scott, Thackeray, Dr. Johnson's dictionary, the volumes of Pope and Milton and Dante and Shakespeare were dusted off and closed up carefully again. Curtains came down in dingy heaps and went up again stiff and sweet-smelling; rugs were heaved forth in dusty confusion and returned flat and gay with flowers once more; the kitchen was no longer dingy and desolate but a place of heavenly order where it was tempting to linger" (*CS*, 324). After her stay, with order restored, she returns home where "at once she set to work restoring to order the place which no doubt had gone somewhat astray in her absence" (*CS*, 325). Her demands for order, based on unchanging tradition, are strict and inclusive. As with Por-

2. Simpson, *The Brazen Face of History*, 241.

ter's grandmother in "Portrait: Old South," she lives in intimate contact with her memory, basing everything she does on its dictates.

But Sophia Jane's life is out of balance, primarily because memories utterly dominate her perspective, overruling all other concerns and values. Her situation reverses that typically found in Porter's early stories, where characters attempt to repress their deep selves of memory: Sophia Jane instead gives herself entirely to the demands of memory and represses all challenges to what she sees as its realm of completeness and finality. With Aunt Nannie, her black maid and companion, Sophia Jane spends much of her time talking about the past, extolling bygone days and devaluing all else. "They talked about the past, really—always about the past," the narrative consciousness writes. "Even the future seemed like something gone and done with when they spoke of it. It did not seem an extension of their past, but a repetition of it." While not blind to the changing attitudes and patterns of life about them—indeed they are very much aware that the pressures of time and modernity are transforming the South—Sophia Jane and Aunt Nannie steadfastly refuse to confront these changes and to adopt a realistic view of the times. "They would agree that nothing remained of life as they had known it, the world was changing swiftly," the narrator writes, "but by the mysterious logic of hope they insisted that each change was probably the last; or if not, a series of changes might bring them, blessedly, back full-circle to the old ways they had known" (*CS*, 327).

As we have already noted, Porter saw herself, as she did Thomas Hardy, as an Inquirer, a person who forever challenged and pressured accepted traditions with questions and doubts. Under the grip of their commitment to memory and tradition, however, Sophia Jane and Aunt Nannie smother all of their questions and uneasiness to live by duty rather than inquiry. The narrator characterizes their musings:

Who knows why they loved their past? It had been bitter for them both, they had questioned the burdensome rule they lived by every day of their lives, but without rebellion and without expecting an answer. This unbroken thread of inquiry in their minds contained no doubt as to the utter rightness and justice of basic laws of human existence, founded as they were on God's plan; but they wondered perpetually, with only a hint now and then to each other of the uneasiness of their hearts; how so much suffering and confusion could have been built up and maintained on such a foundation. The grandmother's rôle was authority, she knew that; it was her duty to portion out activities, to urge or restrain where necessary, to teach morals, manners, and religion, to punish and reward her own household according to a fixed code. Her own doubts and hesitations she concealed, also, she reminded herself, as a matter of duty. Old Nannie had no ideas at all as to her place in the world. It had been assigned to her before birth, and for her daily rule she had all her life obeyed the authority nearest to her. (*CS,* 327–28)

In her dutiful commitment to her memories and the tradition they embody—there is no dialogue between her memory and her present self—Sophia Jane cuts herself off from the possibility of fulfillment and completion, both as a person and, as we have also characterized her, as an artist. Her willfulness on the one hand gives her great strength and power, as we can see in her heroic efforts to raise her grandchildren and her successes at running a farm amid personal and economic adversity. Her grandchildren note her strength: "She was the only reality to them in a world that seemed otherwise without fixed authority or refuge" (*CS,* 324). On the other hand, her power borders on tyranny. In the iron grip of memory, she strives to impose her will upon others just as her inner self imposes itself upon her. She demands loyalty and obedience, and with the seat of all value resting firmly upon herself, she rejects any divergent opinion or perspective. Driven by this consuming confidence in her own self-sufficiency, Sophia Jane, the narrator writes, "developed a character truly portentous under the discipline of trying to change the characters of others." Her husband, along with probably everyone else in the household, came to fear "her deadly willfulness, her certainty that her ways were not only right but beyond criticism, that her feelings were important, even in the lightest matter, and must not be tampered with or treated casually" (*CS,* 335).

Porter's grandmother, as represented in the fiction and nonfiction, thus finally emerges as a complex and ambiguous character. Porter on one level clearly emulated her, and in the following description from "Portrait: Old South" she clearly characterizes herself as much as her ancestor: "Grandmother was by nature lavish, she loved leisure and calm, she loved luxury, she loved dress and adornment, she loved to sit and talk with friends or listen to music; she did not in the least like pinching or saving and mending and making things do, and she had no patience with the kind of slackness that tried to say second-best was best, or half good enough" (*CE,* 162). The life of dignity and decorum pointed to the order and stability that, in a world gone awry, Porter sought to achieve with her art. Yet Porter at the same time resisted her grandmother, seeing her "deadly willfulness" as a representation of the danger of a life tyrannized by the past, of a monologic rather than a dialogic existence. Instead of opening herself to all experience, including the multiple voices in her memory and not merely the single voice of authoritative tradition, the grandmother entombs herself from the ever-changing diversity of life and embraces instead a single-minded vision of fixed order and value. For Porter such single-mindedness invited destruction for both the individual and the artist. Writers given to such limited thinking, Porter believed, usually wrote fiction either blatantly propagandist or sickeningly nostalgic (or some dreadful combination of the two). The grandmother's heavy-handed raising of the children suggests the former, whereas her and Nannie's sewing suggest the latter. Nannie and Sophia Jane delight in sewing patchworks from cut "scraps of the family finery, hoarded for fifty years." This is a fitting metaphor for the artist's delving into memory to reinvent and reshape a larger pattern of meaning. But whereas Porter saw the artist's efforts as a process of challenge and interplay that ultimately enlarged consciousness, for Nannie and Sophia Jane their sewing is merely a means to apotheosize the past, strengthening its grip on their thinking. Fittingly, their patchworks, outlined "with a running briar stitch in clear lemon-colored floss," serve no function in the household. "They had contrived enough bed and couch covers, table spreads, dressing table scarfs, to have furnished forth several households," the narrator writes. "Each piece as it was finished was lined with yellow silk, folded, and laid away in a chest, never again to see the light of day" (*CS,* 326).

Porter's conflicting feelings toward her grandmother shed light on her own struggles with incorporating her memories into the development of her identity and art. In fact, so central is her grandmother to Porter's thinking—it is no coincidence that Porter entitles the opening work of "The Old Order," a sketch of Sophia Jane, "The Source" and that she begins "Portrait:

Old South" with the declaration, "I am the grandchild of a lost War"—that I believe Porter came to see her grandmother as the embodiment of the predominant voice of her own hidden self of memory. As such, her grandmother stands as a disturbing double whose presence demands both recognition and interaction. She represents in her complexity both the potential for meaningful creation and growth and the possibility of falling prey to a destructive tyranny of the past. To advance as a person and as an artist, Porter believed she had to incorporate her grandmother and her grandmother's ways into her own life—to maintain an ongoing and open-ended dialogue with her—without becoming entirely like her and thereby closing herself off from the other voices of the world and of her past.

This persistent dialogue with her grandmother and the southern tradition that she represents in many regards marks the development of Porter's mature fiction. As we have seen, Porter's commitment to dialogic encounters with memory, particularly those involving her imaginative revisions of her upbringing, emerged only after a number of years of personal and artistic struggle. In the thirties, however, having established a conception of the artistic imagination that remained essentially consistent for the rest of her career, Porter began to reassess her intellectual and imaginative development with her stories about Miranda. Although anything but strict autobiography, these stories explore the growth and development of a woman from childhood to adulthood whose struggles with imagination and consciousness (if not always the outer circumstances that initiate these inner struggles) strongly resemble Porter's own. Porter's observation about the strength of Eleanor Clark's autobiographical vision in *Rome and a Villa* at the same time expresses what Porter herself was striving for with the Miranda stories: "This whole book is the distillation of a deep personal experience; it is autobiography in the truest sense, in terms of what outward impact set the inner life in motion toward its true relation to the world: the search for what is truly one's own, and the ability to recognize it when found, and to be faithful in love of it" (*CE*, 80). In examining Miranda's "inner life in motion," I want to explore three works—"The Old Order," "Old Mortality," and "Pale Horse, Pale Rider"—and I will arrange my discussion roughly around Miranda's chronology (rather than the chronology of publication). I will begin my examination with the story sequence

"The Old Order" and also will end there, with a look at "The Grave," the story that fittingly concludes the entire Miranda cycle.

Much of "The Old Order" focuses on Miranda's childhood and early development, particularly her efforts to order her understanding of reality into a coherent narrative framework. Her attempts at achieving coherence largely involve coming to terms with the stories people have told her, a task calling for the ongoing testing of the stories against her own experiences and against stories that conflict in their presentation of the past and the present. As the title of the story sequence indicates, Miranda's primary task is figuring out what to make of the South's "old order" as embodied in her family and its conception of itself and, most crucially, of the world created by her grandmother. The grandmother's understanding of things, as we have already noted, is rigid and confining, defined by unchanging patterns of southern tradition. There is very little room for individual resistance to her ways, as Miranda quickly discovers: "'This way and no other!' Grandmother always said when she was laying down the law about all kinds of things. 'It must be done *this* way, and no other'" (*CS,* 354). To Miranda and her siblings such rigidity both comforts and limits, providing their lives with structure, but structure that cannot be challenged, at least openly.

Porter underscores Miranda's need for a narrative structure to describe the multiplicity of her experiences in "The Circus." Here the young Miranda, as Edward Schwartz has pointed out, does not understand the conventions that underlie the activities at the circus. Like George Posey in Allen Tate's *The Fathers,* a man who receives "the shock of the world at the end of his nerves," Miranda on this first trip to the circus suffers frightening torment in not having a mediating structure to help her understand what she sees.[3] Initially the surroundings fascinate Miranda—the narrator comments that "she could not look hard enough at everything"—but her fascination quickly turns to bewilderment and then even to panic. Lacking the guiding hand of her grandmother and the consistent routine of life at home, Miranda understands little of what is going on around her, since the circus operates by conventions that turn her everyday world topsy-turvy. Nobody

3. Schwartz, "The Fictions of Memory," 205; Tate, *The Fathers,* rev. ed., in Tate, *"The Fathers" and Other Fiction,* 185.

offers her any meaningful or sympathetic help. Typical is Dicey's response to Miranda's asking why a pack of boys squat underneath the bleachers leering upward: "You jus mind yo' own business and stop throwin' yo' legs around that way. Don't you pay any mind. Plenty o' monkeys right here in the show widout you studyin dat kind" (*CS,* 344).

Even more disturbing are the circus acts, which appear to Miranda as frantic onrushes of sights and sounds. Their audacious flauntings of the norms of everyday activities mock the rigid decorum by which Miranda until now has unquestioningly lived. (Not insignificantly, her grandmother had apparently understood this threat and had resisted Miranda's attending the circus. She finally allowed her to go because the outing was occasioned by a family reunion, an activity embodying the solidarity of the family and Miranda's place within it.) Even the brass band sends Miranda close to hysteria: "An enormous brass band seemed to explode right at Miranda's ear. She jumped, quivered, thrilled blindly and almost forgot to breathe as sound and color and smell rushed together and poured through her skin and hair and beat in her head and hands and feet and pit of her stomach. 'Oh,' she called out in her panic, closing her eyes and seizing Dicey's hand hard. The flaring lights burned through her lids, a roar of laughter like rage drowned out the steady raging of the drums and horns." When she opens her eyes, she sees a clown on a tightrope tantalizing the crowd. Everyone else knows what to make of his derring-do, and the onlookers roar with delight. Miranda, though, is terrified by the high-wire act, frightened even by the clown's costume. Having never seen a clown before, she sees not a comic entertainer but "a creature in a blousy white overall with ruffles at the neck and ankles," its made-up face not silly but terrifying, a "bone-white skull and chalk-white face, with tufted eyebrows far apart in the middle of his forehead, the lids in a black sharp angle, a long scarlet mouth stretching back into sunken cheeks, turned up at the corners in a perpetual bitter grimace of pain, astonishment, not smiling" (*CS,* 344). When the clown stumbles on the wire, apparently purposefully as part of the act, Miranda shrieks "with real pain." After the clown blows kisses as he dangles on the wire held up only by his ankle, Miranda covers her face and shrieks out even harder, "the tears pouring over her cheeks and chin" (*CS,* 345). Adding to her terror is the ugly grimace a dwarf gives her as she and Dicey leave the circus early. Miranda realizes by his look (his grimace mirrors Miranda's distorted face) that the dwarf is not, as she had suspected, a misshapen animal whose ugliness is entirely discrete from her but a human being who suffers as she does. Miranda sees the dwarf as a fitting image of the horror and ugliness that human existence, including her own, can acquire and of the cruelty that can unexpectedly explode from people—all of which until this night was essentially unknown to Miranda, a girl more accustomed to seeing people at their civilized best, behaving by the rules of her grandmother.

At home after the circus Miranda hears the other children speak about the acts she had missed. For them the circus was all delight. Their versions of the death-defying acts glow in a magic aura because, unlike Miranda, they understand the circus as a world governed by its own rules and conventions. What happens at the circus has little to do with their own everyday lives. It is the stuff of dreams, and they describe the acts accordingly: "More clowns, funnier than the first one even . . . beautiful ladies with bright yellow hair, wearing white silk tights with red satin sashes had performed on white trapezes; they also had hung by their toes, but how gracefully, like flying birds! Huge white horses had lolloped around and round the ring with men and women dancing on their backs! One man had swung by his teeth from the top of the tent and another had put his head in a lion's mouth. Ah, what she had not missed!" (*CS,* 346). Upon going to bed, Miranda tries to transform her vision of the circus into that held by the others, but her frightening memories shatter her efforts: "She tried, as if she were really remembering them, to think of the beautiful wild beings in white satin and spangles and red sashes who danced and frolicked on the trapezes; of the sweet little furry ponies and the lovely pet monkeys in their comical clothes. She fell asleep, and her invented memories gave way before her real ones, the bitter terrified face of the man in blowsy white falling to his death—ah, the cruel joke!—and the terrible grimace of the unsmiling dwarf. She screamed in her sleep and sat up crying for deliverance from her torments" (*CS,* 347).

Without being able either to place the circus in the world she has up until now known and constructed or to understand the conventions that undergird it, Miranda sees the circus as embodying forces of misrule and disorder that throw her and her grandmother's orderly life into utter disarray. For Porter, such horrifying disorder underlay all existence and had to be acknowledged, but to confront the chaos without the mediating structures provided by the rituals of family, community, and religion was to risk being overwhelmed by despair and terror. If, returning to Lacy Buchan's observation in Allen Tate's *The Fathers,* "civilization [is] the agreement, slowly arrived at, to let the abyss alone," then Miranda sees at the circus that the abyss is never far from consciousness, there to be faced, often unexpectedly, in all its horror.[4]

"The Circus" not only suggests the need for frameworks by which to structure experience but also underscores a damaging flaw in the grandmother's systematic ordering: her vision of self and reality too easily glosses over the terror underlying experience with saccharine nostalgia, what the narrator of "The Last Leaf" characterizes as "an out-of-date sentimental way of thinking" (*CS,* 349). Other stories from "The Old Order" also point to this flaw. In "The Witness," for instance, Uncle Jimbilly, a former slave, tells stories describing the horrors of slavery that cut against the family's tales glorifying plantation life on which Miranda and her siblings had been brought up. He tells the children:

> Dey used to take 'em out and tie 'em down and whup 'em, wid gret big leather strops inch thick long as yo' ahm, wid round holes bored in 'em so's evey time dey hit 'em de hide and de meat done come off dey bones in little round chunks. And wen dey had whupped 'em wid de strop till dey backs was all raw and bloody, dey spread dry cawnshucks on dey backs and set 'em afire and pahched 'em, and den dey poured vinega all ovah 'em . . . Yassuh. And den, the ve'y nex day dey'd got to git back to work in the fiels or dey'd do the same thing right ovah agin. Yassah. Dat was it. If dey didn't git back to work dey got it all right ovah agin. (*CS,* 341)

As the title of the sketch suggests, Uncle Jimbilly stands as a disturbing witness whose testimony refutes much of the grandmother's rosier recollections of the past. Not surprisingly, Miranda (six years old in the story) and

4. Tate, *The Fathers,* rev. ed., in Tate, *"The Fathers" and Other Fiction,* 186.

her older brother (eight) and sister (ten) stand mystified by Uncle Jimbilly's stories, not knowing how to integrate his version of slavery into their previous understanding of it. "They knew, of course, that once upon a time Negroes had been slaves; but they had all been freed long ago and were now only servants," the narrator says of the children's fairy tale–like conception of the antebellum past. For all his crazy rantings and empty threats, Uncle Jimbilly nonetheless delivers a telling rebuke to the family's glorified past, nudging the children out of their innocence. As they listen to his terrifying tales, the three children find themselves displaced from their former ease and confidence into embarrassment and guilt, feelings entirely new within the context of their family heritage.

If Uncle Jimbilly disrupts the children's understanding of their family's history, of its narratives of "happy darkies" during the time of slavery, Aunt Nannie in "The Last Leaf" undermines their present-day security in the benevolence of black-white relations and indeed of the stability of familial bonds. Aunt Nannie may be, as the title of the story suggests, the final leaf of her generation to fall, but she also may be, in another reading of "Leaf," the concluding page of the grandmother's narrative. As the last page of the grandmother's story, Aunt Nannie suggests not the narrative's closure and completeness but its dissolution and disorder: her moving out of the family house into a house of her own refutes the stereotypical role she, along with other blacks, was forced to play in the grandmother's (and the South's) narrative, thereby subverting its portrayal of family order and interracial harmony. In her new home Aunt Nannie sheds the persona of trustworthy servant for that of a strong and independent African. Although Nannie remains neat and precise in her ways, the narrator comments that she "was no more the faithful old servant Nannie, a freed slave: she was an aged Bantu woman of independent means, sitting on the steps, breathing the free air. She began wearing a blue bandana wrapped around her head, and at the age of eighty-five she took to smoking a corncob pipe. The black iris of the deep, withdrawn old eyes turned a chocolate brown and seemed to spread over the whole surface of the eyeball. As her sight failed, the eyelids crinkled and drew in, so that her face was like an eyeless mask" (CS, 349). Once the wearer of a mask of servility, Nannie now embraces her lost heritage, her new identity signified by the transformation of her features into those of an African tribal mask. Nannie's metamorphosis only hastens the dissolution of the family order that she and the grandmother had once held together so well. "Almost immediately after she went," the narrator comments, "everything slackened, lost tone, went off edge" (*CS,* 350).

Besides glossing over complex and problematic issues of race, the grandmother's organized system rigidly opposes, in its emphasis on stability through tradition and social ritual, freethinking intellectual pursuits. The grandmother's anti-intellectualism (and more generally, the South's) is one of her firmest bulwarks against the inroads of modernism that threaten to subvert the established order. As the family's legends and organization, undergirded by nostalgia and closed-mindedness, come under pressure by the testimonies of Uncle Jimbilly and Aunt Nannie, so too does its anti-intellectualism, usually called into question by the demystifying presence of an outsider. The limits of the grandmother's vision and the pressures exerted upon it by "modern" thinking—such as that of scientific investigation—are central in "The Fig Tree." In this story Miranda stands between her grandmother's obsession for establishing a coherent community, characterized by her command always to act under her orders ("This way and no other!" [*CS,* 354]) and her great-aunt Eliza's obvious disinterest in standards of social behavior and her compulsion instead for structuring life according to scientific observation. If Sophia Jane always focuses her attention on the family and its codes, making sure as best she can that everyone acts by what she sees as the appropriate standards, Eliza always has her eyes at either the microscope or the telescope, seeking to discover how things are put together and work. Miranda, not surprisingly, stands transfixed by Eliza, for she has never seen anyone so openly disregard the family's codes of conduct. At the family farm Miranda abandons her customary interests in barnyard animals because she finds Eliza so captivating. The narrator comments that "Great-Aunt Eliza's ways and habits kept Miranda following her about, gazing, or sitting across the dining-table, gazing, for when Great-Aunt Eliza was not on the roof before her telescope, always just before daylight or just after dark, she was walking about with a microscope and a burning glass, peering closely at something she saw on a tree trunk, something she found in the grass; now and then she collected fragments that looked like dried leaves or bits of bark, brought them in the house, spread them out on a sheet of white paper, and sat there poring, as still as if she were saying her prayers" (CS, 360). Sophia Jane has her religion of tradition and community; Eliza has hers of science and intellectual inquiry.

Significantly, Eliza's system, rather than Sophia Jane's, solves Miranda's crisis, her fear that she has mistakenly buried a chick alive. Following her grandmother's strictures about the burial of dead animals, Miranda had given the chick a proper burial "in a little grave with flowers on top and a smooth stone at the head" (CS, 354). The "weep-weep" Miranda had heard after the burial and had believed to be the chick's cries, Eliza later makes clear, are merely the calls of tree frogs. Eliza's revelation sends Miranda into a "fog of bliss" (CS, 362), and she takes hold of her great-aunt's hand, an action signifying her allegiance to this strong-minded woman whose knowledge helps her to understand the world as she never had before. Her hand-in-hand embrace suggests her freeing, at least for the moment, from her grandmother's grip.

Miranda's apparent newfound freedom, however, may in fact be merely continued servility, with only the tyrants changing. Sophia Jane and Eliza, indeed, share some striking and disturbing similarities, as Miranda notices during one of their frequent arguments. Miranda intently watches the foes at battle, intrigued less by Sophia Jane's and Eliza's words than by their manner, at once authoritarian and childish. She sees, the narrator writes, "two old women, who were proud of being grandmothers, who spoke to children always as if they knew best about everything and children knew nothing, and they told children all day long to come here, go there, do this, do not do that, and they were always right and children never were except when they did anything they were told right away without a word. And here they were bickering like two little girls at school, or even the way Miranda and her sister Maria bickered and nagged and picked on each other and said things on purpose to hurt each other's feelings." She backs away, feeling "sad and strange and a little frightened" (CS, 359). Eliza's obsession with science, mirroring that of the grandmother's with tradition, the narrator makes clear, is in some ways as rigid and distorting in its single-mindedness. In "The Loss of the Creature," Walker Percy discusses how the wonder of the concrete presence of existence can be entirely lost to those who strive to explain everything away by scientific theory. "Instead of the marvels of the universe being made available to the public, the universe is disposed of by theory," Percy writes. "The loss of sovereignty takes this form: As a result of the science of botany, trees are not made available to every man. On the contrary. The tree loses its proper density and mystery as a concrete existent and, as merely another *specimen of* a species, becomes itself nugatory."[5] Eliza so suffers: for her the world is more an equation to be solved than an environment to be lived in. The dining room table, for instance, becomes a laboratory instead of a place for repast and conversation. She gets her greatest joy not from eating but from picking her food apart to determine its structural characteristics. The narrator comments that customarily at meals "she would dissect a scrap of potato peeling or anything else she might be eating, and sit there, bowed over, saying 'Hum,' from time to time" (*CS,* 360). More tellingly, in her obsessive quest for facts, Eliza remains almost entirely oblivious to the feelings and concerns of others, living in a world essentially unto herself. Amid Miranda's overwhelming joy at the story's end, when she revels in her awareness that she has not buried the chick alive and grasps her great-aunt's hand, Eliza maintains her cool scientific detachment, acting more like an academic lecturer than a close family relation: " 'Just think,' said Great-Aunt Eliza, in her most scientific voice, 'when tree frogs shed their skins, they pull them over their heads like little shirts, and they eat them. Can you imagine? They have the prettiest little shapes you ever saw—I'll show you one some time under the microscope' " (*CS,* 361–62).

Sophia Jane and Eliza represent opposing approaches to organizing one's life, depicting the tension between traditionalism and modernism with which Miranda must come to terms as she grows up. At the end of "The Fig Tree," Eliza has shown Miranda an entirely new way of understanding things: Miranda sees that despite her grandmother's admonitions, there is a way other than her grandmother's "this way." She stands awed by her awareness that reality can be structured, and narrated, in ways she has never seen before, and a new world of possibility looms before her, a realization about the here and now not unlike what she discovered about the

5. Walker Percy, "The Loss of the Creature," in Percy, *The Message in the Bottle: How Queer Man Is, How Queer Language Is, and What One Has to Do with the Other* (New York, 1975), 63.

heavens when she looked for the first time at the moon through Eliza's telescope: "Oh, it's like another world" (*CS,* 361). Eliza's modernism is indeed for Miranda "like another world," and at the story's conclusion Miranda appears anxious to explore this new world as fully as possible with Eliza as her guide. Miranda's fulfillment, however, lies not in simple discipleship with Eliza, for as we have already noted, Eliza has limitations every bit as problematic as Sophia Jane's. Although Miranda's allegiance to Eliza no doubt will introduce more freedom into her life, such freedom, as seen in Eliza, creates new problems and struggles. Put in the context of the other Miranda stories, particularly "Old Mortality," Miranda must learn to draw from the opposing ways of her grandmother and her great-aunt, rejecting neither but embracing both, integrating into her growing consciousness a dialogue between them that pressures and illuminates both figures and their outlooks—a difficult endeavor, but one of rich rewards.

In "Old Mortality," Miranda again faces the dilemma of coming to grips with the predominant traditionalism of her family and the modernism of one of the family's "rebels," in this case Cousin Eva. Miranda's problem focuses primarily on the question of how to interpret the life of Aunt Amy, a woman who died young and whose life, depending upon who is telling the story, was filled with either mystery and glamour (the family's version) or with deceit and sexual obsession and repression (Cousin Eva's view). On one level, the structure of "Old Mortality" follows Miranda's move away from her family's traditionalism, embodied here in its idealization of Amy, to her own independent view of things, a move that at the same time also represents a repudiation of Eva's modernism, portrayed in her psychoanalytic reading of Amy. This stepping free into a new world of interpretations, however, comes with its own dangers, temptations, and distortions.

Much of Part 1 of "Old Mortality" deals with the story of Amy as told by Miranda's family and the power that it—and other family stories—have over Miranda and her sister, Maria. Most of Miranda's elders share a strong love for their family legends and enthusiastically celebrate them in deeply felt tales. "They loved to tell stories, romantic and poetic, or comic with a romantic humor," the narrator writes. "They did not gild the outward circumstance, it was the feeling that mattered" (*CS,* 175). For both Miranda and Maria, the feeling evoked by the stories seizes their attention and enchants their imaginations. They have little use, in contrast, for the mementos and keepsakes of Amy and bygone days. Unlike the family stories, these items carry little mystery or wonder. "Photographs, portraits by inept painters who meant earnestly to flatter, and the festival garments folded away in dried herbs and camphor were disappointing when the little girls tried to fit them to the living beings created in their minds by the breathing words of their elders," the narrator comments at one point. At another she writes that Miranda and Maria, in looking at the old photographs of their family, "found it impossible to sympathize with those young persons, sitting rather stiffly before the camera, hopelessly out of fashion; but they were drawn and held by the mysterious love of the living, who remembered and cherished these dead. The visible remains were nothing; they were dust, perishable as the flesh; the features stamped on paper and metal were nothing, but their living memory enchanted the little girls" (CS, 175, 176).

Both Miranda and Maria associate the wondrous aura of the family legends with the romance of the theater and literature they so much adore. "Their Aunt Amy belonged to the world of poetry," the narrator characterizes their thinking. "The romance of Uncle Gabriel's long, unrewarded love for her, her early death, was such a story as one found in old books: unworldly books, but true, such as Vita Nuova, the Sonnets of Shakespeare and the Wedding Song of Spenser; and poems by Edgar Allan Poe" (CS, 178). Hearing their elders speak gloriously not only about ancestors but about previously seen stars of stage and performance (Jenny Lind, Bernhardt, and Rubenstein, for instance) brings the girls to see beyond the mundane, opening them to an awareness of "a life beyond a life in this world, as well as in the next; such episodes confirmed for the little girls the nobility of human feeling, the divinity of man's vision of the unseen, the importance of life and death, the depths of the human heart, the romantic value of tragedy" (CS, 179). That the stories they hear from their family are about people who really lived and whose presence deeply touched the lives of those who now tell their stories particularly enchants Miranda, as she imagines the mysteries that someday she hopes will enliven her everyday existence, an existence characterized by "dull lessons to be learned, stiff shoes to be limbered up, scratchy flannels to be endured in cold weather, measles and disappointed expectations" (CS, 178). So taken is Miranda by Amy's story that she faithfully envisions a life for herself every bit as glamorous as her aunt's. Over Maria's objections that she and Miranda will never be strikingly beautiful, Miranda nonetheless "secretly believed that she would one day suddenly receive beauty, as by inheritance, riches laid suddenly in her hands through no deserts of her own. She believed for quite a while that she would one day be like Aunt Amy, not as she appeared in the photograph, but as she was remembered by those who had seen her" (CS, 177). Miranda's wishes are apparently not unlike those of Amy herself, who strove to shape her life into one of a romantic narrative. After her ride to Mexico following her brother's duel, Amy returned gravely ill but overjoyed, to her parents' horror. Amy laughs happily at their distress, explaining: "Mammy, it was splendid, the most delightful trip I ever had. And if I am to be the heroine of this novel, why shouldn't I make the most of it?" (CS, 189).

Despite their love of the family legends and their willingness to believe in them, Miranda and Maria eventually come to discover discrepancies between the world in which they live and that of the family narratives. These discrepancies undercut the stories' credibility and power, a situation analogous to the girls' problems in fitting the physical mementos, aspects of the real world, into the family's imaginative narratives. The most obvious example of the family lore's unreliability is their father's steadfast assertion that all of the family's women "in every generation without exception, [were] as slim as reeds and graceful as sylphs." Even the girls know that their great-aunt Keziah was so large and bulky that she "quite squeezed herself through doors, and . . . when seated, was one solid pyramidal monument from floor to neck" (CS, 174). Further evidence comes when Maria asks her father about a reference to Amy as a "singing angel" in the poem Gabriel had inscribed on her tombstone. To Maria's question if Amy did in fact sing, her father responds curtly: "Now what has that to do with it? It's a poem" (CS, 181). Miranda's and Maria's frustration with resolving the tension between reality and romance mirrors Amy's, for her unhappiness lay in the undermining of her romantic vision by the everyday demands of routine life and by the resistance of her friends and family to measure up to the roles she had created for them in the narrative by which she wanted to live. "Mammy, I'm sick of this world," she confided to her mother after her father remonstrated with her about her daring dress and her later flirtation at the dance that led to her brother's duel. "I don't like anything in it. It's so *dull*" (*CS,* 188).

Equally disturbing is Miranda and Maria's growing awareness that while the family stories might enlarge their everyday world with an added dimension of romance and intrigue, they can also, in their overriding emphasis on the past, in effect destroy the present and the future. This is the destructive power wielded by Sophia Jane and Nannie in "The Old Order" when they hold roost over the family with their authoritarian rules and their endless storytelling. Miranda particularly notices that no matter how thrilling a musical or stage performance the family sees "there was always a voice recalling other and greater occasions" (*CS,* 179). Although Miranda enjoys hearing about stars and shows from the past, she also realizes that by her elders' standards whatever happens in the present never measures up to what has happened in the past. The present is always a dim shadow of a more glorious past, not a particularly comforting thought for a young girl about to embark on her life. Typical of her budding resentment toward the past's stranglehold on the present is her response to an old gentleman who downplays a performance of Paderewski in light of his earlier hearings of Rubenstein. The narrator reports that the gentleman "could not but feel that Rubenstein had reached the final height of musical interpretation, and, for him, Paderewski had been something of an anticlimax." The gentleman dominates the postperformance discussion, talking along while "holding up one hand, patting the air as if he were calling for silence." Everyone but Miranda listens to the man without disfavor. Her response smacks of bitterness: "They had never heard Rubenstein; they had, one hour since, heard Paderewski, and why should anyone need to recall the past? Miranda, dragged away, half understanding the old gentleman, hated him" (*CS,* 179).

In Part 2, Miranda and Maria, a few years older and a bit wiser, confront even more obviously both the distortions of the family legends and the crushing potential of the past, when worshiped unreservedly, to thwart personal growth by devaluing the present. Now at a convent school in New Orleans, the girls still read avidly, particularly romances, but they no longer automatically see the narratives as relevant to their own lives. The story begins with immediate evidence of their more discriminating visions. Like

Part 1, Part 2 opens with legendary history—here of the evil goings-on within the cells and dungeons of Catholic convents, as described in the pulp novels Miranda and Maria have been reading. But the girls are more aware of the distortions and exaggerations, more cognizant of the gulf separating the world of the imaginative narratives from that of everyday life. "It was no good at all trying to fit the stories to life, and they did not even try," the narrator writes, speaking of the girls' reading about convent life and their own experience in one. "They had long since learned to draw the lines between life, which was real and earnest, and the grave was not its goal; poetry, which was true but not real; and stories, or forbidden reading matter, in which things happened as nowhere else, with the most sublime irrelevance and unlikelihood, and one need not turn a hair, because there was not a word of truth in them" (*CS,* 194).

Despite their greater discrimination and more realistic appraisal of happenings about them, Miranda and Maria still feel the power of the legend of Aunt Amy, though much of that power dissipates when they meet Uncle Gabriel at the racetrack. Gabriel is anything but the dashing figure the girls had imagined. From afar he appears as "a vast bulging man with a red face and immense tan ragged mustaches fading into gray," and close up he is even more disappointing, described as "a shabby fat man with bloodshot blue eyes, sad beaten eyes, and a big melancholy laugh, like a groan." Miranda and Maria stand stunned, wondering to themselves if that could really be their Uncle Gabriel: " 'Is that Aunt Amy's handsome romantic beau? Is that the man who wrote the poem about our Aunt Amy?' Oh, what did grown-up people *mean* when they talked, anyway?" (*CS,* 197). Also dashed are Miranda's romantic conceptions of horse racing. After Miss Lucy, Uncle Gabriel's horse, wins her race, Miranda sees that the mare has paid dearly for her effort: she suffers from a nosebleed and struggles for breath with eyes wild and knees trembling. Horrified by the horse's distress, Miranda reinterprets the race in an entirely new light: "So instantly and completely did her heart reject that victory, she did not know when it happened, but she hated it and she was ashamed that she had screamed and shed tears for joy when Miss Lucy, with her bloodied nose and bursting heart had gone past the judge's stand a neck ahead. She felt empty and sick and held to her father's hand so hard that he shook her off a little

impatiently and said, 'What is the matter with you? Don't be so fidgety' "
(*CS*, 199).

During their visit to Uncle Gabriel's home, Miranda and Maria see how
the past utterly consumes the present when a person lives entirely by his or
her memories. They see that Gabriel's zest for life died along with his first
wife. Gabriel wallows in long-lost dreams of happiness with Amy, dreams
that overshadow all else. An extreme version of the elders in Part 1 who
had focused their lives almost entirely on their memories, Gabriel continually measures what happens to him in light of his memories of his days with
Amy, recalling her with almost every breath: he names his racehorse after
Amy's mare, he introduces Miranda and Maria as Amy's nieces and Harry
as Amy's brother, and he asks his wife, Honey, whether she thinks his nieces
bear a striking resemblance to Amy. Earlier at the racetrack Gabriel noted
that none of his horses had ever come up to their namesake, Amy's original
Miss Lucy, and so too in Gabriel's mind does everything else in his life pale
beside his days with Amy. His heavy drinking underscores his unhappiness
and self-pity.

In Part 3, Miranda, now eighteen, has rejected her elders and their
ways. Against her father's wishes she has eloped and left the convent school.
As bold a step as that was, Miranda nonetheless is not entirely free from her
family and its legends, as the very situation of the opening scene of the
section, her returning home for Uncle Gabriel's funeral, indicates. On the
train she meets one of her relatives, Eva, and as they talk Amy's legend once
again comes under close scrutiny, a scrutiny that catalyzes Miranda's con-
tinuance of her quest for complete freedom and the power to narrate her
own life.

Eva is a thoroughgoing modernist who has striven to free herself from
her upbringing and her family. A leader in the women's suffrage movement, Eva evaluates life with cold Freudian cynicism, and she targets the
family (both her own and families in general) for vicious attack. At one
point, after angrily telling Miranda about the humiliation she had suffered
at the family's hands because of her weak chin, she concludes by saying that
"the whole hideous institution should be wiped from the face of the earth.
It is the root of all human wrongs." Much to Miranda's surprise Eva
launches into a bitter tirade about Amy that debunks her legendary stature.

Claiming that her interpretation is "the other side of the story" (*CS*, 217), Eva asserts that Amy was no romantic heroine but simply one of the many spoiled young women of her social set who were consumed by only one thing—sex. "It was just sex," Eva explains. "Their minds dwelt on nothing else. They didn't call it that, it was all smothered under pretty names, but that's all it was, sex" (*CS*, 216). Eva goes on to say that even though Amy was more spirited than her friends, she nevertheless "was simply sex-ridden, like the rest. She behaved as if she hadn't a rival on earth, and she pretended not to know what marriage was about, but I know better. None of them had, and they didn't want to have, anything else to think about, and they didn't really know anything about that, so they simply festered in-side—they festered" (*CS*, 216). Even more disturbing are Eva's suspicions that Amy's relations with another man were the cause of her hastily arranged marriage to Gabriel and that she may have committed suicide in the face of unhappiness and scandal.

Although Eva perceives the family's stories of Amy as falsely romantic and hers as objectively balanced, Miranda thinks otherwise. After Eva speaks of the demented socialites, Miranda imagines "a long procession of living corpses, festering women stepping gaily towards the charnel house, their corruption concealed under laces and flowers, their dead faces lifted smiling." She then concludes about Eva's argument: "Of course it was not like that. This is no more true than what I was told before, it's every bit as romantic" (*CS*, 216). Not only every bit as romantic as the family's, Eva's obsession with the past is also every bit as consuming. For all of her efforts to assert her independence and to free herself from the past, Eva is chained to her childhood by her Freudian vision. Her outburst about Amy reveals as much about the psychic damage inflicted upon her by the family as it does about the damage she inflicts upon herself as an adult utterly fixated upon the past. Whatever the truth of Eva's characterization of Amy and Amy's friends, her description of them, in an irony she herself does not see, is actually a portrait of herself—a festering, sex-obsessed woman. Miranda notes, depressingly, that a warped personality undergirds Eva's strength: "Why was a strong character so deforming? Miranda felt she truly wanted to be strong, but how could she face it, seeing what it did to one?" (*CS*, 215).

Back at home, after being snubbed by her father who still has not forgiven her for her elopement, Miranda sees with eye-opening clarity the generational gulf separating her from Eva and her father. Despite their differences, Eva and Harry quickly fall into friendly talk, utterly ignoring Miranda. The narrator describes them as two people "who knew each other well, who were comfortable with each other, being contemporaries on equal terms, who occupied by right their place in this world, at the time of life to which they had arrived by paths familiar to them both" (*CS*, 219). Common memories bond Eva and Harry together (even if at other times they put these memories into different contexts and to different uses), and they delight in "going over old memories and finding new points of interest in them" (*CS*, 220). Over the roar of the car's engine, Miranda cannot hear the stories Eva and her father tell, but ablaze with her sense of difference, she does not care, for she vows from this day forward to be the author of her own stories. "She knew too many stories like them," the narrator writes of Miranda as she watches Eva and her father chat, "she wanted something new of her own. The language was familiar to them, but not to her, not any more" (*CS*, 220). Miranda vows, "in her arrogance, her pride" (*CS*, 219) to go her own way, depending upon no one but herself for guidance and support. Her vow gives way to bitter resentment over what she sees as her elders' domination: "She resented, slowly and deeply and in profound silence, the presence of these aliens who lectured and admonished her, who loved her with bitterness and denied her the right to look at the world with her own eyes, who demanded that she accept their version of life and yet could not tell her the truth, not in the smallest thing. 'I hate them both,' her inner and secret mind said plainly, *I will be free of them, I shall not even remember them*'" (*CS*, 219).

Miranda's fierce rage for independence quickly extends itself: she will seek to liberate herself not only from her elders but also from her entire family, even those of her own generation. She will not return to her husband. She wants to be free of all ties to others, ties that she now sees not as enriching but as confining. "She would have no more bonds that smothered her in love and hatred," the narrator reports her thinking. "She knew now why she had run away to marriage, and she knew that she was going to run away from marriage, and she was not going to stay in any place, with anyone, that threatened to forbid her making her own discoveries, that said

'No' to her" (*CS*, 220). Hers will be a quest for truth that she will structure and narrate exclusively on the basis of her own feelings and experiences:

> What is the truth, she asked herself as intently as if the question had never been asked, the truth, even about the smallest, the least important of all the things I must find out? and where shall I begin to look for it? Her mind closed stubbornly against remembering, not the past but the legend of the past, other people's memory of the past, at which she had spent her life peering in wonder like a child at a magic-lantern show. Ah, but there is my own life to come yet, she thought, my own life now and beyond. I don't want any promises, I won't have false hopes, I won't be romantic about myself. I can't live in their world any longer, she told herself, listening to the voices back of her. Let them tell their stories to each other. Let them go on explaining how things happened. I don't care. At least I can know the truth about what happened to me, she assured herself silently, making a promise to herself, in her hopefulness, her ignorance. (*CS*, 221)

Miranda's hopefulness is obvious here, but what of her ignorance? Her ignorance lies primarily in her naïveté: although she claims that she will not be romantic about herself, that is exactly what she is. She conceives herself as a solitary quester for truth, in effect the romantic artist. Naïve, too, is Miranda's thinking that she can free herself from her family merely by not remembering them. Memory does not work so simply, and the members of her family, no matter how much she consciously resists them, will always be active participants in her inner life. Moreover, Miranda naïvely believes that the narrative she wishes to construct can be entirely distinct from and unaffected by that of her family, that she can simply erase from her consciousness all traces of meaning and interpretation from others and begin with a clean page.[6] Miranda's angry rebellion against her family may be necessary to loosen its tight control of her thinking, but it is merely an initial step toward a fulfillment that lies far ahead. To reach her goal, Mir-

6. In this quest to unground meaning, as George Cheatham has shown, Miranda resembles the modernist who seeks "to deny the past's impingement on the present, to deny all confirming priorties." See Cheatham, "Death and Repetition in Porter's Miranda Stories," *American Literature*, LXI (1989), 610–24.

anda must use and draw from her past, engaging rather than repressing her memories.

In "Pale Horse, Pale Rider," Miranda struggles to live the ultimate freedom that she had vowed to achieve at the end of "Old Mortality." It is no easy struggle, and ultimately Miranda falls prey, ironically, to the same disorder from which she has been fleeing: the usurpation of the present and future by an all-consuming memory focused on the past. Now six years older and a newspaper reporter, Miranda finds her independence under assault from a variety of forces. For one, other people apply strong pressure on her to conform to society's standards. Miranda's visit from the agents selling liberty bonds typifies this pressure. Disregarding her complaints of poverty, one of the agents tells Miranda that she can pay weekly like most other people are doing, and he warns her that she has much to lose by not signing up for the program. "You're the only one in this whole newspaper office that hasn't come in," he lies to her. "And every firm in this city has come in one hundred percent. Over at the *Daily Clarion* nobody had to be asked twice" (*CS,* 274). Amid the agents' badgering, Miranda can only think about what she would like to say to them: "Suppose I were not a coward, but said what I really thought? Suppose I said to hell with this filthy war? Suppose I asked that little thug, What's the matter with you, why aren't you rotting in Belleau Wood? I wish you were" (*CS,* 273). Here suffering in her speechlessness, Miranda later suffers for speaking her mind. After her negative review of his acting, an indignant entertainer verbally assaults her at the newspaper office. He attempts to discredit her by suggesting that her opinions deviate wildly from the mainstream, and he waves before him a number of tear sheets praising him. Although Miranda stands up to this man, his attack takes its toll, one of the many pressures that, taken together, Miranda finally finds overwhelming. "There's too much of everything in this world just now," she tells a friend after the entertainer has left. "I'd like to sit down here on the curb, Chuck, and die, and never again see—I wish I could lose my memory and my own name" (*CS,* 289).

That the oblivion Miranda here calls for entails the loss of memory points to memory itself as a pressure that haunts Miranda's bid for freedom. Despite her efforts to simplify her life by focusing on the present moment and the hopeful future, Miranda discovers the past difficult to escape. As

Miranda lies gravely ill, the narrator comments that with her mind with-drawn into itself under the onslaught of bodily pain, she lives with a single-mindedness absent from her everyday life: "There were no longer any mul-tiple planes of living, no tough filaments of memory and hope pulling taut backwards and forwards holding her upright between them" (*CS,* 304). Potentially healthy in its interplay and dialogue, this dynamic tension be-tween past and present in Miranda's everyday life is instead troublesome and disruptive, depleting rather than enriching. Not surprisingly, she typi-cally resists memory's intrusion and downplays its significance. When Adam asks her to tell him about her past, she responds: "There's nothing to tell, after all, if it ends now, for all this time I was getting ready for something that was going to happen later, when the time came. So now it's nothing much." To his query about whether she had ever been happy, she responds: "I don't know. I just lived and never thought about it." She then adds, as much to turn the conversation away from herself as to highlight her past, that she remembers things she liked and hoped for. She does not elaborate, however, except obliquely in a later question to Adam that speaks of immediate sensations anyone could experience rather than of specific events from her past. "Don't you love being alive?" Miranda asks. "Don't you love weather and the colors at different times of the day, and all the sounds and noises like children screaming in the next lot, and automobile horns and little bands playing in the street and the smell of food cooking?" (*CS,* 302).

Adam is yet another pressure weighing upon Miranda. Clearly Mir-anda has conflicting feelings toward her lover: a part of her yearns for a relationship of stability and commitment, whereas another part knows the impossibility of such love. At a nightclub Miranda notices with envy a couple who sit together in a world entirely unto themselves, a world Mir-anda would like to construct with Adam. "Something was done and settled between them, at least," the narrator reports her thinking of the couple. "It was enviable, enviable, that they could sit quietly together and have the same expression on their faces while they looked into the hell they shared, no matter what kind of hell, it was theirs, they were together" (*CS,* 296). At the same time, Miranda knows, with Adam's impending departure to the front and her growing sense of her own illness, that such a world is naïvely and romantically conceived, destined to crumble before the demands of reality. Thus, while she savors her and Adam's dreams of romance, Miranda also envisions a grim future for the two of them, represented by the tawdriness of the nightclub. "Life is completely crazy anyway," the narrator reports her thinking, "so what does it matter? This is what we have, Adam and I, this is all we're going to get, this is the way it is with us. She wanted to say, 'Adam, come out of your dream and listen to me. I have pains in my chest and my head and my heart and they're real. I am in pain all over, and you are in such danger as I can't bear to think about, and why can we not save each other?' " (*CS,* 296). As memory and hope pull her taut, so too do the conflicting pulls of cynicism and romanticism. According to the narrator, every move toward Adam is also a move away from him: "There was only the wish to see him and the fear, the present threat, of not seeing him again; for every step they took towards each other seemed perilous, drawing them apart instead of together, as a swimmer in spite of his most determined strokes is yet drawn slowly backward by the tide. 'I don't want to love,' she would think in spite of herself, 'not Adam, there is no time and we are not ready for it and yet this is all we have' " (*CS,* 292).

The pressures upon Miranda culminate with her illness, which is so severe that her world collapses entirely into the inner reaches of self. In her delirium, she experiences the bliss of oblivion, in effect ironically achieving her goal of complete independence, free from the demands and impositions of other people. Shorn now of the everyday pressures and tensions that had wracked her spirit, Miranda retracts into a mere particle of self-preservation:

> Silenced she sank easily through deeps under deeps of darkness until she lay like a stone at the farthest bottom of life, knowing herself to be blind, deaf, speechless, no longer aware of the members of her own body, entirely withdrawn from all human concerns, yet alive with a peculiar lucidity and coherence; all notions of the mind, the reasonable inquiries of doubt, all ties of blood and the desires of the heart, dissolved and fell away from her, and there remained of her only a minute fiercely burning particle of being that knew itself alone, that relied upon nothing beyond itself for its strength; not susceptible to any appeal or inducement, being itself composed entirely of one single motive, the stubborn will to live. This

fiery motionless particle set itself unaided to resist destruction, to survive
and to be in its own madness of being, motiveless and planless beyond
that one essential end. (*CS*, 310–11)

In the midst of her bliss, with a glorious vision of sunlight, meadow, and
sea opening before her, Miranda sees a large company of people, everybody
from her past, all of whom stand wondrously beautiful. "Their faces were
transfigured," the narrator writes, "each in its own beauty, beyond what she
remembered of them, their eyes were clear and untroubled as good weather,
and they cast no shadows." The figures, "alone but not solitary," encircle
Miranda, who now experiences the joy of being utterly unto herself and yet
part of a larger group that puts no demands on her: "Miranda, alone too,
questioning nothing, desiring nothing, in the quietude of her ecstasy, stayed
where she was, eyes fixed on the overwhelming deep sky where it was
always morning" (*CS*, 311).

Miranda's ecstatic oblivion is short-lived, however. Shots of medication
pull her back into her body, her joyful vision vanishing before the "terrible
compelling pain" that races through her veins and "the sweetish sickening
smell of rotting flesh and pus" that fills her nostrils (*CS*, 321). Miranda
awakes transformed, utterly dominated in thought and vision by her near-
death experience. She now views and judges everything in light of that
experience, forging a perspective derived entirely from her memories. In
this she ironically acts precisely as the elders of her family had done—
precisely as she has pledged to avoid acting. Adding to the irony is the fact
that Miranda's idealized version of eternal mornings and beautiful people
mirrors the romanticized past that her family had celebrated. As nothing
contemporary had ever measured up to the glories of the past for Miranda's
elders, the same is now true for Miranda. The world appears dull and dingy,
even in broad daylight, since by her new vision "there was no light, there
might never be light again, compared as it must always be with the light
she had seen beside the blue sea that lay so tranquilly along the shore of her
paradise" (*CS*, 314). She recoils from both her own body and the world
about her. "The body is a curious monster, no place to live in, how could
anyone feel at home there?" the narrator reports Miranda thinking. "Is it
possible I can ever accustom myself to this place? she asked herself. The

human faces around her seemed dulled and tired, with no radiance of skin and eyes as Miranda remembered radiance; the once white walls of her room were now a soiled gray" (*CS,* 313). To ease her despair she frequently closes her eyes to remember her ecstasy, but each time she opens them, she is shocked once again, seeing "with a new anguish the dull world to which she was condemned, where the light seemed filmed over with cobwebs, all the bright surfaces corroded, the sharp planes melted and formless, all objects and beings meaningless, ah, dead and withered things that believed themselves alive!" (*CS,* 314).

So dominated is Miranda by her near-death experience that in effect she becomes entirely alienated from the present world, viewing it "with the covertly hostile eyes of an alien who does not like the country in which he finds himself, does not understand the language nor wish to learn it, does not mean to live there and yet is helpless, unable to leave it at his will" (*CS,* 313). Her alienation brings her the freedom that she has long sought, but at a terrifying cost—the utter devaluation of life, including her own, before her memory of oblivion. Not unlike the drug addict whose need consumes all else, Miranda is blinded to life's wonder in the here and now by her visionary experience. Rather than bringing her near-death experience into active interplay with both her present self and her other memories (such as her love for Adam), she elevates it to an unchallengeable standard by which all else is judged. The effects are devastating. Her heart, once "tender" and "capable of love," is "hardened" and "indifferent" (*CS,* 315), and she now sees life devoid of meaning with everyone—except herself—deceived by a vast conspiracy into believing that there is nothing better than to be alive. At the end of the story she banishes thoughts of Adam from her consciousness because she knows that recognizing her deep feelings for him, even though he now lies dead and buried, will undermine the cold indifference with which she now faces the world. For Miranda love has become "bitter desire," and life's rich heterogeneity has become drab sameness. The narrator says of Miranda's thoughts, "No more war, no more plague, only the dazed silence that follows the ceasing of the heavy guns; noiseless houses with the shades drawn, empty streets, the dead cold light of tomorrow. Now there would be time for everything" (*CS,* 317). Miranda has time for everything because everything has become nothing.

In the epiphany at the end of "The Grave," Miranda recovers much of the wonder and mystery of life that she had lost at the conclusion of "Pale Horse, Pale Rider." Now about twenty-nine, Miranda has her visionary insight while strolling through a marketplace in a foreign country (apparently Mexico). When a market vendor holds before her a tray of sweets shaped like tiny animals, Miranda suddenly sees again a long-forgotten experience she had with her brother, Paul, twenty years before. Miranda's experiences that day had deeply disturbed her, giving her a brief and forbidding glimpse into what the future held for her as a woman, but in her revived memory of the occasion, she transforms the events into a celebration of self and memory.

On that disturbing day with Paul, Miranda's displacement from the world of childhood began when, after slipping onto her thumb a ring discovered in one of the family's graves, she immediately found herself inexplicably turning against her tomboyish ways and toward the customs of southern womanhood embodied in the family legends. "She wanted to go back to the farmhouse," the narrator reports her thinking, "take a good cold bath, dust herself with plenty of Maria's violet talcum powder—provided Maria was not present to object of course—put on the thinnest, most becoming dress she owned, with a big sash, and sit in a wicker chair under the trees. . . . These things were not all she wanted, of course; she had vague stirrings of desire for luxury and a grand way of living which could not take precise form in her imagination but were founded on family legend of past wealth leisure" (CS, 365). Further displacing her was the sight of unborn rabbits in the womb of the pregnant rabbit Paul had shot and cut open. What had once only been vague intuitions of sexual birth now became disturbingly real manifestations of blood and death:

Having seen, she felt at once as if she had known all along. The very memory of her former ignorance faded; she had always known just this. No one had ever told her anything outright, she had been rather unobservant of the animal life around her because she was so accustomed to animals. They seemed simply disorderly and unaccountably rude in their habits, but altogether natural and not very interesting. Her brother had spoken as if he had known about everything all along. He may have seen all this before. He had never said a word to her, but she knew now a part at least of what he knew. She understood a little of the secret, formless intuitions in her own mind and body, which had been clearing up, taking form, so gradually and steadily she had not realized that she was learning what she had to know. (*CS*, 366–67)

Miranda's initial fascination with the rabbits quickly faded under the pressure of this disturbing realization. Whereas she had first seen the unborn rabbits as "wonderful little creatures" and had felt "pity and astonishment and a kind of shocked delight," she now saw a "bloody heap" and stood "quietly and terribly agitated" (*CS*, 366, 367). So disturbing were Miranda's thoughts about what she had seen and felt that after a few days of "confused unhappiness" (*CS*, 367) she let her memories of the day's events sink quietly into her consciousness where they became lost amidst the vast accumulation of other impressions.

Twenty years later, when the vendor holds the tray of sweets before her and she smells "the mingled sweetness and corruption" of the marketplace, Miranda's memory of the day, until then merely a vague recollection of a hunt for treasure amid opened graves, suddenly "leap[s] from its burial place before her mind's eye" to emerge "plain and clear in its true colors as if she looked through a frame upon a scene that had not stirred nor changed since the moment it happened" (*CS*, 367). Initially, her vision strikes her with the anguish she had felt when the events had occurred twenty years before, but as her mind quickly contextualizes the events, striving to understand their significance in light of what she has experienced and learned in the intervening years, her disquiet gives way to wonder: "The dreadful vision faded, and she saw clearly her brother, whose childhood face she had forgotten, standing again in the blazing sunshine, again twelve years old, a pleased sober smile in his eyes, turning the silver dove over and over in his hands" (*CS*, 367–68).

Miranda's vision of Paul celebrates the victory of the individual, and of the artist, to forge wholeness, order, and beauty from the secrets of memory. Memory, as the vision underscores, deepens experience, challenging a person to a larger understanding of self and world. Rather than in Miranda's brooding alienation at the close of "Pale Horse, Pale Rider," independence and growth for Porter lie in Miranda's wholeness at the end of "The Grave," achieved by engaging the inner reaches of memory with the self's multitudinous experiences in the world. From this dialogic interplay of memory and self, an ongoing process of reconstruction and reformulation (suggested in Miranda's final vision of Paul "turning the silver dove over and over in his hands"), a person gains insight and constructs meaning. The wholeness of self here mirrors the wholeness of art, with adventures transformed into experience, chaos into coherence. "That is what the artist does," Porter wrote on December 30, 1942, to her nephew Paul: "He sees, he is the witness, the one who remembers, and finally works out the pattern and the meaning for himself, and gives form to his memories" (L, 260). That working out is Miranda's achievement at the end of "The Grave," the triumphant close of the Miranda cycle.

# 7
## FASCISM, TOTALITARIANISM, AND THE ORDEAL OF *SHIP OF FOOLS*

In some undated notes Katherine Anne Porter discussed what she saw as the four stages through which writers typically pass: the apprentice, the journeyman, the master, and the virtuoso. "Every stage is full of traps, but the last the most perilous of all," Porter wrote. "It is the point at which many fail, for if virtuosity is what they were aiming for, then almost at once, on being reached, it turns into a headlong showing off, everything gone bad but the technique and a straight-drop into charlatism and self-parody" (McKeldin). Porter's comments here have relevance to her own career, for her final major work, *Ship of Fools,* in some ways can be understood as a failed work of virtuosity—a work of complex and deft technique, but one finally forced and overwrought. This is not to suggest that with *Ship of Fools* Porter drops straight into charlatism and self-parody. Indeed, as in many of her earlier works, she engaged her memories in an effort to forge a work of order and clarity and no doubt was entirely sincere in her attempt. Porter always held fast to her artistic integrity and never catered to popular taste or fancy. And yet *Ship of Fools* is flawed, its tone and texture in many ways differing quite markedly from those of much of her earlier work. Two factors, which I want to explore in some depth in this chapter, I believe undermined the more open-minded dialogic vision of her best short fiction: her almost obsessive determination to make *Ship of Fools* her masterwork and her growing cynicism during the forties and fifties about world affairs and politics.

The origins of *Ship of Fools* lie in Porter's 1931 sea voyage with Eugene Pressly from Veracruz to Bremerhaven. In a long letter to Caroline Gordon dated August 28, 1931, Porter kept a running journal of the trip, what she called in that letter "a kind of log." With it, she wrote in a later letter to Gordon on December 14, 1931, "I meant to give you as clear accounts as I could of the voyage; to amuse you, and to console myself for not having seen you" (*L*, 49, 70). Porter's description of the trip underscores how much she based the characters and events of the novel upon actual people and occurrences. Apparently deeply affected by the crossing, Porter for the next several years continued to make notes and observations, in preparation for what she thought was to be a long story. In 1937 and 1938, under the title "Promised Land," she attempted unsuccessfully to write a story of the voyage that was to be published with the works that were later collected in *Pale Horse, Pale Rider: Three Short Novels*—"Pale Horse, Pale Rider," "Noon Wine," and "Old Mortality." After several more years of thinking and taking notes, Porter came to see the 1931 voyage as the basis for a novel, and in 1940 during a stay at Yaddo she began work, giving it the working title "No Safe Harbor."

Initially Porter's writing went very well. By 1942 she had completed over two hundred pages, and she hoped, as did her publisher, Harcourt, Brace, that the novel would be completed that year or the next. Despite periods of intense effort Porter failed to finish the novel at this time. Rather than calling it quits and salvaging what she could for stories, as she had done when her other attempts at novels had bogged down, Porter stayed with this manuscript, returning to it off and on for close to twenty more years. In 1945 and 1954 she made concerted efforts to complete the novel but lost momentum and left the manuscript unfinished. Finally in 1961, after secluding herself in an inn, she garnered her creative energies and completed her book, published a year later as *Ship of Fools*. Her most arduous and painful struggle as a writer was finally over. "I finished the thing," Porter said of *Ship of Fools,* in an interview with Roy Newquist in which she spoke of her final push, "but I think I sprained my soul" (*C*, 117).

There are a number of reasons for Porter's problems in completing *Ship of Fools*. As even a quick reading of her work clearly indicates, Porter was foremost a master of short fiction. Her stories are securely controlled and tightly crafted, usually focusing on a single character who at the story's climax reaches some type of sudden insight. The novel, however, with its customary emphasis on characters' evolving growth and development, was troublesome for Porter. Particularly troublesome was a novel with the scope of *Ship of Fools,* a work, as Joan Givner observes, written "on a large panoramic canvas" that attempted no less than to "solve the riddle of what had gone wrong with the whole Western world in the twentieth century." Givner rightly adds, "It was a daunting technical problem." Porter's problems with writing novels—or any long work, as evidenced in her failure to finish her biography of Cotton Mather—were not limited to matters of form and structure but also included trouble in maintaining the ongoing commitment needed to complete an extended work. As Darlene Unrue points out, Porter's habit of writing—quick bursts, usually long enough to finish a story, followed by extended periods of inactivity—was not propitious for writing novels.[1]

Then of course there were the everyday problems. During many of the years that Porter was struggling with *Ship of Fools,* she was frequently moving about, accepting various teaching and lecturing engagements primarily because she needed the income. Her lack of a secure home base only added to the feelings of rootlessness and isolation that haunted her during most of her lifetime. Her growing health problems, in part the result of her smoking and drinking habits, only made matters worse. Then, whenever she had found the time and inspiration to settle down to work, she felt badgered by the demands of friends and acquaintances. All in all, the period following Porter's triumph with *Pale Horse, Pale Rider* in 1939 until the publication of *Ship of Fools* in 1962 was a time of personal artistic frustration.

In large part because she had a terrible time maintaining enthusiasm and momentum, Porter was easily distracted from working on her novel. Usually she could get significant amounts of writing done only during times of inspired self-control, frequently when she had isolated herself in some out-of-the-way place. Of the twenty-one years that passed between the beginning and the completion of *Ship of Fools,* she probably spent a total of

1. Givner, *Katherine Anne Porter: A Life,* 407; Unrue, *Truth and Vision,* 164.

no more than two years' time actually writing. Givner cites a revealing letter that Porter wrote to Glenway Wescott on July 5, 1956, that underlines her problems in keeping consistently at work.[2] After listing several distractions that she says had kept her from writing, Porter admitted that these annoyances were not after all serious problems and that she had listed them merely to cover up her boredom with the novel in progress. "I suppose I write them," Porter wrote, speaking of her distractions, "to keep from breaking out and saying how I am slogging at this devilish book, and how bored I am with it, because the plan is so finished, there is nothing to do but just type it down to the end, and OH GOD! how I have to beat myself over the head to get started every morning—and even so I am late, and wake every day with my heart sinking, thinking I'll *never* make it. But I must and will, and I shall *never* write another novel, that is flat!" (McKeldin). Given Porter's feelings here and all the other problems involved in the composition of *Ship of Fools,* certainly it is less surprising that Porter took so long to write the novel than it is that she finished it at all.

Porter's vow to Wescott that she "must and will" complete *Ship of Fools* points to the overwhelming compulsion she felt, despite her own misgivings and inertia, to get the job done at whatever cost. This compulsion, I believe, worked against her own better artistic judgment that told her, as hinted at in her comments to Wescott, that the novel was too planned and mechanical, lacking in its great length the continual passion of inspiration, even if it always was in the firm grip of artistic control. Behind Porter's determination to complete *Ship of Fools* was her awareness that she had expended too much time and energy, not to mention money (several advances from her publisher), to let it die incomplete. In an interview with Newquist, Porter spoke of her troubled times with the novel, asserting that all along she knew that she had no choice but to proceed. She told Newquist that once she had begun writing and realized how long the novel was going to be she felt like calling it quits. "But I had painted myself into a corner, committed myself to it, and I had to go on," Porter said. "I'd work on it and push it away. I separated myself from it for two or three years at a time; I'd quit in the middle of a paragraph and start again months or years later, and I thought

2. Givner, *Katherine Anne Porter: A Life,* 407.

it was going to look like a piece of restored pottery dug out of a prehistoric midden. Yet I would come back and finish the dangling sentence where I'd left it, and little by little, I decided I was just being obstinate, cutting off my nose to spite my face, and that I was going to write a long book no matter what it might take" (*C,* 115–16).

Much of this determination to complete *Ship of Fools* also had to do with her professional pride and her desire for the widespread recognition as a major writer that she felt she deserved but had not received. Porter was hauntingly aware of the bias by publishers and critics against writers of the short story—put simply, the belief that as fine as they might be with short fiction, writers must at some point fulfill their promise with a novel. Porter frequently spoke out against this prejudice, and her comments in a letter dated July 20, 1956, to James F. Powers represent her feelings: "You know, I never had anything against short story writers writing novels, if they wanted to or felt they could, or should. My whole argument was against a short story writer being compelled to write novels when he didn't know how, or wasn't ready" (*L,* 511). At the same time she herself also could not entirely escape the pressure to write a novel, and this pressure only intensified once she had started *Ship of Fools* and had her publisher and the reading public, together with a number of her friends (many of whom had written novels), awaiting its completion. Haunting, too, must have been her memories of her earlier failed attempts with novels. Porter at times viewed the whole project as hopeless: in a letter dated September 9, 1953, to her editor Donald Brace, not long after the publication of *The Days Before,* she wrote that "so far as writing as a profession or a probable means of existence is concerned, I am through. We can both see it as no good. The only thing I want in the world so far as publishing is concerned is to get out of debt to Harcourt Brace" (*L,* 444). She never, though, in her deepest despair entirely gave up hope. In large part to prove to herself and to others that she could do it, together with some goading and support from her friends, particularly Seymour Lawrence during the final stages of writing, Porter finished *Ship of Fools* and soon thereafter found fame and fortune. But the tortuous writing process and her grinding obsession to succeed clearly took their toll on the spirit of Porter and likewise on that of her novel. One senses that much of the bitterness and heavy-handedness of *Ship of Fools* arises from its extended, trouble-plagued composition.

Porter's other obsession during the period she was writing *Ship of Fools*—the dangers of totalitarianism—also greatly affected the novel's final shape and tone. Porter was deeply influenced by the rise of the totalitarian state in Europe during the twenties and thirties and by the onset of World War II, and both darkened her vision considerably, pushing her views on politics and society, particularly later in life, toward progressively extreme positions. Although Porter's political views, as Thomas Walsh points out, frequently varied according to whom she was writing, it is clear that by the early thirties her previous enthusiasm for and then later ambivalence toward communism and the Soviet Union was giving way to disenchantment.[3] In a letter dated January 30, 1933, to Peggy Cowley, Porter wrote of her changing political allegiances: "Dear Peggy, I was a Communist twelve years ago and I couldn't go on with it, and I can't now. . . . It[']s occupied a good part of my thoughts since I was twenty[-]two years old, but the more I see of its directions the more I feel it is exchanging one bad form of government for another." Although she said she had never been and never would be a supporter of the capitalist system, she argued that the widespread support of the Soviet Union by American intellectuals was simply trendiness. "Why weren't they thinking about all this ten years ago?" she wrote. "Then was a time when it was a dangerous undertaking, their voices would have meant something then." She added that she would not join the bandwagon. In opposition to blind worship of the Soviet Union, she pledged, echoing the Agrarians, "I take my stand." She said that she knew that in the Soviet Union "there is already a privileged class, a ruling class and a working class" and that "the bureaucracy there is worse than it is in Germany, and that its propaganda is thoroughly dishonest, and that it strangles its artists in this harness of propaganda" (McKeldin). Porter's negative view of the Soviet Union and its American sympathizers only hardened with time. With the country at war, she wrote to Freda Kirchwey on February 5, 1942, that she was both anti-Nazi and anti-Communist,

3. Walsh, *Katherine Anne Porter and Mexico,* 181–82.

adding that "the people I hate and find detestable in their political morals, political tactics, and general life point of view are the American Communists of either wing [Stalinist and Trotskyite]; I think their acts are treasonable at this time, and even if they are anti-Fascist, they are also anti-American; the sole reason that they are not as dangerous as the Fascists who find so easy entrance into this country is, they are not so numerous and they are more easily watched" (*L,* 221–22).

Noteworthy and revealing in both of the these letters is Porter's linking of the Soviet Union with Germany, that is, of communism with fascism and nazism. Les K. Adler and Thomas G. Patterson have pointed out that beginning in the thirties a number of American intellectuals began noting similarities between Fascist and Communist states. This linkage downplayed, if it did not completely ignore, the different origins and ideologies of the two systems and instead foregrounded what was seen as the totalitarian methods of rule that characterized both. As the nation moved toward and then into war and then later into the cold war, this linkage became more pervasive and rigid, developing into a potent force that profoundly shaped American perceptions of and attitudes toward foreign affairs and political ideology. Characteristic of this perspective are a statement in a 1941 editorial in the *Wall Street Journal* that "the American people know that the principal difference between Mr. Hitler and Mr. Stalin is the size of their respective mustaches" and President Harry S Truman's 1947 remark that "there isn't any difference in totalitarian states. I don't care what you call them, Nazi, Communist or Fascist."[4]

Porter herself was clearly given to such thinking, and there is no doubt that her views on the Soviet Union in particular and political systems in general were profoundly shaped by the rise of fascism in Europe and particularly the coming to power of Hitler and the Nazis. Her 1931–1932 trip to Germany, during which she witnessed firsthand the rising power and menace of the Nazis, galvanized her ambivalent views into a thoroughgoing antifascism. By the mid-thirties her antifascism had developed into a more encompassing antitotalitarianism. To Janice Ford, who had appar-

4. Les K. Adler and Thomas G. Patterson, "Red Fascism: The Merger of Nazi Germany and Soviet Russia in the American Image of Totalitarianism, 1930's–1950's," *American Historical Review,* LXXV (1970), 1046–64, 1051.

ently written Porter about her fears of what was happening in Germany, Porter responded on February 22, 1935, that she was "greatly tempted to believe that blood-thirstiness was never so great among human beings as it is now" (McKeldin). She told Ford, however, that she should not let the situation get her too nervous, but her argument to this end quickly broke down, becoming a forbidding portrait of how widespread and dangerous the situation actually was:

> You, as a Jew, I, as a born and practising heretic, are both considerably safer right this blessed minute than we would have been at any given day of the long and bitter past. At least there are several places to go and we know how to get there. . . . This may not last long, because the baiting and the hunting break out in fresh places every day, but at least the situation exists this minute, and who expects security? Not even technocrats, Fascists, Communists, et al. There'll come along a fresh crowd with a different maggot in its collective brain, and stand *them* up against a wall. . . . You're right, it[']s the catchingest disease there is. (McKeldin)

Porter goes on to say that she accepts the fact that the desire to kill is a constant of human nature and that she has no "quarrel with what cannot be undone in our miserable hearts." She adds, "But I'm sick of hearing of would-be killers trying to cover their tracks by giving all sorts of noble, high-sounding scientific, sociological, economic, political, ethical reasons why they should be permitted to murder other human beings" (McKeldin).

Porter's antitotalitarianism hardened considerably during the forties and fifties, growing into an obsession that pitted almost all of her political energies against manifestations of the totalitarian state. She now unequivocally saw fascism and communism as essentially the same form of government. To Dr. William Ross, president of Colorado State College, Porter wrote on March 4, 1951, of the totalitarian menace, her words echoing those of President Truman: "I'm entirely hostile to the principle of Communism and to every form of totalitarian society, whether it calls itself Communism, Fascism or whatever. I feel indeed that Communism and Fascism are two names for the same thing, that the present struggle is really a civil war between two factions of totalitarianism" (*L,* 394).

The totalitarian threat for Porter was not limited to foreign shores. Indeed, she saw the United States as moving dangerously toward totalitarian rule, its democratic ideals under threat from corrupt politicians, powerful business interests, and covert Fascist agents. Not long after the United States entered World War II, Porter wrote on December 16, 1941, to her nephew Paul that the war was "a horrible dirty business in which no humane principles were at all involved, only the same old power politics played by the same unscrupulous men, almost the very same, who ran the first World War." National interests, particularly those of business and trade, had prevented nations from taking an earlier stand against the Fascist threat and so preventing the war. Such interests had also deformed the democratic ideals of the United States. "This war will decide whether we are going to have another chance for a real democracy here or will this country be turned over again to the Morgans, the Fords and the Standard Oil Company," she wrote. "First we have this war with the foreign enemy, and then there is a second war to be fought here afterward with the internal enemy" (*L,* 215). Porter's comments here on the pervasive power of capitalist business interests to shape international affairs and to pervert democratic principles demonstrate her growing dismay that the federal government, which once represented the people, now represented big business. She feared that the government bureaucracy, particularly the State Department and the Federal Bureau of Investigation, was bent on protecting the interests of American industry over all else, even the rights of individual liberty. To Kirchwey, Porter wrote on February 5, 1942, that she felt little call to protest political oppression abroad when "we have a good many more important things to protest against in our own internal affairs" (*L,* 222). "The *root* of the evil," she added, "is here at home and in our own state department and business firms" (*L,* 223), and she called for the investigation of a number of matters:

> We should learn more about the activities of the German Dye Works (I. G. Farben) in this country and the exact nature of its connection with Standard Oil: we should insist that all firms, Italian, German, and Japanese as well as their allies, that have been put on a banned list should really be suppressed and not to continue to advertise their wares by radio—

Bayer's products for the first that comes to mind. . . . The actual present state of trade relations between all countries should be examined and made public. About two years ago the United Chambers of Commerce in America stated clearly that so long as business was to be had in Germany, they would do business with that country. And if Germany won, naturally they would carry on business and trade with her. . . . There is no reason to believe these men have changed their minds or their methods. (*L,* 222)

Particularly during the war but also for some time afterward Porter greatly feared infiltration of important government and business positions by Fascists and their sympathizers. "When that Dope Goering remarked en passant that America would be an inside job, well, I could only hope it wasn't so," Porter wrote on February 28, 1942, to Donald Elder. "But now I lie awake nights fearing it may be true . . . God knows the air is full of signs and portents" (*L,* 228). In this same letter Porter encouraged Elder to continue his efforts at getting a job in defense work, despite whatever problems he was encountering. "Don't let the Nazis get everything," Porter urged him, speaking of defense jobs. "As you know it is a part of their strategy to get office or jobs in key places, and it wouldn't surprise me if FBI didn't do a good deal to help them. For this reason FBI would naturally put as many stumbling blocks in the way of such as you as they can devise. . . . Get over or around them someway [*sic*], Don. Make it your business to get over them" (*L,* 229–30). As her words here suggest, Porter saw the FBI, most notably in its surveillance and questioning of American citizens, as a dangerous manifestation of totalitarian control. She mentioned to Elder her response to reading an article in the *New Yorker* in which labor leader Harry Bridges told of his hoodwinking of the FBI agents who had him under surveillance: "It was frightfully amusing, and I mean frightfully. I laughed with my hair on end" (*L,* 228).[5]

So strong were Porter's fears of government infiltration by subversive elements that in 1942 she apparently provided damning information— most of it made up—to the FBI, which was then investigating her friend Josephine Herbst. As several critics have suggested, this troubling incident

5. See St. Clair McKelway, "A Reporter at Large: Some Fun with the F.B.I.," *New Yorker,* October 11, 1941, p. 53.

is fraught with the tensions underlying Porter and Herbst's uneasy relationship, together with the anxieties Porter suffered concerning women friends and artistic rivals.[6] Perhaps even more significant, Porter's cooperation with the FBI points to her increasing obsession with antitotalitarian politics, an obsession that at times drastically undermined her judgment, artistic and otherwise, and led her into extreme and often contradictory positions.

Whatever her motives for and the circumstances of her apparent betrayal of Herbst, Porter nonetheless after the war continued to lash out at what she saw as the federal government's growing power over individual citizens and their rights. Despite her fear of Communists, Porter in 1951 denounced Senator Joseph McCarthy as a Fascist because she saw his congressional committee's investigations destroying individual liberties (L, 396). These same fears of government control prompted her to refuse to sign an oath of allegiance that was a condition of her employment as a visiting lecturer at Colorado State College. In a letter dated March 4, 1951, to William Ross, Porter angrily denounced the oath, saying it was a form of blackmail initiated by "cheap politicians who prey on public fears in times of trouble and force their betters into undignified positions." Even though she did not explicitly say that the oath was a tool of totalitarian control, her words certainly suggest just that. She called for resistance rather than complacence, saying that one has a duty "to see through [the politicians behind the oath] and to stop them in their tracks in time and not to be hoodwinked or terrorized by them, not to rationalize or excuse that weakness in us which leads to criminal collusion with them for the sake of our jobs or the hope of being left in peace. That is not the road to any kind of safety." She then sounded an ominous warning: "We're going to be made sorry very soon for our refusal to reject unconditionally the kind of evil that disguises itself as patriotism, as love of virtue, as religious faith, as the crusader against the internal enemy. These people are themselves the enemy" (L, 395).

While Porter's antitotalitarianism made her staunchly anti-Communist and anti-Fascist, she came to see fascism as the greater threat. She explained in her March 4, 1951, letter to Ross that though communism and fascism

6. Givner, *Katherine Anne Porter: A Life*, 3–12; Elinor Langer, *Josephine Herbst* (Boston, 1984), 251–56; Walsh, *Katherine Anne Porter and Mexico*, 194–96.

are similar in their methods of control, "Fascism is older, more insidious, harder to identify, easier to disguise. No one can be a Communist without knowing what he is doing. A man may be a most poisonous Fascist without even in the least recognizing his malady" (*L,* 394). As her words suggest, Porter came to see communism as a clearly developed political philosophy; fascism, on the other hand, despite the existence of Fascist states with specific ideologies, she saw as less a coherent political system than a manifestation of universal evil. Particularly after the war, Porter in effect eviscerated political ideology from fascism, using the term loosely, usually to identify abuses of political power that undermined individual liberty and signaled the drift toward totalitarianism. To Kay and James F. Powers, Porter wrote on December 14, 1947, of communism's visibility and fascism's various disguises:

> The trouble is, we don't need to fear getting involved with Communists: we do know who and where they are and what they are up to: no one is a Communist through ignorance or by accident. It is a political theory which you must know and believe in to practise. But Fascism comes out of the very virus of evil in the soul of man, it is the oldest evil under a new name. It has exactly the same goal as Communism but under a thousand disguises, and I hear perfectly "innocent" people talking it without knowing what they say or where they picked it up. And this is much more to be feared. I much prefer a running fight in the open to an enemy ambushed in the church, in the state department, in the press, in the very air we breathe. It is a true poison, and—unless mankind in general grows less maggoty-minded than he is—I don't doubt that in this war, the totalitarian idea under the name of Fascism will win over the same thing called Communism. That we must choose over one or the other is the falsest of all alternatives. (*L,* 353)

By such thinking, Porter, even during the war, saw fascism's greatest danger to the United States not in military victories but in the slow destruction of the American system by oppressive practices that were insidiously being worked into the social and political structure. Porter wrote on July 20, 1943, to her nephew Paul that she feared not that the war would be lost but that "the very thing we are fighting in Europe is seeping up here among us like a kind of miasma out of the very earth under our feet." She foresaw a future of ongoing struggle against fascism: "Winning the war with bombs and tanks and armies is easy beside the long war every human being that was brought up a free man must fight perhaps for the next half dozen centuries. . . . There never was such a concerted assault on human liberty as we see now, since the first idea of human liberty was ever fought for. And our worst enemies are here at home, most dangerous because you can't walk over them with an army" (*L,* 271).

One of the Fascist enemies Porter saw threatening the United States was the Catholic church. As we have already seen, Porter's relationship with the Church through the years was anything but simple or consistent. Shortly after her conversion to Catholicism during her first marriage, Porter bitterly attacked the Church's activities in Mexico. By the late twenties and into the thirties Porter, though not actively involved in the Church or by any means living piously, apparently had softened her views somewhat, focusing her attention less on the Church's institutional power than on matters of faith, particularly the uses to which people put their faith. In her own case, Catholicism was one voice among many teeming in her consciousness—one voice that in interplay with other voices contributed to her understanding of self and world. During this time Porter began telling people she was a born Catholic, and in much of her fiction, most significantly "The Jilting of Granny Weatherall," "Flowering Judas," and the Miranda stories, she depicted Catholicism as an important force in the affairs of her characters. While these works are anything but religious parables—indeed "The Jilting of Granny Weatherall" can be read as a deliberate reversal of the typical religious story of deathbed conversion—nonetheless with them Porter actively engaged her Catholic past, pressuring it, placing it in new contexts, responding to its challenge. Particularly noteworthy in this regard are the Miranda stories (Miranda's family is Catholic), which on one level are Porter's imaginative reconstruction of her own life, derived in part from her ongoing evaluation of her own youthful experiences. While not a practicing Catholic when she wrote these stories, Porter was still not denying or forgetting Catholicism's significance to her.

In her brief discussion of Porter's relationship with the Catholic church,

Givner observes that although Porter never wavered in her preference for Catholicism (during those times when she was feeling an allegiance toward a particular faith), she throughout her life repeatedly turned to and from the Church in a pattern suggesting both her bedrock independence and her skepticism.[7] During the forties and fifties, however, Porter's turn from the Church was so dramatic and extreme, fired by the associations she was making between the Catholic church and European fascism, that one sees in this rejection more obsessive paranoia than open-minded skepticism. Judging from Porter's letters and notes, her fierce attacks on the Church as a Fascist enterprise began shortly after World War II. In her letters from the early forties, Porter rarely if ever exhibited the ferocity toward the institutional Church that she soon would be doing, and indeed at times she even identified herself as a Catholic. In an undated letter (probably written in 1941 or 1942) to a woman who in 1941 had had romantic feelings for Porter and had pestered her while they were both at Yaddo, Porter wrote of what she saw as the woman's "erotic-religious experience," after which she added a telling statement of her own religious identity: "Remember I am a Catholic, and familiar with every kind and manifestation of sainthood; and with a great many of the extraordinary methods by which it is achieved" (McKeldin). Porter's unqualified identification of herself as a Catholic was in all likelihood made in part to establish her credentials for discussing what she saw as the woman's spiritual problems. Even so, Porter's words nonetheless underscore her strong intellectual and emotional ties with the Church. More representative of her allegiances with Catholicism are her comments in a letter dated August 14, 1940, to Caroline Gordon, in which she talks about her reading of Augustine and Aquinas. Here she is clearly less interested in the institutional role of the Church than she is in the power and beauty of its great thinkers and in the ways these thinkers have helped her to understand and shape experience. After admitting that she reads Augustine less for doctrine than "for poetry and the great story of his human and spiritual pilgrimage through this world," she tells Gordon, anticipating her friend's surprise, that her bedside reading of late has been Aquinas: "Presently I am reading—how can you believe this, knowing my other

7. Givner, *Katherine Anne Porter: A Life,* 100–102.

worldly activities—a condensed version of St. Thomas at night before I sleep; it is sometimes quite a while before I can sleep; but St. Thomas helps me to get all kinds of odds and ends of experience into some sort of relation to each other and to the whole of things. I don't know if that is what he aimed at in his teachings, I rather fancy not, from the history of controversy, but I hope he is glad to be useful even in humble ways, and even at this very late day" (McKeldin).

Quite different is Porter's commentary on Roman Catholicism after the war. Her focus now rests almost exclusively on the institutional power of the Church, a power that she declares Fascist and, by extension, totalitarian. She makes it clear that she wants nothing to do with the Church and that she no longer considers herself a Catholic. To James F. Powers, Porter wrote on November 5, 1947, that as a Catholic she had always been anticlerical and that she had eventually left the Church "for purely political and moral reasons." No doubt to Powers' surprise, Porter then launched into a bitter attack on the Church's political power and what she saw as its insidious fascism: "I am horrified at the growth of power of the church in this country in the past twenty-five years, co-inciding perfectly with the growth of Fascism everywhere. All the ancient plagues of Europe are converging upon us, and even those serio-comic so-called witch-hunts are the preliminary skirmishes between Communism and Fascism in this country, dreary parodies so far of the tragic situation in Europe. I fear Fascism most, for it has the Pope at its head, and is Protean in its forms, and I hear people talking Fascism and acting it without knowing what name to call it by" (*L,* 350). As suggested in this letter, Porter envisioned a prolonged ideological battle in the United States between communism and fascism, with the Catholic church as the primary bulwark of Fascist power. She commented further on this political imbroglio in a letter dated May 1, 1949, to Elizabeth Ames. Porter wrote that as she was writing the letter she was listening to a radio broadcast of a public meeting of Catholics who were attacking communism and invoking the world to come to God, "that is," Porter wryly comments, "to the Catholic Church." Porter continues, "And they chill my blood as much, in a way more, than the Communists, because the Church is Fascist, and somehow, religion and totalitarianism seem more popular in this country than atheism and totalitarianism. . . . Militarily, we may be in danger from Communism, but morally we are deeply in danger of being taken over by Catholicism. . . . It is growing incredibly impudent in this country" (*L,* 372).

The danger Porter saw in the political power of the Catholic church in America lay primarily in the Church's appeals to nationalism and its claim of chosenness, actions Porter believed echoed the tactics of the Nazis in Germany. Her comments to Ames indicate the threat to freedom that she saw when religion was incorporated into national policy and identity. In this situation religion easily could become a powerful foundation for totalitarian control. In her letter to Ames, Porter wrote of her dismay when she heard the Catholic meeting close with a choral singing of "The Star Spangled Banner": "I'll swear, I believe when all is said and done, I prefer the Communists. They hate the country and will break up everything if they can, but at least they *don't* sing the 'Star Spangled Banner' at their meetings" (*L,* 372–73). Porter clearly saw the Catholic church's claim of being *the* church of God as a threat to individual liberty, specifically the freedom of thought and expression. The request of the Reverend John F. Fahey, who had written Porter asking about her religious views for his research on a work about writers and their religion (Fahey had read Harry Sylvester's article in the *Atlantic Monthly,* "Problems of the Catholic Writer," in which Sylvester said Porter was a former Catholic), struck a raw nerve with Porter.[8] She apparently perceived his request and his research as representative of the Catholic church's attempts to pry into individuals' affairs and to solidify its claims of superiority, by judging writers by their theology rather than their art. She wrote testily to Fahey on October 5, 1948: "To answer your question: I am not a Catholic and cannot be judged as such; and have made it a rule never to discuss religious differences with any one, for I believe firmly in absolute freedom of religious faith and expression for every human being of every known and (to me) unknown denomination, and I am truly disturbed by any threat from any source to this freedom. I claim also my inalienable right to my own private thoughts and feelings on this subject" (*L,* 358). In a draft of her letter to Fahey, she

8. Harry Sylvester, "Problems of the Catholic Writer," *Atlantic Monthly,* CLXXXI (Janurary, 1948), 109–13.

addressed the issue of evaluating a work of literature by its moral vision, asserting the primacy of aesthetics over ideology. Porter wrote, "Certainly one of the great functions of any art is communication; certainly it has a moral function; but its real reason for being is that it preserves unbroken the line of continuous *human* feeling and satisfies the esthetic instinct from age to age on the human level: so that a work of beauty and nobility remains forever new and never loses its preciousness as work of art, when the creed and forms of government and the very race and the language of a period have disappeared" (*L,* 358).

In some notes on religion and politics, dated July 18, 1948, Porter discussed the guiding principles, expressed both positively and negatively, that she felt had to be maintained in political and governmental affairs. Although she did not mention Roman Catholicism here specifically, there seems little doubt, given the context and her other comments from this period, that Catholicism, together with its links with fascism, was very much on her mind in these observations. Porter divided her comments into two sections, "Negative" and "Positive." The negative section has four unelaborated statements of what "there is no such thing as": "one sole true revealed Religion," "A Chosen People," "a Master Race," and "a Natural Ruling Class." The positive section affirms the reasoning behind her selection of the four negative statements. "Every religion is exactly as valid and true as every other religion," the first elaboration begins, to which a proviso is added: "Church and State should be entirely separate." Porter continues by saying that all religious property should be taxed, no religious group should receive any governmental support, there should be absolute religious freedom, and church members should be free to criticize the government to the same extent as all other citizens. The second statement asserts: "No group of people would be allowed any privileges or exemption in law or in society on the grounds of being mystically chosen or in some special relation to God separate from the rest of the human race: Example, the Jews' claim to Palestine." The third elaboration says that no nation or people should have any claims for leadership or territory based "on the ground of natural superiority." The final point of discussion asserts: "No power shall be allowed to become hereditary or inalienable in any department of government or society. Candidates for place in government would be chosen after rigorous tests, based on intelligence, capacity for higher education, and moral qualities. All education and government would be purely secular, and based on the four major premises stated above" (McKeldin). Central to all four of Porter's declarations is her reaction against what she frequently called the "herd mentality," that is, the domination of the individual and the destruction of his or her rights by a group of people that deems itself superior. As suggested by the placement of her discussion in her first section, Porter saw the claim of a sole true religion—what she frequently found in the thinking of Catholics and, as revealed in her example in her second elaboration in the positive section, of Jews—was potentially the source of all the other problems. Indeed, the three other assertions can be understood as transformations, rewordings in different contexts, of the first. Reading specifics into Porter's comments, in light of what she was saying elsewhere about Catholicism, one can see in these notes Porter working through her argument of the Fascist threat to democracy posed by the Catholic church.

Porter's attacks on the Catholic church and more generally on fascism and totalitarianism suggest how obsessive her thinking had become and bear witness to a general souring of Porter's personal, social, and political views. Always one who valued her privacy, Porter from the beginning had believed the gravest threat of totalitarianism was its destruction of a person's right to privacy. By the mid-fifties this fear so dominated Porter's thinking that many of her once strongly held values and beliefs crumbled under its pressure. Her comments in a letter dated August 30, 1956, to W. Chapman, an editor at *House and Garden* who had written Porter asking if she would write an essay on privacy for the magazine, indicate her intense feelings in the fifties. Early in her letter Porter spoke of how important it is for people to be able to keep their inner lives free from intrusion by other people. "It is so good for everybody concerned in any human arrangement," Porter wrote, "to have the boundaries clearly drawn, the rights and privileges of each well understood, with a shaping controlling discipline that knows when to be tactful—like giving the children time to stop fighting before you walk in." Porter then launched into a feverish discussion of the totalitarian threat to privacy, saying that her recent rereading of George Orwell's *1984,* "surely one of the most frightening books ever written," has made her see that threat as even more terrifying than she had previously perceived it.

Haunted by Orwell's vision of the totalitarian state, Porter wrote that "the real horror of the totalitarian form of government is the brutal suppression of a human being[']s most important liberty—the right to a private life—whatever it may be." She elaborated:

> This is the first human dignity to be attacked by the Lenins, the Mussolinis, the Hitlers, the Francos: somehow even worse than the corklined torture chambers, the labor camps, the exterminating gases, (for these are tragic, but final) were those dreadfuly [sic] little stories from Germany about the local or neighborhood *Gauleiters* snooping around kitchens, looking in the sauce pans to see that no contraband was being prepared for supper. . . . and children set up to spy on their parents, and the parents unable to control them for fear they should be denounced. . . . I feel that the practise of a private life in this country is getting to be more and more suspect: one who wishes to be alone for whatever reason is supposed to be up to no good: has taken to drink or some other secret immorality, is sidestepping his social responsibilities, is a neurotic, or Escapist—this last a really serious accusation. (McKeldin)

As this letter suggests, Porter's valorization of the right to privacy was undermining a number of her egalitarian sympathies and ideals.

One such belief that so suffered was her faith in America's democratic system of government. As we have seen, Porter during the forties and fifties frequently attacked what she saw as the abuses of power by corrupt politicians and big business, but during this time her underlying loyalty to and confidence in democracy waned considerably. A strong supporter of democratic principles in the early forties, Porter by the mid-fifties was bitter and disillusioned, if not paranoid. During World War II and shortly thereafter Porter for the most part voiced her loyalty to the American system at the same time that she was vehemently criticizing its corruption. In her December 16, 1941, letter to her nephew Paul, in which she bemoaned the havoc that abusive power politics and corporate interests had wreaked upon national and world affairs, she nonetheless forthrightly stated: "I believe in our form of government, I think it the best ever devised in human affairs, in spite of the abuses, in spite of the perversions that have deformed it in practice" (*L,* 215). For democracy to work, Porter suggests in this letter, people must be willing to fight not only external enemies but also internal ones, who in many ways pose the graver threat. This is a central idea in her essay "An Act of Faith: 4 July 1942," which argues that maintaining our freedoms is an ongoing struggle in times of both war and peace. After saying that the war on the battlefield will not be lost, Porter writes that "the people of this country are going to have the enormous privilege of another chance to make of their Republic what those men who won and founded it for us meant for it to be" (*CE,* 195). We must never take our freedoms for granted, Porter adds, but must always stand up for them, for there are at all times enemies of the system who are working to abolish them. Our liberties, Porter writes, "are implicit in our theory of government, which was in turn based on humanistic concepts of the importance of the individual man and his rights in society. They are not mere ornaments on the façade, but are laid in the foundation stone of the structure, and they will last so long as the structure itself but no longer. They are not inalienable: the house was built with great labor and it is made with human hands; human hands can tear it down again, and will, if it is not well loved and defended. The first rule for any effective defense is: Know your enemies" (*CE,* 196).

Following her own advice, Porter actively campaigned in New York for Franklin D. Roosevelt's 1944 reelection. "Yesterday I was called by telephone from New York to come up and help speak at a meeting where four or five thousand people are expected," Porter wrote on October 28, 1944, to her nephew Paul. "I shall go to a Negro Democratic meeting here tomorrow. So I do know I am doing my little part as well as I can, with you and all like you in mind" (*L,* 294). Porter had little sympathy for the Republicans—"Deweyites and Nazi bundsmen" she characterized them in her August 27, 1944, letter to Monroe Wheeler (McKeldin)—and she believed that President Roosevelt's successful reelection was crucial for maintaining America's democratic freedoms.

For all this enthusiasm, Porter's confidence in the democratic system and the struggle to preserve it nonetheless waned considerably after the war. If Porter championed Franklin Roosevelt as democracy's savior in 1944, by 1947, with Truman in the White House and the cold war under way, she saw the government floundering, infiltrated by Fascists and Communists alike and controlled by weak-kneed liberals who were blind to the internal threats. In a letter to the editor of the *Nation* dated May 11, 1947, Porter wrote that Communists were systematically occupying important positions of power in all sectors of society, "not only in departments of government here and abroad, but in our universities, the press, the publishing business, industry, the motion pictures." She continued, "You find them everywhere; they mean business and they are dangerous." But, she added, in regard to the government's enthusiastic drive against the Communists, including the introduction of repressive legislation undermining individual liberties, the Fascists had made even more inroads into the government. She wrote that "the Rankins of this country are as bitter enemies of democratic government as any Communist, and the legislation proposed by them seeks the suppression of all liberty of speech or opinion; if they are not stopped here and now, we shall find ourselves with a 'subversive-thoughts' law on our books" (*CE,* 203). Porter then lashed out at the liberals in the government, whom she said had been hoodwinked by the Fascists and Communists into believing that "only a democracy has no right to defend itself from its enemies." When calls are made to curb the Fascists and Communists, liberals always resist, claiming that democracy must be preserved by defending what Porter characterizes as "the most cynical and base of our so-called liberties." Unless liberals come around quickly to see the danger of the current threat, Porter warns, they will in all likelihood be "driven underground to form a resistance movement to fascism or communism—the end will be the same—in our own country" (*CE,* 203–204).

Porter's letter to the *Nation* reveals the extreme—and contradictory—political positions toward which her fear of totalitarianism was pushing her, positions that, as we saw earlier, probably were significant in her apparent betrayal of Josephine Herbst to the FBI. While railing against what she saw as the Fascist suppression of Communists, an action that more generally threatened civil liberties, she at the same time called for a tough suppression of the Fascists. Liberals who called for the protection of civil liberties were to her eyes weak and naïve, and yet she attacked the congressional investigation of Communists because those very same civil liberties were threatened. Ironically, she ends her letter by calling for liberals to snap out of their innocence and start weeding out Fascists and Communists in a pogrom one can only characterize, from Porter's perspective, as Fascist. Her closing observations smack of the dangerous polemics she had earlier in the letter (and elsewhere in her writings) railed against. "Why is it such a crime for a democracy in the United States to put fascist and Communist conspirators in jail, or at least to deprive them of their confidential posts in departments of our government?" she asks. "Does being a democrat morally oblige a man to consent to his own murder?" Referring specifically to the conflict between Fascists and Communists in Italy but more generally also to this conflict in the United States, Porter adds: "Stalin played a sinister game with Hitler when Germany was the center of power for fascism. The Vatican is now that center, and the Communists are playing their old game again. How many jolts of this kind can the liberals of this country take, I wonder, and still preserve their dazzled innocence?" (*CE,* 204). In essence Porter attacks totalitarian tactics from a totalitarian position. The true democrat for Porter appears here as the person willing to fight to protect democracy from totalitarian enemies by willingly engaging in totalitarian methods—an irony that in her enthusiasm Porter failed to see.

Her attacks on liberals in her letter to the *Nation* signal the hardening of Porter's conservatism and point to what might best be characterized as the aristocratic elitism that in the coming years progressively dominated her outlook. By the mid-fifties Porter had all but abandoned her previous sympathies for oppressed minorities and was seeing such groups, together with the "common" citizenry, as threats that were every bit as dangerous as the Fascists and Communists to the system of government she desired—democracy by name but actually something closer to oligarchy. Her championing of privacy took on new meaning, emphasizing the right of individuals to choose with whom they associate as much as their right to hold their own thoughts and values. In her August 30, 1956, letter to W. Chapman, Porter wrote that "the crown of civilization is the pure liberty to choose what one needs of silence, solitude, long uninterrupted hours for work, for reading, for study." She then underscored that this liberty "is bound up with another freedom not less important, and one equally threatened—the right to choose one's own society as well as to be chosen by it: the blessed liberty of keeping the company of one's own kind, and the right to defend one[']s privacy against the invasive, the prying, the dull, on the one hand, and quite simply—and this is the real point—any one at all, that one doesn't care for and doesn't want around!" Porter added that those who resent people who hold fast to a private life also resent those who want to keep company only with their own. Of the criticism that people like herself had to bear, Porter wrote that the resentful others believe "it is 'snobbish' or 'undemocratic' to be able to tell one person from another, or to be a little particular who one invites into the house; it is a curious example of how a political theory—misunderstood, misinterpreted, mis-practised—can subtly undermine the prime individual liberties it was meant to foster and safeguard" (McKeldin). Her charge here that a theory of freedom in the wrong hands can undermine the rights of the individual could of course be leveled at her own conservative logic, both here and in her letter to the *Nation*.

Perhaps what Porter in the fifties found most appalling about American democracy was what she saw as the dangerous extremes to which its central philosophical formulation that "all men are created equal" was being taken in justifying the leveling of all classes and races into an undifferentiated mass in regard to breeding, education, and talent. Her calls for the right to be able to choose the people with whom she associated embodies her resistance to this democratic leveling—a resistance she believed necessary for maintaining her version of democracy, a democratic elitism. In some notes dated September 23, 1956, entitled "7 stages of degeneration or Circular Democracy," Porter depicted democracy's demise as an endless repetition of leveling:

1 We are equals.
2 I am as good as you are.
3 You are as good as I am!
4 You are no better than I am.
5 You are worse than I am.
6 I am as bad as you are.
7 We are equals—
(McKeldin)

In some other notes, undated but in all likelihood written at about the same time, Porter wrote that while politically she believed in democracy, she was "no leveller in any department of human affairs." She was particularly strident against the glorification of the common man:

> I have alway[s] felt a long step towards true democracy would be made when in America certain people stop calling other people "Common." I have no use for the Common Man, above all the wilfully, or even fraudulently common. I feel pretty certain that no man [penciled in margin, "of even little intelligence or feeling"] really regards himself as common, or even ordinary. He is always talking about some one else. Whoever wishes to regard himself as common, or even to *be* that, let him be: but he should be correspondingly modest and not attempt to force his lowered standards of feeling and thinking and being on his society. (McKeldin)

We are here back to Porter's fear of the "herd mentality" and the "collective mind" that contributed heavily to the shaping of her antitotalitarianism in the thirties and forties. But now these threats come from American democracy. In her 1965 interview with Hank Lopez, Porter critiqued what she saw as the democratic fallacy. After reiterating her belief that F. Scott Fitzgerald wrote about people of no importance, Porter added: "Somebody said I shouldn't feel like that, that everybody was important. Well, that's just one of the fallacies of the world. That's one of the things we say when we're being democratic. Eighty percent of the people of this world, as Ford Madox Ford said, are stuff to fill graves with. The rest are the ones that make it go round" (*C*, 132).

Porter in the fifties spoke out not only against the democratic masses but also against minority groups trying to sway the masses. In light of her cynical views of democracy and her passionate regard for privacy (particularly her understanding of privacy as in part the right to choose one's company), it should come as no surprise that Porter had little sympathy for the civil rights movement, despite having spoken out earlier in her career, especially during the thirties, about the plight of blacks in America. In a 1958 interview with the Richmond *News Leader* Porter chastised the Supreme Court for its "moral irresponsibility" in its 1954 *Brown* v. *Board of Education* decision. She told the paper that she belonged "to the school of thought

that believes the Supreme Court acted recklessly and irresponsibly in pre-
cipitating this crisis at the worst possible time when we already had enough
crises on hand" (*C,* 39). Clearly she saw blacks' struggle for civil liberties as
a threat to her own (the right of privacy in particular) and indeed as a threat
to the entire democratic process. "The down-trodden minorities," she told
the paper, "are organized into tight little cabals to run the country so that
we will become the down-trodden vast majority if we don't look out." The
ultimate result of the Court's actions and the general drift in American
politics "was the oppression of the human spirit through the multiple making of petty, niggling laws," a destructive manifestation of democratic leveling that she characterized as the tendency "to put the human spirit in a
mould . . . to compress the individual into the lowest common denominator
in human life." In a rather stunning statement Porter suggested that in some
ways American democracy was heading toward totalitarianism. Asked
what most disappointed her about present-day America, Porter responded
that it was "the way we have of taking on all the evils we were supposed to
be fighting in Nazism, Fascism and Communism." She then added: "Although it's always been true that, in the strangest way, you tend to become
like the thing you fight" (*C,* 39–40).

Deeply ironic is Porter's final observation here, for it was not the
American political and judicial system that was becoming Fascist or totalitarian in its granting of civil liberties to blacks, but Porter herself in her
railing against minorities and their threat to America. Indeed, her comments to the Richmond *News Leader* barely mask an ugly racism that was
now an important part of Porter's thinking and that was not unlike that
which characterized Nazi thought. Toward Jews and blacks her racism was
most virulent. Givner notes that Porter's anti-Semitism is starkly clear in
some of the marginal comments she made in her books. In Albert Memmi's
*Portrait of a Jew,* for instance, Porter wrote that "everybody except the Jews
knows the Jews are not chosen but are a lot of noisy, arrogant, stupid, pretentious people and then what?" Alongside Memmi's photograph on the
dust jacket she commented: "This writer is completely typically Jewish,
nose and mouth especially—But it is not a question of features. It is a *look,*
an expression, a manner, that identifies them. And it is not a question of

ugliness."[9] Porter's racist attitudes toward blacks surface in a number of her letters from the fifties and sixties. Not untypical are her comments to Cyrilly Abels on June 15, 1963:

> I can't tell you how I don't want to come back to the US. . . . And certainly never to Washington. I shall never again live in a negro-infested place. They have made the air unbreathable there. I have nothing in the world against them except that I do not want to be over-run by them; you know that I have always believed and said that we must make an end to our second-class citizenship, which includes every kind of nationality and color. We have also Indians—the worst treated of any—Hawaiian, Eskimos, Puerto Ricans, and our own submerged neglected poor whites of the southern mountains, so I feel no particular partiality for the advancement of the negro at the expense of the freedoms of everybody else in the country. I think the situation there is disgraceful and it is everybody's fault. A small minority should not be allowed to blackmail and disrupt a whole tremendous nation. Oh how right Thomas Jefferson was when he said, around 1800 or before, that we should free all the Negroes, send them back to Africa and provide for them until they were resettled. But as always, such humane good sense is simply too unexciting to be practised. . . . And as for the negroes themselves, you couldn't pay them to go to Africa. They wish to stay here and enjoy the benefits of a civilization they are incapable of creating, to befoul all they touch in our world, and to push themselves into places they have neither earned nor merited. . . . This does not surprise me. What I cannot understand is the government of such a nation allowing such anarchy. . . .
>
> Well, this seems a long way from Venice, or even Europe, which has also its troubles, but such as I can understand better even if they do dismay me. It is just possible the world is getting ready to plunge back into another Dark Age, and this time a Black Age. We will not be the first to see a great world destroyed by sav[a]ges. (McKeldin)

A great world being destroyed is also a crucial theme of *Ship of Fools* (most people on the ship, furthermore, could be characterized as ruthless

9. Quoted in Givner, *Katherine Anne Porter: A Life,* 451.

savages), and its centrality suggests the extent to which Porter's social and political obsessions shaped the novel. In the grip of her single-minded ideas that dwelled on the hidden evil within the heart of humanity and its visible manifestations in tyrannical politics and interpersonal relations, Porter in *Ship of Fools* reworked many of the themes and concerns of her previous fiction, creating a more sinister and forbidding fictional world. The narrative perspective of *Ship of Fools,* compared with that of her fiction of the twenties and thirties, is much harsher and more unforgiving. If Porter's richest short fiction, particularly the Miranda stories and other works dealing with southern life, were written with a dialogism suggesting that a person's vision grows through the interplay of opposing viewpoints, *Ship of Fools* was written with a single-minded monologism typified by Porter's ugly racism and paranoia about the threat to private liberties by a society being overrun by Fascists and Communists. In other words, Porter's late vision, in large part shaped in response to totalitarianism, became itself totalitarian.

As we have seen, Porter's concern about totalitarianism began not long after her trip to Germany in 1931. Her growing fears about the German threat in particular and totalitarianism in general may in large part explain her attempt in the early thirties to revise her story "Holiday," the first draft of which she apparently completed in 1924. Not published until 1960, "Holiday" can be read as a parable of the totalitarian state, with the Müller family representing the emerging power of Germany under Fascist ideology. Bonding the Müllers together, as the narrator notes, is a tribal identity that banishes all outsiders to the margins. Insiders deemed physically or mentally unfit, like Ottilie, are also disempowered. There is little room for individual identity within the tight-knit and systematically organized family. All work as one, and the corporate identity supersedes the individual's. The narrator observes that the entire family, even the men who married into the family, give the impression of being "one human being divided into several separate appearances" (*CS,* 417). Nor is there much space for private emotions and enthusiasms. Although the family grieves deeply at Mother Müller's death, preserving family order and stability means that the established routine must be broken only briefly. On the day of the funeral the narrator knows that "already the thoughts of the living were turning to tomorrow, when they would be at the work of rebuilding and replanting and repairing—even now, today, they would hurry back from the burial to milk the cow and feed the chickens" (*CS,* 433).

For all of the family's flaws, the narrator nonetheless finds much to affirm about the Müllers. Certainly impressive is the family's efficiency in running their very successful farm. "These were solid, practical, hard-bitten, land-holding German peasants," the narrator remarks, "who struck their mattocks into the earth deep and held fast wherever they were, because to them life and land were one indivisible thing" (*CS,* 413). Likewise impressive is the family's cohesiveness as manifested in its communal solidarity and identity, even if this bonding means that individual concerns and development at times are sacrificed to the group's needs. As a tight-knit unit, the family marshals great strength in the face of adversity, seen particularly in the healing grief they share among themselves at Mother Müller's death. Although they in effect enslave one of their own, the narrator notes that seen from a different angle the family actually places Ottilie "in the bosom of her family," allowing her to become "one of [the family's] most useful and competent members." The narrator continues, "They with a deep right instinct had learned to live with her disaster on its own terms, and hers; they had accepted and then made use of what was for them only one more painful event in a world full of troubles, many of them much worse than this." She adds that "in some way that I could not quite explain to myself, I found great virtue and courage in their steadiness and refusal to feel sorry for anybody, least of all for themselves" (*CS,* 428).

If on the level of parable the Müller family represents the organization of a Fascist state, then the narrator's ambivalence toward the Müllers may suggest that in the early thirties Porter herself shared similar feelings. These feelings, it should be added, would have been close to the mainstream in American opinion toward Fascist Europe. Until 1935, when public opinion turned decidedly against Mussolini after Italy's invasion of Ethiopia, American popular opinion by and large held European fascism in high esteem. Fascism was defended, if at times uneasily, for its efficiency, discipline, and progress in a modern world floundering with weak leaders and inefficient bureaucracies.[10] Porter, too, may have early on felt the pull of fascism's energy and vitalism, but she was also, as we know, always concerned about the threat to individual freedom and the danger of unbridled nationalism. And so if Porter was indeed somewhat attracted to fascism in the early thirties, she at the same time recognized its dark underpinnings. These conflicted feelings suggest the narrator's ambivalence about the Müllers' treatment of Ottilie, a character who, depending on one's line of vision, is either embraced or exiled by the family.

In later work from the thirties Porter exhibited little ambivalence toward anything that smacked of fascism or totalitarianism. In "Pale Horse, Pale Rider," for instance, two government agents hound Miranda about why she has not bought any war bonds. One agent, in an obvious allusion to Hitler, wears "a square little mustache" (CS, 272), and the two men's pressuring of Miranda with thinly veiled threats suggests the insidious power of the government to crush individual thinking and to demand unquestioned allegiance. Intimidation is their primary weapon. Startled at one point by the nasty tone of one agent's voice, Miranda catches the man's stare, a stare that she sees is "really stony, really viciously cold, the kind of thing you might expect to meet behind a pistol on a deserted corner" (CS, 272). As the narrator makes clear, the two agents are unexceptional men who have been transformed into goons by the fearsome power of the government that stands behind them. Both men, Miranda notices, "had a stale air of borrowed importance which apparently they had got from the same source" (CS, 271). When she looks closely at the older of the two, she sees a "pursy-faced man, gross-mouthed, with little lightless eyes," whom she readily imagines working otherwise as a crafty confidence man trying to entice customers and promote his wares. He stands before Miranda trying to do just that—to con her—and frighteningly, he speaks with the authority of a man who can punish anyone who does not do as he suggests. His argument for buying liberty bonds is quite simple: "You can't lose by it, and you can lose a lot if you don't" (CS, 273). But of course in promising to purchase liberty bonds Miranda loses a lot too—her individual liberty.

10. John P. Diggins, *Mussolini and Fascism: The View from America* (Princeton, N.J., 1972), Chapters 1–4.

The government agents embody the menace of government control demanding allegiance and uniformity. So struck is Miranda by this threat that at the end of the story when she awakens from her near-death experience and sees a joyless and bleak world, she conceives herself as a victim of society's conspiracy. Hers is a despairing vision of the ultimate totalitarianism—a world of gray uniformity from which, as she notes, "there was no escape" and in which everyone, "Dr. Hildesheim, Miss Tanner, the nurses in the diet kitchen, the chemist, the surgeon, the precise machine of the hospital, the whole humane conviction and custom of society," stands in league against her. In the face of all these conspirators, Miranda only smiles and says what is expected of her, for she knows "it will not do to betray the conspiracy and tamper with the courage of the living; there is nothing better than to be alive, everyone has agreed on that; it is past argument, and who attempts to deny it is justly outlawed" (*CS*, 314–15). Although Miranda's vision here is wildly askew (as we have seen in our earlier discussion of the story, she is more the victim of her dreams than of her friends and of society), nonetheless her frightening fantasy of the totalitarian state in all likelihood suggests Porter's own worst nightmare about society and points ahead to her later paranoia about the totalitarian menace that gripped her in the late forties and the fifties.

If a totalitarian society looms large in the imagination of Miranda at the end of "Pale Horse, Pale Rider," an unequivocally real totalitarian state—or at least an incipient one—forms the backdrop of "The Leaning Tower," a story Porter began in the early thirties and revised and completed in 1940. The story is set in Germany in 1931, a time when the country was beset with deep economic depression and when Hitler and his National Socialist party were making great strides in popularity and power. While Hitler would not gain the chancellorship until 1933, aspects of totalitarianism were already taking hold in Germany, with Hitler wielding power and influence with his party's platform emphasizing German nationalism and anti-Semitism. Hitler's paramilitary organization, the Sturmabteilungen (SA), was also then quite active, not only in marching through the streets and holding rallies but also in engaging in street battles with opponents of Hitler, particularly the Communists. During this time Hitler drove home in his speeches three concepts—"blood, authority of personality, and a fighting spirit"—a powerful combination that together galvanized first his party and later the nation.[11] Charles Upton, the young American protagonist of "The Leaning Tower," witnesses manifestations of all three concepts during his brief stay in Berlin.

The influence of Nazi thinking pervades the Berlin of "The Leaning Tower," even though neither Hitler nor the SA has an obvious presence. Upton sees the powerful appeal of the Hitler mystique—Hitler's "authority of personality"—when he goes to get a haircut. The barber wants to cut Upton's hair long on top and clipped to the skin along the sides—the Hitler cut, which was fast becoming the obligatory style. "His own was cut that way," the narrator observes of the barber, "the streets were full of such heads, and a photograph, clipped from the newspaper and stuck in the corner of the mirror, showed a little shouting politician, top lock on end, wide-stretched mouth adorned by a square mustache, who had, apparently, made the style popular" (CS, 451). Only prolonged resistance to the barber's wishes gets Upton the haircut he wants, the entire episode indicating the power of the Hitler cult and its demands for conformity.

In his conversations with his fellow roomers at Rosa's boardinghouse, Upton comes face-to-face with the rigid racial bias—the "blood" in Hitler's speeches—underlying German nationalism and cementing Nazi ideology. Hans and Otto, two German boarders, rarely miss an opportunity to praise what they claim are the glories of the Germanic race, and they are always quick to defend the race from criticism. When the boarders discuss the physical characteristics of different nationalities, Otto breaks in to declare earnestly that "no matter how it came about, the true great old Germanic type is lean and tall and fair as gods" (CS, 481). Both Hans and Otto build their philosophic positions from this unassailable premise of Germanic splendor and achievement. No other race measures up to their own. They time and again characterize various nationalities with degrading stereotypes that underscore their differences from the Germanic paragon. Hans says that for all their elegant manners and tastes, the French are "a race of monkeys," while the Poles, physically beautiful, "have contributed exactly

11. Pierre Stephen Robert Payne, *The Life and Death of Adolf Hitler* (New York, 1973), 234.

nothing to world-culture" (*CS*, 484, 482). Underlying such thinking is of course pride in racial purity, the desire to protect it, and the consequent distrust of outsiders. After Otto concludes that Charles is decadently rich, he eyes him "from head to foot as if he were some improbable faintly repellent creature of another species." He goes on to warn him: "Ah, well, seriously, I advise you to observe our curious customs, and do nothing, not the smallest thing, to attract the attention of the police. I tell you this because you are unfamiliar with the country—they are not fond of outlanders here" (*CS*, 470).

In his speeches of the early thirties Hitler exhorted Germans to embrace "a fighting spirit" for their battles with German Communists. In "The Leaning Tower," the Germanic "fighting spirit" manifests itself as the desire to fight for world domination, seen most forcefully in the comments of Hans. Hans's ideas on foreign policy are quite simple: attack before being attacked. "Why," he responds to Charles' challenge, "because [your enemy] always attacks when you are not looking, or when you have put down your arms for an instant. So you are punished for carelessness, really, for not troubling to learn the intentions of your enemy. You are beaten, and that is the end of you, unless you can gather strength and fight again" (*CS*, 485–86). Hans coolly looks ahead to the next world war, saying that unlike what happened in World War I, Germany will make no errors this time. To Tadeusz' assertion that a people can be defeated militarily and still exert profound worldwide influence, Hans disdainfully responds that influence is "a purely oblique, feminine, worthless thing." He adds that power rather than influence is the lifeblood of a nation: "Power, pure power, is what counts to a nation or a race. You must be able to tell other peoples what to do, and above all what they may not do, you must be able to enforce every order you give against no matter what opposition, and when you demand anything at all, it must be given you without question. That is the only power, and power is the only thing of any value or importance in this world" (*CS*, 486).

Comments such as Hans's cast a dark pall over "The Leaning Tower," with the terror of totalitarian thinking enshrouding scene and situation, the dream vision of Miranda at the end of "Pale Horse, Pale Rider" made real in Berlin. Even so, both in "The Leaning Tower" and the other two stories just examined, the totalitarian menace, while certainly threatening, does not entirely overwhelm the stories, making them little else but bleak exposés of an oppressive political system. At this time Porter was not so consumed with the dangers of totalitarianism that she felt she had to make her fiction blatantly propagandist. Her fear of totalitarianism had not yet drastically undermined her openness to life's richness and her confidence in the dialogic nature of human understanding. Crucial to the thrust of these stories is their focus on the protagonists' struggles for growth and fulfillment rather than on the workings of totalitarian politics, although certainly these workings do impinge upon the protagonists' efforts. Darlene Unrue has said that "The Leaning Tower" is less an attack on the specific social and political developments transforming Germany in the thirties than it is an exploration of Charles Upton's disillusionment with his ideals.[12] Even if Unrue downplays the threat of nazism a bit too much, she nonetheless correctly locates the center of the story in Upton's problems, not Germany's. Similarly, the entanglement of disillusionment and enlightenment of the narrator in "Holiday" and of Miranda in "Pale Horse, Pale Rider" shapes these stories. While the tone grows progressively sinister in the succession of stories, reflecting Porter's increasing concerns about totalitarianism and the ongoing deterioration in world affairs throughout the thirties and early forties, all three nonetheless suggest that the evil of totalitarianism, for all its attractiveness to a weak-minded and complacent humanity, can still be resisted and overcome by clear-sighted vision and determined effort. The narrator of "Holiday," for instance, though attracted to the Müllers' way of life, in the end understands its limitations; Miranda, it seems, will in all likelihood awaken from her nightmare of a totalitarian society, helped along by her friends "to put in order her disordered mind" (CS, 314); and even Charles Upton has enough sense to resist the pressures of the German nationalists.

Before the fifties, when Porter was beset by a deep despair and paranoia about the tide of totalitarianism, she put great stock in the power of reason and intelligence to overcome humanity's proclivity toward evil and its most disturbing social and political manifestation, fascism. In some undated

12. Unrue, *Truth and Vision*, 139–40.

notes, in all likelihood from the late thirties or early forties (her reference to Hitler clearly suggests that he is alive and in power), Porter discusses the role of reason in correcting the misguided ways of twentieth-century humanity. She begins by observing that behind the dominant movements in Western art and politics is "the deliberate turning away from the use of reason to the world of fantasy and dream of myth and sleep." After mentioning several artists she finds representative—James Joyce, Gertrude Stein, the dadaists, the surrealists, and D. H. Lawrence—she singles out one politician: Hitler. "Hitler," she writes, "is Surrealism in action, applied to politics," and she characterizes what she sees as the underlying logic of nazism and its corrective: "The subjective mind, which is mad and reasonless, but perfectly logical in its own right: beginning with a false premise it proceeds flawlessly to its false conclusion. The work of reason is to find out and master the fantasy" (McKeldin). Porter concludes her notes by saying that the true function of both art and government is finally the same: to correct with the waking mind the flawed logic of the subjective mind's dreams. Such faith in rationality, I believe, stands behind Porter's fiction of the thirties and early forties.

By the fifties, with Porter well into and bogged down with *Ship of Fools*, that faith was for the most part gone. As we have seen, Porter's concern with totalitarianism by this time had become obsessive. She no longer looked to rationality as an answer to totalitarian thinking but instead focused on totalitarianism's overwhelming power over and corruption of all aspects of life, including the reasonable mind. Certainly, and particularly early on, Porter saw *Ship of Fools* as fulfilling what she said in her notes cited above was art's function: to expose and correct the ill-conceived logic of the subjective mind that was shaping twentieth-century culture. *Ship of Fools* assuredly exposes the ills arising from humanity's flawed thinking, but it offers little if any corrective, other than perhaps the suggestion embodied in the simple fact of the novel's existence: there is a possibility of order and beauty in the literary artifact. No clear answer to the madness on the ship, however, emerges from within the novel's action. Even the most dignified and reasonable character, Dr. Schumann, falls prey to psychological fantasies. If Givner is right that with *Ship of Fools* Porter sought to "solve the riddle of what had gone wrong with the whole Western world in the twentieth century," then what she ended up with was less an answer to the riddle than a seemingly endless repetition of that riddle—humanity's collusion with evil.[13]

The very structure of *Ship of Fools* is dominated by repetition, a point that Porter herself frequently underscored. To her publisher Seymour Lawrence, Porter wrote on April 29, 1956, that the novel (still unfinished at this point) was structured not by developing action but by recurring theme. She wrote, "There is no plot: there is only a theme which is illustrated from every point of view I am able to command, over and over and over, in a series of subplots or incidents which keep the characters in movement and the theme developing as we go" (*L*, 489). In a 1963 interview with Barbara Thompson, Porter suggested that the structure of *Ship of Fools* had less to do with narrative unfolding than with symphonic harmony. "A novel is really like a symphony, you know, where instrument after instrument has to come in at its own time, and no other," she said, and she elaborated on the specific problems with structure she faced in *Ship of Fools:* "It was the question of keeping everything moving at once. There are about forty-five main characters, all taking part in each other's lives, and then there was a steerage of sugar workers, deportees. It was all a matter of deciding which should come first, in order to keep the harmonious moving forward" (*C,* 97–98). Harmony came, as she suggested in her letter to Lawrence, in having all the novel's incidents voicing the same theme, and this theme, she told Thompson, was "betrayal and treachery, but also self-betrayal and self-deception—the way that all human beings deceive themselves about the way they operate. . . . We don't really know what is going to happen to us, and we don't know why. Quite often the best we can do is to keep our heads, and try to keep at least one line unbroken and unobstructed. Misunderstanding and separation are the natural conditions of man" (*C,* 97). Expanding on this idea of betrayal and treachery, Porter described *Ship of Fools* in a letter dated February 20, 1958, to Cyrilly Abels as "a long exposition of the disastrous things people do to each other out of ignorance, prejudice, presumptuousness, self-love and self-hate, with religion, or politics, or race, or social distinctions, or even just nationality or a difference in customs . . .

13. Givner, *Katherine Anne Porter: A Life,* 407.

and—this is the other side of the question, out of inertia, moral apathy, timidity, indifference, and even a subconscious criminal collusion, people allow others to do every kind of wrong, and even, if the wrongdoers are successful, finally rather approve of them, perhaps envy them a little" (*L,* 546–47).

In her interview with Thompson, Porter emphasizes humanity's irrational and disordered existence. Noting that the physical universe has a recognizable and systematic structure, Porter adds that "human life itself is almost pure chaos. Everyone takes his stance, asserts his own rights and feelings, mistaking the motives of others and his own" (*C,* 97). Such chaos, together with humanity's outward indifference toward and secret collusion with evil, opens the way for the terrors of totalitarianism and, as *Ship of Fools* specifically underscores, of fascism and nazism. Perhaps most terrifying about the world of *Ship of Fools* is the utter failure of genuine human community based on love, respect, and trust. Every relationship—those between acquaintances, friends, lovers, and family (with the possible exception of that between the newlyweds, whose idyllic bond will in all likelihood soon become tainted and troubled like everyone else's)—is somehow marred by an ugly failing, a situation perhaps best explained by the narrator's observation on Frau Schmitt's understanding of human interaction: "She had always believed so deeply that human beings wished only to be quiet and happy, each in his own way: but there was a spirit of evil in them that could not let each other be in peace. One man's desire must always crowd out another's, one must always take his own good at another's expense. Or so it seemed. God forgive us all" (*SF,* 152).

Any number of relationships on board illustrate the justice of Frau Schmitt's observation, but perhaps the most chilling is Dr. Schumann's with La Condesa, because of the doctor's otherwise obvious dignity and nobility. For all of Dr. Schumann's goodness, his relationship with La Condesa reveals that his idealism is at heart a destructive asceticism of self-denial and detachment from human affairs. Dr. Schumann maintains his stability and ideals only through withdrawal and repression. While he falls desperately in love with La Condesa, he hates her just as desperately because his love undermines the foundation on which his life is built: a strict indifference to and detachment from the affairs of other people and his own emotions. At one point his anger at and fear of both La Condesa and his feelings for her explode so intensely that he envisions her as a spirit from hell bent on destroying his virtue. A terrifying rage grips him: "He had a savage impulse to strike her from him, this diabolical possession, this incubus fastened upon him like a bat, this evil spirit come out of her hell to accuse him falsely, to seduce his mind, to charge him with fraudulent obligations to her, to burden his life to the end of his days, to bring him to despair" (*SF,* 316). Although he does not see it here, later Dr. Schumann comes to understand that his actions toward La Condesa embody a diabolical impulse that betrays everything for which he outwardly stands. While being prodded by Herr Graf, Dr. Schumann has an epiphanic insight of himself that shatters—at least momentarily—his ascetic detachment, showing it to be moral cowardice rather than moral heroism:

> The Doctor suffered the psychic equivalent of a lightning stroke, which cleared away there and then his emotional fogs and vapors, and he faced his truth, nearly intolerable but the kind of pain he could deal with, something he recognized and accepted unconditionally. His lapse into the dire, the criminal sentimental cruelty of the past days was merely the symptom of his moral collapse: he had refused to acknowledge the wrong he had done La Condesa his patient, he had taken advantage of her situation as prisoner, he had tormented her with his guilty love and yet had refused her—and himself—any human joy in it. He had let her go in hopelessness without even the faintest promise of future help or deliverance. What a coward, what a swine, Dr. Schumann told himself, calmly, bathed in the transfiguring light of Herr Graf's contempt; but not only, not altogether, if he did not choose to be! (*SF,* 373)

Even though, as the final words above suggest, Dr. Schumann almost immediately begins to reinvoke his cherished view of himself, the damage to his serenity and his self-worth has already been done. Dr. Schumann will never be able entirely to forget the startling image of himself with which Herr Graf has brought him face-to-face.

Dr. Schumann's shattering insight has disturbing implications extending far beyond his own situation. Indeed, his downfall suggests that the work of intelligence and rationality is merely another sham behind which people hide from themselves and others. In light of Porter's earlier faith in reason to combat evil lurking within and without, Dr. Schumann's actions point to the dramatic turn in the writer's thinking toward pessimism and cynicism, a darkening that envisioned the evils of humanity as so pervasive and encompassing that the means that she once saw for achieving enlightenment and virtue have themselves now become embodiments of chaos. The implications of Dr. Schumann's "lightning stroke" stretch even further, calling into question the enterprise of the novel itself. For if rationality is compromised by human failings, so too may art—a creation of the reasonable mind—be tainted, specifically *Ship of Fools*. By this line of thinking, Dr. Schumann's idealism and attempts at self-control mirror the narrator's, with the suggestion that the narrative and its creator may be every bit as befouled as the good doctor and his work, motivated ultimately as much by self-deception as by virtue. *Ship of Fools,* then, both depicts and itself embodies a world—and a fictional construct—gone bad.

The radical hardening and harshening of Porter's views resulting from her obsession with totalitarianism can be seen, on a simple level, in even a cursory comparison of her 1931 letter to Caroline Gordon chronicling her trip from Mexico to Germany with the novel that evolved from this voyage. Porter's letter to Gordon lacks the bitterness, the anger, and the fixation upon evil that mark *Ship of Fools*. Although she briefly mentions the indifference the travelers show each other and some of their prejudiced comments arising from their fervent nationalism, she does not dwell on these matters, and indeed, the letter for the most part is overwhelmingly upbeat. "It seems to me now I am having the loveliest time of my life," she writes at one point, and at another she talks about how recuperative being among a large group of people is. She says that while in Mexico, living by "anarchic freedom," she had so withdrawn from human contact that "I was beginning to dread the appearance of a human face, any kind of face, the more clear space I had around me the more I needed, so that I managed quite habitually to keep two or three rooms between me and any one else, and I wanted the whole orchard to myself when I took a walk." But on board the ship she quickly broke out of her shell: "Already I am accustomed to faces, all kinds, I sit here and write with the whole life of the ship revolving on the decks, and it is even comfortable to me" (*L,* 52). Invigorated by life on board, she mentions two stories she sees emerging from her experiences and observations from the voyage: one "about a little fat man dancing a waltz" (apparently to be structured by the idea that the waltz momentarily breaks down the barriers that otherwise separate people) and another, to be called ". . . And a Pleasant Journey," about selling her house and leaving it (*L*, 50). Neither these proposed stories nor Porter's letter to Gordon as a whole suggests the joyless and forbidding world Porter later created in *Ship of Fools*.

Progressive bitterness and anger do not necessarily signal the weakening of artistic vision, but in Porter's case I believe they did. Ushered along by her totalitarian obsession, Porter's dark vision of the fifties marked a closing off of her openness to the wealth and variety of experience and a withdrawal into a stultifying and paranoid cynicism. Near the end of *Ship of Fools,* with the ship approaching its destination, the narrator notes that the people at the captain's table no longer converse: "They were no longer interested in anything the others had to say—their minds were closing in and folding up once more around their own concerns, their only common hope being to leave that ship and end that voyage and to take up their real and separate lives once more" (*SF,* 493). As they had during their preparations for embarking from Mexico, the travelers now each "chose to maintain his pride and separateness within himself" (*SF,* 11). In her writing of *Ship of Fools* Porter likewise suffered, giving herself over unquestioningly to her obsessive thinking. Porter may have seen *Ship of Fools* as an attempt to correct twentieth-century chaos and madness, but what the novel finally became was something close in spirit to Dr. Schumann's calculated detachment and idealism—not a corrective for but an embodiment of the very problem it supposedly combated. With its high-minded authoritarianism, *Ship of Fools* itself points to the totalitarian madness that Porter came to see in everyone but herself. One thinks most obviously here of her blindness in failing to see the connection between her own ugly racism and that of Nazi ideology.

After the publication of *Ship of Fools* Porter liked to tell interviewers that she too was a passenger on board the *Vera,* that is, that she suffered from the same human failings as did the characters in the novel. Most assuredly she did, but she never fully acknowledged the degree to which she tended toward authoritarianism. Nor did she ever see that the fixations and paranoia that characterized much of her thinking during the time when she was writing *Ship of Fools* severely undermined the richness of her creative imagination and her fiction. *Ship of Fools* represents a decline from Porter's earlier stories, a decline that ironically brought her the fame and fortune she had always wanted. But such reward of course says more about the American reading public than about Porter's literary achievement. Her greatest works—"The Jilting of Granny Weatherall," "Flowering Judas," the Miranda stories, "Noon Wine," and a few other stories—come from an earlier period and were written in a different genre, and they tower above the novel that Porter strove so hard and so obsessively to make her masterwork.

# BIBLIOGRAPHY

Adler, Les K., and Thomas G. Patterson. "Red Fascism: The Merger of Nazi Germany and Soviet Russia in the American Image of Totalitarianism, 1930's–1950's." *American Historical Review,* LXXV (1970), 1046–64.

Agee, James. "Dixie Doodle." *Partisan Review,* IV (February, 1938), 8.

Allen, Charles A. "Katherine Anne Porter: Psychology as Art." *Southwest Review,* XLI (1956), 223–30.

Baker, Howard. "The Upward Path: Notes on the Work of Katherine Anne Porter." *Southern Review,* n.s., IV (1968), 1–19.

Bakhtin, Mikhail. *The Dialogic Imagination: Four Essays.* Edited by Michael Holquist. Translated by Caryl Emerson and Michael Holquist. Austin, Tex., 1981.

———. *Problems of Dostoevsky's Poetics.* Edited and translated by Caryl Emerson. Minneapolis, 1984.

———. *Rabelais and His World.* Translated by Helene Iswolsky. Bloomington, Ind., 1984.

Bayley, Isabel, ed. *Letters of Katherine Anne Porter.* New York, 1990.

Bishop, John Peale. *The Collected Essays.* Edited by Edmund Wilson. New York, 1948.

Bloom, Harold, ed. *Katherine Anne Porter.* New York, 1986.

Bradbury, John M. *Renaissance in the South: A Critical History of the Literature, 1920–1960.* Chapel Hill, N.C., 1963.

Brinkmeyer, Robert H., Jr. "'Endless Remembering': The Artistic Vision of Katherine Anne Porter." *Mississippi Quarterly,* XL (1986–87), 5–19.

Broughton, Irv. "An Interview with Allen Tate." *Western Humanities Review,* XXXII (1978), 317–36.

Bufkin, E. C., ed. "An *Open Mind* Profile: Katherine Anne Porter Talks with Glenway Wescott and Eric F. Goldman." *Georgia Review,* XLI (1987), 769–95.

Cheatham, George. "Death and Repetition in Porter's Miranda Stories." *American Literature,* LXI (1989), 610–24.

Clifford, Craig, and Tom Pilkington, eds. *Range Wars: Heated Debates, Sober Reflections, and Other Assessments of Texas Writing.* Dallas, 1989.

Cobb, Joann P. "Pascal's Wager and Two Modern Losers." *Philosophy and Literature,* III (1979), 187–98.

Corey, Jim. "*Ship of Fools:* Katherine Anne Porter in Decline." *Four Quarters,* XXXIV (Spring–Summer, 1985), 16–25.

Cowley, Malcolm. *Exile's Return: A Literary Odyssey of the 1920's.* New York, 1951.

Curley, Daniel. "Katherine Anne Porter: The Larger Plan." *Kenyon Review,* XXV (1963), 671–95.

———. "Treasure in 'The Grave.'" *Modern Fiction Studies,* IX (1963), 377–84.

DeMouy, Jane Krause. *Katherine Anne Porter's Women: The Eye of Her Fiction.* Austin, Tex., 1983.

DeVoto, Bernard. "The Skeptical Biographer." *Harper's,* CLXVI (January, 1933), 181–92.

Diggins, John P. *Mussolini and Fascism: The View from America.* Princeton, N.J., 1972.

Emmons, Winfred S. *Katherine Anne Porter: The Regional Stories.* Austin, Tex., 1967.

Flanders, Jane. "Katherine Anne Porter and the Ordeal of Southern Womanhood." *Southern Literary Journal,* IX (Fall, 1976), 47–60.

Flaubert, Gustave. *The Letters of Gustave Flaubert, 1830–1857.* Translated and edited by Francis Steegmuller. Cambridge, Mass., 1980.

"Foreword." *Fugitive,* I (April, 1922), 2.

Geertz, Clifford. *The Interpretation of Cultures.* New York, 1973.

Givner, Joan. "The Genesis of *Ship of Fools.*" *Southern Literary Journal,* X (Fall, 1970), 14–30.

———. "Her Great and Sober Craft: Katherine Anne Porter's Creative Process." *Southwest Review,* LXII (1977), 217–30.

———. *Katherine Anne Porter: A Life.* Rev. ed. Athens, Ga., 1991.

———, ed. *Katherine Anne Porter: Conversations.* Jackson, Miss., 1987.

———. "Porter's Subsidiary Art." *Southwest Review,* LIX (1974), 265–76.

Gordon, Caroline. "Katherine Anne Porter and the ICM." *Harper's,* CCXXIX (November, 1964), 146–48.

Gottfried, Leon. "Death's Other Kingdom: Dantesque and Theological Symbolism in 'Flowering Judas.'" *PMLA,* LXXXIV (1969), 112–24.

Graham, Don, James W. L. Lee, and William T. Pilkington, eds. *The Texas Literary Tradition: Fiction, Folklore, History.* Austin, Tex., 1983.

Gray, Richard. *The Literature of Memory: Writers of the Modern South.* Baltimore, 1977.

———. *Writing the South: Ideas of an American Region.* Cambridge, Eng., 1986.

Gretlund, Jan Nordby. "Flannery O'Connor and Katherine Anne Porter." *Flannery O'Connor Bulletin,* VIII (1979), 77–87.

———. "Katherine Anne Porter and the South: A Corrective." *Mississippi Quarterly,* XXXIV (1981), 435–44.

———. "Three on Katherine Anne Porter." *Mississippi Quarterly,* XXXVI (1983), 117–30.

Gunn, Drewey Wayne. *American and British Writers in Mexico, 1556–1973.* Austin, Tex., 1974.

Gwin, Minrose. "Mentioning the Tamales: Food and Drink in Katherine Anne Porter's *Flowering Judas and Other Stories.*" *Mississippi Quarterly,* XXXVIII (1984–85), 49–57.

Hafley, James. "'María Concepción': Life Among the Ruins." *Four Quarters,* XII (November, 1962), 11–17.

Hagopian, John V. "Katherine Anne Porter: Feeling, Form, and Truth." *Four Quarters,* XII (November, 1962), 1–10.

Hamovitch, Mitzi Berger. "Today and Yesterday: Letters from Katherine Anne Porter." *Centennial Review,* XXVII (1983), 278–87.

Hardy, John Edward. *Katherine Anne Porter.* New York, 1973.

Harpham, Geoffrey Galt. *The Ascetic Imperative in Culture and Criticism.* Chicago, 1987.

Hartley, Lodwick, and George Core, eds. *Katherine Anne Porter: A Critical Symposium.* Athens, Ga., 1969.

Hendrick, George. "Katherine Anne Porter's 'Hacienda.'" *Four Quarters,* XII (November, 1962), 24–29.

Hendrick, Willene, and George Hendrick. *Katherine Anne Porter.* Rev. ed. Boston, 1988.

Hennessy, Rosemary. "Katherine Anne Porter's Model for Heroines." *Colorado Quarterly,* XXV (1977), 301–15.

Hilt, Kathryn, and Ruth M. Alvarez. *Katherine Anne Porter: An Annotated Bibliography.* New York, 1990.

Hoffman, Frederick J. *The Art of Southern Fiction.* Carbondale, Ill., 1967.

James, Henry. "The Beast in the Jungle." In *The New York Edition of the Novels and Tales of Henry James.* Vol. XVII of 26 vols. New York, 1909.

Johnson, James William. "Another Look at Katherine Anne Porter." *Virginia Quarterly Review,* XXXVI (1960), 598–613.

Jones, Anne Goodwyn. "Gender and the Great War: The Case of Faulkner and Porter." *Women's Studies,* XIII (1986), 135–48.

―――. *Tomorrow Is Another Day: The Woman Writer in the South, 1859–1936.* Baton Rouge, 1981.

Jorgensen, Bruce W. "'The Other Side of Silence': Katherine Anne Porter's 'He' as Tragedy." *Modern Fiction Studies,* XXVIII (1982), 395–404.

King, Richard H. *A Southern Renaissance: The Cultural Awakening of the American South, 1930–1955.* New York, 1980.

Langer, Elinor. *Josephine Herbst.* Boston, 1984.

Lawson, Lewis A. *Another Generation: Southern Fiction Since World War II.* Jackson, Miss., 1984.

Liberman, M. M. *Katherine Anne Porter's Fiction.* Detroit, 1971.

―――. "Some Observations on the Genesis of *Ship of Fools:* A Letter from Katherine Anne Porter." *PMLA,* LXXXIV (1969), 135–37.

Lopez, Enrique Hank. *Conversations with Katherine Anne Porter: Refugee from Indian Creek.* Boston, 1981.

Machann, Clinton, and William Bedford Clark, eds. *Katherine Anne Porter and Texas: An Uneasy Relationship.* College Station, Tex., 1990.

McKelway, St. Clair. "A Reporter at Large: Some Fun with the F.B.I." *New Yorker,* October 11, 1941, pp. 53–57.

McMurtry, Larry. *In a Narrow Grave: Essays on Texas.* 1968; rpr. New York, 1989.

Madden, David. "The Charged Image in Katherine Anne Porter's 'Flowering Judas.'" *Studies in Short Fiction,* VII (1970), 277–89.

Miller, J. Hillis. *Poets of Reality: Six Twentieth-Century Writers.* Cambridge, Mass., 1965.

Moddelmog, Debra A. "Narrative Irony and Hidden Motivations in Katherine Anne Porter's 'He.'" *Modern Fiction Studies,* XXVIII (1982), 405–13.

Morgan, Janice, and Colette T. Hall, eds. *Gender and Genre in Literature: Redefining Autobiography in Twentieth-Century Women's Fiction.* New York, 1991.

Nance, William L. "Katherine Anne Porter and Mexico." *Southwest Review,* LV (1970), 143–53.

―――. *Katherine Anne Porter and the Art of Rejection.* Chapel Hill, N.C., 1964.

Nietzsche, Friedrich. *Untimely Meditations*. Translated by R. J. Hollingdale. Cambridge, Mass., 1983.

O'Connor, Flannery. *The Habit of Being: Letters*. Edited by Sally Fitzgerald. New York, 1979.

————. *Mystery and Manners: Occasional Prose*. Edited by Sally Fitzgerald and Robert Fitzgerald. New York, 1969.

Ong, Walter J. "Voice as Summons for Belief." In *Literature and Belief,* edited by M. H. Abrams. New York, 1958.

Partridge, Colin. "My Familiar Country: An Image of Mexico in the Work of Katherine Anne Porter." *Studies in Short Fiction,* VII (1970), 597–614.

Payne, Pierre Stephen Robert. *The Life and Death of Adolf Hitler*. New York, 1973.

Percy, Walker. *The Message in the Bottle: How Queer Man Is, How Queer Language Is, and What One Has to Do with the Other*. New York, 1975.

Perry, Robert L. "Porter's 'Hacienda' and the Theme of Change." *Midwest Quarterly,* VI (1965), 403–15.

Porter, Katherine Anne. "Children and Art." *Nation,* March 2, 1927, pp. 233–34.

————. *The Collected Essays and Occasional Writings of Katherine Anne Porter*. New York, 1970.

————. *The Collected Stories of Katherine Anne Porter*. New York, 1965.

————. *The Never-Ending Wrong*. Boston, 1977.

————. "Notes on the Texas I Remember." *Atlantic Monthly,* CCXXXV (March, 1975), 102–106.

————. *Outline of Mexican Popular Arts and Crafts*. Los Angeles, 1922.

————. *Ship of Fools*. Boston, 1962.

Prater, William. "'The Grave': Form and Symbol." *Studies in Short Fiction,* VI (1969), 336–38.

Rubin, Louis D., Jr. *The Wary Fugitives: Four Poets and the South*. Baton Rouge, 1978.

Ruoff, James, and Del Smith. "Katherine Anne Porter on *Ship of Fools.*" *College English,* XXIV (1963), 396–97.

Ryan, Marjorie. "*Dubliners* and the Stories of Katherine Anne Porter." *American Literature,* XXXI (1960), 464–73.

Schwartz, Edward G. "The Fictions of Memory." *Southwest Review,* XLV (1960), 204–15.

Simpson, Lewis P. *The Brazen Face of History: Studies in the Literary Consciousness in America*. Baton Rouge, 1980.

————. *The Dispossessed Garden: Pastoral and History in Southern Literature.* 1975; rpr. Baton Rouge, 1983.

Singal, Daniel Joseph. *The War Within: From Victorian to Modernist Thought in the South, 1919–1945.* Chapel Hill, N.C., 1982.

Squires, Radcliffe. *Allen Tate: A Literary Biography.* New York, 1971.

Stein, William Bysshe. "'Theft': Porter's Politics of Modern Love." *Perspective,* XI (1960), 223–28.

Stout, Janis P. "Miranda's Guarded Speech." *Philological Quarterly,* LVI (1977), 259–78.

————. *Strategies of Reticence: Silence and Meaning in the Works of Jane Austen, Willa Cather, Katherine Anne Porter, and Joan Didion.* Charlottesville, Va., 1990.

Sullivan, Walter. *Death by Melancholy: Essays on Modern Southern Fiction.* Baton Rouge, 1972.

————. *A Requiem for the Renascence: The State of Fiction in the Modern South.* Athens, Ga., 1976.

Sylvester, Harry. "Problems of the Catholic Writer." *Atlantic Monthly,* CLXXXI (January, 1948), 109–13.

Tanner, James T. F. *The Texas Legacy of Katherine Anne Porter.* Denton, Tex., 1990.

Tate, Allen. *Collected Poems, 1919–1976.* New York, 1977.

————. *"The Fathers" and Other Fiction.* Baton Rouge, 1977.

————. *Mere Literature and the Lost Traveller.* Nashville, 1969.

————. "A New Star." *Nation,* October 1, 1930, pp. 352–53.

————. "One Escape from the Dilemma." *Fugitive,* III (April, 1924), 34–36.

Titus, Mary. "The 'Booby Trap' of Love: Artist and Sadist in Katherine Anne Porter's Mexico Fiction." *Journal of Modern Literature,* XVI (1990), 617–34.

————. "'Mingled Sweetness and Corruption': Katherine Anne Porter's 'The Fig Tree' and 'The Grave.'" *South Atlantic Review,* LIII (1988), 111–25.

Todorov, Tzvetan. *The Conquest of America: The Question of the Other.* Translated by Richard Howard. New York, 1984.

Torgovnick, Marianna. *Gone Primitive: Savage Intellects, Modern Lives.* Chicago, 1990.

Twelve Southerners. *I'll Take My Stand: The South and the Agrarian Tradition.* 1930; rpr. New York, 1962.

Unrue, Darlene Harbour, ed. *"This Strange, Old World" and Other Book Reviews by Katherine Anne Porter.* Athens, Ga., 1991.

————. *Truth and Vision in Katherine Anne Porter's Fiction.* Athens, Ga., 1985.

Walsh, Thomas F. "Braggioni's Jockey Club in Porter's 'Flowering Judas.'" *Studies in Short Fiction,* XX (1983), 136–38.

————. "Deep Similarities in 'Noon Wine.'" *Mosaic,* IX (1975), 83–91.

————. "The Dream of Self in 'Pale Horse, Pale Rider.'" *Wascana Review,* XIV (1979), 61–79.

————. "Identifying a Sketch by Katherine Anne Porter." *Journal of Modern Literature,* VII (1979), 555–61.

————. *Katherine Anne Porter and Mexico: The Illusion of Eden.* Austin, Tex., 1992.

————. "The Making of 'Flowering Judas.'" *Journal of Modern Literature,* XII (1985), 109–30.

————. "The 'Noon Wine' Devils." *Georgia Review,* XXII (1968), 90–96.

————. "Xochitl: Katherine Anne Porter's Changing Goddess." *American Literature,* LII (1980), 183–93.

Warren, Robert Penn. "The Genius of Katherine Anne Porter." *Saturday Review,* VII (December, 1980), 10–11.

————, ed. *Katherine Anne Porter: A Collection of Critical Essays.* Englewood Cliffs, N.J., 1979.

————. "Uncorrupted Consciousness: The Stories of Katherine Anne Porter." *Yale Review,* LV (1965), 280–90.

Weisenfarth, Joseph. "Negatives of Hope: A Reading of Katherine Anne Porter." *Renascence,* XXV (1973), 85–94.

Welty, Eudora. "The Eye of the Story." *Yale Review,* LV (1966), 265–74.

————. *The Eye of the Story: Selected Essays and Reviews.* New York, 1978.

————. *The Optimist's Daughter.* New York, 1972.

Wescott, Glenway. *Images of Truth.* New York, 1962.

West, Ray B., Jr. *Katherine Anne Porter.* Minneapolis, 1963.

————. "Katherine Anne Porter and Historic Memory." *Hopkins Review,* VI (Fall, 1952), 16–27.

Westling, Louise. *Sacred Groves and Ravaged Gardens: The Fiction of Eudora Welty, Carson McCullers, and Flannery O'Connor.* Athens, Ga., 1985.

White, Hayden. *Tropics of Discourse: Essays in Cultural Criticism.* Baltimore, 1978.

Wilson, Edmund. *Classics and Commercials: A Literary Chronicle of the Forties.* New York, 1950.

# INDEX